D0857429

German Romantic Criticism

The German Library : Volume 21

Volkmar Sander, General Editor

GERMAN ROMANTIC CRITICISM

Edited by A. Leslie Willson

Foreword by Ernst Behler

CONTINUUM · NEW YORK

1982

The Continuum Publishing Company
575 Lexington Avenue, New York, NY 10022

Copyright © 1982 by The Continuum Publishing Company

Foreword © 1982 by Ernst Behler
Introduction © 1982 by A. Leslie Willson

Printed in the United States of America

Library of Congress Cataloging in Publication Data
Main entry under title:

German romantic criticism.

(The German library; v. 21)
Contents: From On the different methods of translation / Friedrich Schleiermacher—From School for
aesthetics / Jean Paul Friedrich Richter—Aphorisms and
fragments / Novalis—[etc.]
 1. Criticism—Germany—Addresses, essays, lectures.
 2. Literature—Addresses, essays, lectures. I. Willson,
 A. Leslie (Amos Leslie), 1923– . II. Series.
 PN99.G4G4   801'.95'0943   82-5016
 ISBN 0-8264-0232-6   AACR2
        ISBN 0-8264-0262-3 pbk

For acknowledgments of previously published material, see page 293,
which constitutes an extension of the copyright page.

Contents

Foreword

The emergence of Romanticism in Germany toward the end of the eighteenth century constitutes a decisive turning point in the history of criticism. Prepared by Lessing, Herder, and Schiller and stimulated by Goethe's poetic creations, a completely new view of literary work and artistic process developed, which diverged sharply from the dominant classicist understanding of aesthetics and poetics. The European classicist tradition had stressed unchangeable norms for art; had codified a hierarchical system of immutable genres; had bound artistic production to an imitation of nature and an adherence to verisimilitude; and had defined poetic unity according to rules. The early Romantic critics made decisive inroads into this classicist view of poetry by recognizing the infinite changeability of genres: their constant mixing and mingling and the frequent emergence of new literary forms. For instance, the novel (which was not represented in Boileau's classicist codex of literary forms) appeared to the early Romantic critics to be the most effective medium for literary expression in their own time. Rebelling against alleged normative rules and pedantic regulations, they asserted the rights of genius and creative imagination. They saw the poetic unity of a literary work as an inner conformity with itself, connecting a multiplicity of phenomena to an absolutely achieved whole. However, this task could not be accomplished by applying external rules, or by focusing on particular instances; it required the shaping power of creative imagination.

Contemporaries such as Adam Müller and Henry Crabb Robinson characterized these new critical accomplishments as a "revolution," meaning of course a "critical" or an "aesthetic" revolution.[1] These assessments certainly coincided with the opinions of Novalis, Friedrich Schlegel, and Hölderlin, who saw their aesthetic and poetic activities, at least in their initial stages, in close association with the French Revolution.[2] The linkage between the outbreak of these two events—the French Revolution as a decisive alteration in Europe's political life and Romanticism as a crucial change in literary and critical habits—is indeed so close that critics have generally been inclined to consider romanticism a revolution in literature. Viewed from this angle, Romantic criticism appears as an attempt to overthrow and demolish the *ancien régime* of classicist theory. But we should keep in mind that the real target of the romantic assault was not classicism, but the aesthetic system of neoclassicism and the classicist tradition of the *ars poetica*. The origins of Romanticism in Germany reveal a strong affinity to Greek and Roman antiquity. At best one can speak of a shift of emphasis in the relationship to classicism, which can be described as a departure from the dominant Roman and Aristotelian influence upon European criticism in exchange for a closer bond with the Greeks and especially the Platonic tradition.

Another characteristic feature of German Romantic criticism is its close connection with the prevailing philosophy of the time, transcendental idealism. In his *Critique of Judgment* of 1790, Kant had laid the groundwork for the Romantic conceptions of the autonomy of art and the uniqueness and distinctiveness of aesthetic judgments in contrast to other judgments, especially scientific and moral ones. With these topics, Kant had decisively changed the ground rules in the debate on art and the beautiful as it had prevailed in European criticism. Until Kant, art had usually been conceived of as one section within the hierarchical compartments of the human mind. Value judgments depreciated the realm of art, which, unlike philosophy and morality, also has a sensual side to its nature. During the course of the eighteenth century, the sense of the autonomy of art certainly increased, but it was not until Kant that the realm of aesthetics assumed its own right.[3] On this basis and in stark contrast to the prevailing ideas of the eighteenth century, Romanticism brought about a new appreciation of artistic creation—a glorification of creative imagination—and made of the artist a spokesman for the godhead, an orphic seer, and prophetic priest.

Kant's theory of the autonomy and distinctiveness of aesthetic judgments in contrast to scientific and moral judgments exerted yet another decisive stimulus for the development of romantic criticism. Kant overcame the relativism inherent in aesthetic judgments by strictly separating them from mere judgments of taste and placing these aesthetic judgments midway between objective ones based on *a priori* principles that are general and universal and judgments of taste that are merely subjective, according to the dictum *De gustibus non est disputandum.* Regarding aesthetic matter, Kant admitted, we cannot come to general judgments, but we still do not surrender to sheer subjectivity. We appeal rather to a common judge, humanity, and expect that our judgment ought to be universal.[4] Friedrich Schlegel and other romantic critics derived from these thoughts their theory of criticism. Schlegel delineated this type of judgment in a much more concrete fashion when he discussed judgments dealing with their objects not in scientific, moral, or social, but in aesthetic terms. Such judgments require intense familiarity with the organization and treatment of their objects. Yet what matters most in these judgments is what Kant had considered the appeal to a higher judge, humanity, and what Schlegel in more artistic fashion rendered as a "representation of the impression" that the work of art has made upon the critic. This should not be achieved in the style of mere impressionistic criticism. It should not result in a "poem about the poem" demonstrating the critic's brilliance, nor should the critic merely convey the "impression that the work made yesterday or makes today on this or that reader, but the impression that it should make on any civilized person at any time."[5]

German Romantic criticism represents a fundamentally dialectical type of thinking, and it was the philosopher Johann Gottlieb Fichte who inspired the romantics in this type of thought and counterthought. In its desire to be entirely by itself and with itself—that is, to be completely free—the reflective principle postulated by Fichte and termed the "Ego" constantly encounters barriers and finds itself in otherness and alienation. After having overcome one barrier, this ego confronts yet another, and so the transcendental thought process moves on for Fichte towards absolute self-consciousness and self-determination. Hegel later described this manner of philosophizing as "a continuous alternation of negation and affirmation, an identity with itself that immediately succumbs to negation, but then is immediately reconstituted." [6] This alternation of affirmation and negation, of emerging from and returning to the self, of expansion and contraction is obvious in Hölderlin's "On the Process of the Poetic Mind"; in the counteracting rhythm of Novalis's "romanticizing" (raising to a higher power) and "logarithmicizing" (reducing to a lower power); and in Friedrich Schlegel's concept of romantic irony, defined as a "constant alternation between self-creation and self-destruction." In a more mystical aspect such dialectical thinking is also operative in Novalis's shifts between introspection and observation of nature—both necessary to full comprehension. [7]

The view of literary history held by Romantic criticism derives its most important inspiration from the famous distinction between Romanticism and classicism introduced by the Schlegel brothers and most emphatically developed in August Wilhelm Schlegel's "Lectures on Dramatic Art and Literature." This distinction, which according to a remark by Goethe was "making its way over the entire world," [8] conveys two basic meanings. First of all, it establishes the intrinsic difference between the historical moment of Greek antiquity and the historical moment of modern Europe. Classical Greek literature represents a closed cycle: it has fully exhausted all the potentialities of poetry in its world and achieved this in classical beauty. With the dawn of modernity, however, art and literature entered upon an endlessly developing process, towards an ideal of beauty that could be reached only by infinite approximations. Reason and inventiveness determine the culture of the moderns. Capable of ever new and unimaginable achievements, they find total perfection *eo ipso* unattainable and a regulative ideal at best.

Second, Schlegel's distinction between classicism and Romanticism emphasizes and rescues from oblivion and rejection that tradition of European literature which had not been recognized by classical standards, the literature of the minnesinger, the troubadours, of Dante, Boccaccio, Cervantes, Ariosto, even Shakespeare—a tradition held in low regard by classicist taste. In this way the distinction between classicism and Romanticism led to an enormous enlargement of historical consciousness among the romantic generation to include the recognition of what had not yet met the standards of classicist taste. It led, that is, to a pluralistic view of human accomplishments. Neglected traditions were soon of interest; e.g., the literary tradition of the romance, the European Middle Ages, the Asian world, the culture of classical India, fairy tales, folklore, sagas, and nonclassical mythologies. Inspired by a predilection for the old, the mysterious, and the marvelous, historical research encompassed popular traditions; mythical residua; primeval history in the form of myths and symbols; genetic investigations into language, grammar, religions, as well as judicial traditions in their particular settings. History appeared as the most important way of comprehending the human condition.

The distinction between classicism and Romanticism was not introduced as an oppositional and hostile one. Though it served to point out the differences between classicism and Romanticism, it was not meant, as in the famous *Quarrel between the Ancients and the Moderns,* as an act of self-manifestation on the part of the moderns against the overwhelming predominance of the ancients. It rather attempted to mediate between the two worlds by bringing the moderns into a competitive relationship with the ancients. One cannot restore the classical age by returning to a past historical era, however perfect it may have been. One must instead produce something timely—which will of necessity be surpassed in the future because of art's incredible variety and inexhaustible perfectibility.

The particular historical self-understanding of the Romantic critics is best illustrated by their futuristic idea of infinite perfectibility. Whereas during the Enlightenment the contemporary age was taken as a standard for previous epochs, the Romantics regarded their age within the all-pervasive process of becoming, and accordingly saw themselves drifting toward ever new possibilities in the future. Under the influence of Kant and Schiller, they presented the idea of infinite perfectibility as an infinite striving toward a state of aesthetic fulfillment where every trace of alienation has been overcome. They saw Romantic poetry as an absolutely "progressive poetry," involved in a process of constant becoming and endless development.[9] The idea of infinite perfectibility also applies to literary criticism and the act of understanding literary works. It corresponds to the inexhaustibility of interpretation, to the infinite potentialities in the understanding of a literary work, which yields new meanings from ever new modes of historical consciousness.

As these remarks imply, the Romantic age of criticism is simultaneously a new chapter in the history of hermeneutics. Wilhelm Dilthey and Hans Georg Gadamer have pointed out[10] that German romanticism was that turning point in the history of hermeneutics when the act of understanding became its own subject, when interpretation turned into an interpretation of interpretation; just as Kant had presented philosophy as an investigation into the conditions for the possibility of philosophy and Fichte had raised philosophy to a philosophy of philosophy. This intensified reflective status of the discipline of interpretation during the period of Romanticism and transcendental idealism was accompanied by a total departure from the classicist theory of literature according to normative genres. The new approach assumed an active interior faculty in the creative mind that produced the inner form of a work. Neoclassicism took the text as something given and self-evident. Romantic hermeneutics, however, became interested in the creative process, in the author's manner of expressing himself, and in his intention. Now reunderstanding, reenacting, and reconstruction became devices for the hermeneutic approach to the aesthetic unity of a work.

In the light of our own experiences, we have perhaps become more cautious with regard to doctrines such as the infinite perfectibility of man or the creative power of imagination, and maybe even skeptical of the glorification of art and the artist during the romantic period of criticism. Yet we clearly realize that with Romantic criticism we are on the threshold of that phase of modernity of which we are still the inheritors.

ERNST BEHLER

NOTES

1. Adam Müller, *Kritische, ästhetische und philosophische Schriften,* ed. Walter Schroeder and Werner Siebert (Neuwied, 1967), 1: 23, 38, 39, 41. Diana Behler, "Henry Crabb Robinson as a Mediator of Early German Romanticism in England," *Arcadia* 12 (1977): 119.

2. Richard Brinkmann, ed., *Deutsche Literatur und französische Revolution. Sieben Studien,* (Göttingen, 1974).

3. René Wellek, "Immanuel Kant's Aesthetics and Criticism," in *Discriminations. Further Concepts of Criticism,* ed. René Wellek, (New Haven, 1970), pp. 122–42.

4. On this subject see Ernst Behler, "Kant vu par le groupe de Coppet. La formation de l'image staëlienne de Kant," in: *Le Groupe de Coppet. Actes et documents du deuxième Colloque de Coppet,* ed. Simon Balayé. 10–13 juillet 1974 (Geneva and Paris, 1977), pp. 144–47.

5. Friedrich Schlegel, *Kritische Ausgabe,* ed. Ernst Behler in cooperation with Jean-Jacques Anstett and Hans Eichner (Paderborn-Darmstadt, 1958 et seq.), 1: 499. See on this theme Hans Eichner, *Friedrich Schlegel* (New York, 1970), pp. 34–43.

6. *Jubiläumsausgabe,* ed. Hermann Glockner (Stuttgart-Bad Cannstadt, 1965), 19: 629.

7. Novalis, *Schriften,* ed. Richard Samuel in cooperation with Hans-Joachim Mähl and Gerhard Schulz (Darmstadt, 1960ff.), 3: 429.

8. *Gedenkausgabe,* ed. Ernst Beutler (Zurich, 1949), 24: 405.

9. Friedrich Schlegel, *Kritische Ausgabe,* 2: 182–83.

10. Wilhelm Dilthey, "Die Entstehung der Hermeneutik (1900)," in, Wilhelm Dilthey, *Gesammelte Schriften,* 3rd ed. (Göttingen, 1961), 5: 317–31. Hans Georg Gadamer, *Truth and Method,* (New York, 1975).

Introduction

It is fitting that a volume dedicated to the literary criticism of the Romantic era in Germany should begin with an essay on the craft of translation and end with one on the origins of language itself. The period of German Romantic art and thought extends from about 1790 to about 1850, with its high point centered in the two decades from 1798 to 1818. What was debated, written, and read in those decades changed the face of literary criticism in the Western world and exerted its influence on realms as various as politics and art history.

The age of Romantic criticism was one of discovery, exploration, and rediscovery. The literary heritage of ages past, once brought to light, was revivified. The classical writers of Greece and Rome received new appreciation and their tenets found new application. Songs and tales of folk origin for the first time became the objects of serious critical discourse. Translation flourished. New directions in literary criticism began, and the science of the study of language, a nascent linguistics, came into being.

The essays that follow here reflect the most penetrating thoughts of the most involved minds of this most inventive time. The ideas propounded by such diverse minds as those of the Schlegel brothers and of Friedrich Hölderlin introduce the panorama of Romantic critical thought. To begin with, consider the theologian Friedrich Schleiermacher (1768–1834), in his early years a friend of Friedrich Schlegel, with whom he shares the distinction of being among the earliest theorists of the science of interpretation known to twentieth-century critics as hermeneutics. Schleiermacher's essay on translation not only probes that complex aesthetic and interpretative act but accosts language itself and speculates about its nature. If "understanding a foreign work [is] a thing known and desired," and if "the native language [is] allowed a certain flexibility," then "translation becomes a natural phenomenon, influencing the whole evolution of a culture and giving a certain pleasure as it is given a certain value." Translation is an act of liberation, an act that enhances both the original work and the linguistic community into which it is transported. It is an essential task for the development of world literature, admirable even when the result of the effort is flawed. It is, in the last analysis, an ongoing human occupation.

Jean Paul Friedrich Richter (1763–1825), who called himself simply Jean Paul and who was best known for his witty, rambling, fantastic novels, much in the mode of Laurence Sterne, published his *School for Aesthetics* in 1804. The work is less a series of lectures on aesthetics than one on poetics, for in it Jean Paul devotes his attention to the nature of poetry. He distinguishes between the extremes of imitation and copying of nature, on the one hand, which he considers materialistic, and the use of excessive fantasy and emotion, which he holds to be nihilistic. A balanced mixture of the two opposing modes is the best for the literary interpretation of the world. For Jean Paul the spirit of Romanticism, with its moonlit dreaming, was the most apt literary vehicle to depict the world and explore the mind of mankind.

The epitome of the Romantic spirit, the quintessential Romantic writer, is Novalis (Friedrich von Hardenberg, 1772–1801), at once a salt-mine inspector and a brooding, imaginative poet. The author of a poetic novel about the development of a poet, *Heinrich von Ofterdingen* (unfinished, published posthumously in 1802), Novalis pronounced his aesthetic and critical ideas in a few brief essays and in the popular form of the aphorism, which was held to be the seed of critical thought. To him, the fantasy of the fairy tale was the basis of all prose literature, which should strive to make the unfamiliar familiar. Poetry's essence was dream. Playful associative literary acts were the most entertaining and enlightening. Novalis would have liked to see the entire world poeticized, for only thus could it be truly realized and relished in its wonder.

Perhaps the greatest Romantic critic, despite his undisciplined

nature an iridescent thinker and probing observer of art and literature, was Friedrich Schlegel (1772–1829), who, like Novalis,
jotted down ideas incessantly. For most of his life close friends
with his brother August Wilhelm, Friedrich spawned critical insights that were then nourished and developed systematically and
adroitly by August Wilhelm. The true founder of hermeneutics,
Friedrich Schlegel elucidated ideas on the role of myth and irony
in prose literature that later found international acceptance and
application as they were propounded fully by his brother. Like
other Romanticists, he emphasized the importance of a historical
sense in the contemplation of literary works, and he spied a unity
of literature worldwide that made it a single and singular work of
art. The hieroglyphic nature of myth achieved prominence in literary expression because of him and eventually developed into
symbolist metaphor. He did not deny the intellect but rather gave
it equal standing with the emotions; the sublime balance of the
two produced true poetry. With his concept of Romantic irony he
recognized the willful and subjective nature of the artist and the
skill with which the artist wrought his world.

Wilhelm von Humboldt (1767–1835), friend of the Schlegels
while they were in Jena, founder of the University of Berlin in
1810, was the humanist among Romantic critics. It was he who
taught German to Madame de Staël, the French Germanophile who
later spread the tenets of German Romanticism throughout Europe. Humboldt lauds the imagination as an essential ingredient
for any poetic work. Fantasy ignites the world when the artist
subordinates his sensual capacity in favor of his imagination, which
destroys and re-creates the world in a work of art. Humboldt con-
sistently emphasizes the unique character of the human being as
an art maker.

With an ebullience reminiscent of Jean Paul, Joseph Görres
(1776–1848) made liberal use of analogy and metaphor in his literary studies, which peaked with his work on the German chapbooks in 1807. René Wellek remarks in the second volume of his
History of Modern Criticism that Görres produced "an early doc-
ument in the study of comparative literature" (p. 281) with that
work. Görres later greeted the collection of folksongs in *Des Kna-
ben Wunderhorn* (gathered by Achim von Arnim and Clemens

Brentano in 1808) with great enthusiasm. He also identified the *Nibelungenlied* as a fragment of an ancient work of prodigious import.

With indefatigable energy and discipline August Wilhelm Schlegel (1767–1845) gave form and substance to the lightning-flash ideas of his younger brother, Friedrich, ideas which he popularized and spread widely in his lectures, particularly those on *Dramatic Art and Literature* which focused on his own favorite genre. Like most of the other Romantic critics, August Wilhelm was an erudite scholar who had a keen sense of history and connection with art in the formation of an organic unity. He maintained critical objectivity, yet admitted and approved a limited subjectivity on the part of the individual critic.

The most gifted poet of the Romantic era, Friedrich Hölderlin (1770–1843), was a solitary man whose increasing isolation from social contact led to thirty-six years of madness. Best known as the author of incomparable odes and elegies on themes of life, death, and love, Hölderlin is also the author of the novel *Hyperion,* in which he gives voice to his longing for the reestablishment of Grecian ideals on European (German) soil. His essay "On the Process of the Poetic Mind," typical of Hölderlin in its grammatical complexity and tenuous thought, is a pronouncement on the wholeness, unity, and harmony desirable in the person and intellect of the poet. First appreciated only in the early decades of the twentieth century, Hölderlin perceives the necessary but intractable relationship between form and content and the supremacy of the mind in its mastery of this essential paradox inherent in all being.

Heinrich von Kleist (1777–1811), like Hölderlin a man who never found his proper niche in society, was a master dramatist and storyteller. His famous short essay "On the Marionette Theater" emphasizes the ethereal—but also real—and intuitive nature of art, in a series of anecdotes that hail the grace, naturalness, and formless innocence that once enhanced man's existence. Günter Grass alludes to Kleist's essay at the end of his own aesthetic study, a short piece entitled "The Ballerina," which points out the enormous control and effort behind apparent grace and beauty.

Adam Müller (1779–1829), essentially a disciple of the Schlegels and of Novalis, approaches literature organically and historically. He recognizes the imperfections in poetry and in poets but asserts that art humanizes the world. One lecture from a series on rhetoric defines and differentiates what he calls winged and iron styles in literature, ending with his praise of Johannes von Müller, who was for him an example of "the seriousness of practical life."

Finally, in an exemplary lecture, Jacob Grimm (1778–1863) speculates on a topic that fascinated poets and critics in the late eighteenth and early nineteenth centuries, the question of the origin of language. Grimm, best known with his brother Wilhelm for their collection of fairy tales, is the critic responsible for the initial development of linguistics and the influential approach to literature and language known as philology.

The essays in this volume present only a small portion of the momentous contributions to the history and development of literary criticism made by the Romantic critics. It was an age of beginnings, of discoveries about language and literature, of innovative speculations and daring assertions about the nature of the poetic arts, and its influence, evident in imitation, denial, elaboration, verification, and application, is felt to the present day throughout the arts and humanities.

A. L. W.

On the Different Methods of Translation

Friedrich Schleiermacher

The fact that speech is translated from one language into another confronts us everywhere under a wide variety of guises. On the one hand this allows people to establish contact who were originally as far apart from each other as the length of the earth's diameter: products of another language that has been dead for many centuries may be incorporated into a language. On the other hand we do not even have to go outside the domain of one language to encounter the same phenomenon. For not only do the dialects spoken by different tribes belonging to the same nation and the different stages of the same language or dialect in different centuries, different languages in the strict sense of the word, not infrequently require a complete translation between them: moreover, even contemporaries who are not separated by dialects, but merely belong to different classes that are not often linked through social intercourse and are far apart in education, often can understand each other only by means of a similar mediation. Are we indeed not often required to translate the speech of another for ourselves, even if he is totally our equal but possesses a different frame of mind or feeling? For when we feel that the same words would, in our mouth, have a totally different sense, or at least a stronger weight here and a weaker impact there, than in his, and that if we wanted to express the same things he meant, we would make use of totally different words and locutions, according to our nature—it seems, if we define this feeling more closely and as it becomes a thought for us, that we translate. Indeed, we must

1

sometimes even translate our own words after a while, when we want to make them really our own again. And this ability is not only exercised to transplant into foreign soil what a language has produced in the field of scholarship and the arts of speech and to enlarge the radius within which these products of the mind can operate by doing so; it is also exercised in the domain of trade between different nations and in the diplomatic commerce individual governments have with each other, in which each is accustomed to talking to the other in its own language only, if they want to ensure that they are treated on a basis of strict equality without having to make use of a dead language.

We do not, of course, wish to incorporate everything that lies within this wide radius into our present observations. The necessity to translate even inside one's own language and dialect, which is more or less an immediate need of the emotions, is too much a thing of the moment in its impact to need any guidance other than that given by the emotions; and if rules were to be promulgated about this, they could only be the rules following which man keeps a purely moral mood for himself, so that his receptivity for the less congenial remains open as well. If we exclude this and concern ourselves for the time being with translation from a foreign language into ours, we shall be able to distinguish two different fields here as well—not totally distinct of course—this is very rarely the case—but separated by boundaries that overlap, and yet separated clearly enough if one keeps their goals in sight. The interpreter plies his trade in the field of commerce; the translator proper operates mainly in the fields of art and scholarship. Those who find this definition arbitrary, because interpreting is usually taken to mean what is done orally and translating what is written, will, I am sure, forgive me for using them, for they are very conveniently tailored to fit the present need, the more so since the two definitions are by no means far removed from each other. Writing is appropriate to the fields of art and scholarship because writing alone gives these works endurance, and to interpret scholarly or artistic products by word of mouth would be as useless as it seems to be impossible. For commerce, on the other hand, writing is but a mechanical means; oral bargaining is the original form here, and all written interpreting should really be considered the notation of oral interpreting.

Two other fields are joined to this one very closely as regards their nature and spirit; yet because of the great multiplicity of objects belonging to them they already make a transition, one to the field of art, the other to that of scholarship. For each transaction that includes interpreting is a fact the development of which is perceived in two different languages. But the translation of writings that are purely narrative or descriptive in nature, which also merely translates the development already described of a fact into another language, can still include much of the interpreter's trade. The less the author himself appears in the original, the more he has merely acted as the perceiving organ of an object; and the more he has adhered to the order of space and time, the more the translation depends upon simple interpreting. Thus the translator of newspaper articles and the common literature of travel is at first in close proximity to the interpreter, and he risks becoming ridiculous when his work makes greater claims and he wants to be recognized as an artist. Alternatively, the more the author's particular way of seeing and shaping has been dominant in the representation, the more he has followed some freely chosen order or an order defined by his impression, the more his work is a part of the higher field of art—and the translator, too, must then bring other powers and abilities to bear on his work and be familiar with his author and his author's language in another way than the interpreter is. On the other hand, every transaction which involves interpreting is the drawing up of a specific case according to certain legal obligations; the translation is made only for participants who are sufficiently familiar with these obligations, and the way these obligations are expressed in the two languages is well defined, either by law or by custom and mutual explanation. But the situation is different, even though formally it may be very similar to what we have just referred to, in the case of transactions by means of which new legal obligations are established. The less these can be subsumed as particular cases under a sufficiently known general rule, the more scholarly knowledge and circumspection are required in formulating them, and the more scholarly knowledge of fact and language the translator will need for his trade. On this double scale, therefore, the translator rises more and more above the interpreter until he reaches his proper field, namely, those mental products of scholarship and art in which the free idiosyncratic combinatory powers of the author and the spirit of the language, in which is the repository of a system of observations and shades of moods are everything, in which the object no longer dominates in any way, but is dominated by thoughts and emotions, in which, indeed, the object has become object only through speech and is present only in conjunction with speech.

What is the basis of this important distinction? Everyone perceives it even in borderline cases, but it strikes the eye most strongly at the outer poles. In the life of commerce one is, for the most part, faced with obvious objects or at least with objects defined with the greatest possible precision; all transactions have an arithmetical or a mathematical character, so to speak, and number and measure help out everywhere; and even in the case of those objects that, as the ancients were wont to say, subsume the more and the less into themselves and are referred to by means of a gradation of words, which weigh now more, now less in common life because their essence is not defined, an established usage of individual words soon arises through law and custom. When, therefore, the speaker does not intentionally construct hidden indeterminacies or make a mistake in order to deceive or because he is not paying attention, he can be understood by everyone who knows the language and the field, and at the most only unimportant differences appear in the use of language. Even so, there are rarely any doubts that cannot be immediately dispelled as to which expression in one language corresponds to an expression in another. Translating in this field is, therefore, almost a mechanical activity, which anyone can perform who has a fair to middling knowledge of both languages, and in which there is little distinction between better and worse as long as the obviously wrong is avoided. But when the products of art and scholarship have to be transplanted from one language to another, two considerations appear that completely change the relationship. For if, in the case of two languages, one word in one language exactly corresponded to one word in the other, if it expressed the same concept to the same extent, if their declensions represented the same relationships, and the ways in which they connect sentences matched, so that these languages were indeed different to the ear only—then all translation in the field of art and scholarship would be as mechanical as it is in the field of commerce insofar as it communicated only the contents of a spoken or written text, and it could be said of every translation that except for the effects produced by sound and melody, it puts the foreign reader in the same relationship to the author and his work as the native reader. But the case with all languages not so closely related that they can almost be considered different dialects only is precisely the opposite, and the farther they are apart in time and genealogical descent, the less a word in one language corresponds completely to a word in another or a declension in one language comprehends exactly the same multiplicity of relationships as another in a different language. Since this irrationality, if I may call it that, pervades all elements of two languages, it should obviously also make an impact on the domain of social intercourse. Yet it clearly exerts much less pressure there, and it has as good as no influence. All words denoting objects and actions that may be of importance have been verified, so to speak, and even if empty, overcautious inventiveness might still wish to guard against a possible unequal value of words, the subject matter itself immediately restores the balance. Matters are completely different in the domains of art and scholarship and wherever thought, which is one with the word, not the thing of which the word is only a possibly arbitrary but fixed sign, dominates to a greater extent. For how endlessly difficult and complex the problem becomes here! What precise knowledge and what mastery of both languages it presupposes! And how often the most expert and best versed in languages, starting from a shared conviction that an equivalent expression cannot be found, differ significantly when they want to show which expression is the closest approximation. This holds true both of the most vivid pictorial expressions in poetic works and of the most abstract terms denoting the innermost and most general components of the highest scholarship.

The second consideration that changes true translation into an activity radically different from mere interpreting is the following: Whenever the word is not completely bound by obvious objects or external facts it merely has to express, wherever the speaker is thinking more or less independently and, therefore, wants to express himself, he stands in a double relationship to language, and what he says will be understood correctly only insofar as that relationship is perceived correctly. On the one hand, every man is in the power of the language he speaks, and all his thinking is a product thereof. He cannot think anything with great precision that would lie outside the limits of language; the shape of his concepts, the nature and the limits of the way in which they can be connected, is prescribed for him by the language in which he is born and educated—intellect and imagination are bound by it. Yet on the other hand, every freely thinking, mentally self-employed human being shapes his own language. For in what other way—except precisely by means of these influences—would it have developed and grown from its first raw state to its more perfect elaboration in scholarship and art? In this sense, therefore, it is the living power of the individual that creates new forms by means of the plastic material of language, at first only for the immediate purpose of communicating a passing consciousness; yet now more, now less of it remains behind in the language, is taken up by others, and reaches out, a shaping force. It might even be said that a person deserves to be heard beyond his immediate environment only to the extent to which he influences language. Any verbal text soon dies away of necessity, if it can be reproduced by a thousand organs in a form that is always the same; only that text can and may endure longer that constitutes a new element in the life of a language itself. Therefore, each free and higher speech needs to be understood twice, once out of the spirit of the language of whose elements it is composed, as a living representation bound and defined by that spirit and conceived out of it in the speaker, and once out of the speaker's emotions, as his action, as produced and explicable only out of his own being. Indeed, any speech of this kind is understood, in the higher sense of the word, only when these two relationships have been perceived together and in their true relation to each other, so that we know which of the two dominates on the whole or in individual parts. We understand the spoken word as an act of the speaker only when we feel at the same time where and how the power of language has taken hold of him, where in its current the lightning of thought has uncoiled, snakelike, where and how the roving imagination has been held firm in its forms. We understand the spoken word as a product of language and as an expression of its spirit only when we feel that only a Greek, for instance, could think and speak in that way, that only this particular language could operate in a human mind this way, and when we feel at the same time that only this man could think and speak in the Greek fashion in this way, that only he could seize and shape the language in this manner, that only his living possession of the riches of language reveals itself like this, an alert sense for measure and the euphony that belongs to him alone, a power of thinking and shaping that is peculiarly his. If understanding in this field is difficult, even in the same language and the author's proper nature, how much more will it not be a high art when one speaks of the products of a distant and foreign language! Whoever has mastered this art of understanding through the most diligent cultivation of a language, through precise knowledge of the whole historical life of a nation and through the living representation of single works and their authors, he and he alone may wish to lay open the same understanding of the masterpieces of art and scholarship to his contemporaries and compatriots. But the risks accumulate when he prepares himself for his task, when he wishes to define his goals more accurately and he surveys the means at his disposal. Should he resolve to bring two people who are so fully separated from each other as the man who speaks his own language, but not that of the author, and the author himself—to bring these two into a relationship so immediate as the one that exists between an author and his original reader? Or does he merely want to lay open for his readers the same understanding and the same pleasure he himself enjoys, with the traces of hardship it carries and the feeling of the strange that remains mixed into it. How can he achieve the second, let alone the first, with the means at his disposal? If his readers are to understand, they must perceive the spirit of the language that was the author's own and be able to see his peculiar way of thinking and feeling; and to realize these two aims the translator can offer them nothing but his own language, which at no point fully corresponds to the other, and his own person, whose understanding of his author is now more, now less clear, and whose admiration and approval of him is now greater, now less. Does not translation, considered in this way, seem a foolish enterprise? That is why people, in despair at not reaching this goal, or, if you prefer, before they had reached the stage at which all this could be clearly thought out, discovered two other methods of becoming acquainted with works in foreign languages, not with a view to gathering their real artistic or linguistic sense, but rather to fill a need and to contemplate spiritual art; in these methods some of these difficulties are forcibly removed, others slyly circumvented, but the concept of translation adduced here is completely abandoned. These two methods are paraphrase and imitation. Paraphrase strives to conquer the irrationality of languages, but only in a mechanical way. It says: Even if I do not find a word in my language that corresponds to a word in the original language, I still want to try to penetrate its value by adding both restrictive and expansive definitions. Thus it laboriously works itself through to an accumulation of empty particulars, caught between a troublesome too much and a painful too little. In this way it may possibly succeed in rendering the content with limited precision, but it totally abandons the impression made by the original, for the living speech has been killed irrevocably, since everybody feels that it cannot originally have proceeded—as it is—from the feelings of a human being. The paraphrast treats the elements of the two languages as if they were mathematical signs that may be reduced to the same value by means of addition and subtraction, and neither the spirit of the language transformed nor that of the original language are given the opportunity to reveal themselves in this method. If, moreover, the paraphrase attempts to mark psychologically the traces of the conjunction of thoughts—where they are unclear and strive to lose themselves—by means of the interjected sentences that it inserts as so many landmarks, in this way it also tries to take the place of a commentary in the case of difficult compositions, and it can, therefore, even less be reduced to the concept of translation. Imitation, on the other hand, submits to the irrationality of languages; it grants that one cannot render a copy—which would correspond precisely to the original in all its parts—of a verbal artifact in another language, and that, given the difference between languages, with which so many other differences are connected, there is no option but to produce an imitation, a whole that is composed of parts obviously different from the parts of the original, but that would yet in its effects come as close to that whole as the difference in material allows. Such an imitation is now no longer that work itself, and in no way should the spirit of the original language be represented in it and be active in it; on the contrary, many things are exchanged for the foreignness that spirit has produced; a work of this kind should merely be, as much as possible and as far as the difference in language, morals, education allows, the same thing for its readers as the original was for its own—to save the analogy of impression one abandons the identity of the work. The imitator, therefore, does not attempt to bring the two parties—the writer and the reader of the imitation—together, because he does not think a direct relationship between them is possible; he merely wants to produce on the reader an impression similar to that received from the original by its contemporaries who spoke the same language. Paraphrase is more current in the domain of scholarship, imitation in that of art; and just as everyone confesses that a work of art loses its tone, its brilliance, its whole artistic essence in paraphrase, just so no one has as yet undertaken the foolish task of producing an imitation of a scholarly masterpiece that treats its content freely. Both methods fail, however, to satisfy the person who, permeated by the value of a foreign masterpiece, wishes to extend its operational radius to those who speak his language and keeps the stricter concept of translation in mind. Neither can therefore be considered more closely here, because they deviate from this concept; they are adduced only to mark the boundaries of the field that is our real concern.

But what of the genuine translator, who wants to bring those two completely separated persons, his author and his reader, truly together, and who would like to bring the latter to an understanding and enjoyment of the former as correct and complete as possible without inviting him to leave the sphere of his mother tongue—what roads are open to him? In my opinion there are only two. Either the translator leaves the author in peace, as much as possible, and moves the reader towards him; or he leaves the reader in peace, as much as possible, and moves the author towards him. The two roads are so completely separate from each other that one or the other must be followed as closely as possible, and that a highly unreliable result would proceed from any mixture, so that it is to be feared that author and reader would not meet at all. The difference between the two methods, and the fact that they stand in this relationship, must be immediately obvious. For in the first case, the translator tries, by means of his work, to replace for the reader the understanding of the original language that the reader does not have. He tries to communicate to the readers the same image, the same impression he himself has gained—through his knowledge of the original language—of the work as it stands; and in doing so he tries to move the readers towards his point of view, which is essentially foreign to them. But if the translation wants to let its Roman author, for instance, speak the way he would have spoken to Germans if he had been German, it does not merely move the author to where the translator stands, because to him he does not speak German, but Latin; rather it drags him directly into the world of the German readers and transforms him into their equal—and that, precisely, is the other case. The first translation will be perfect in its kind when one can say that if the author had learned German as well as the translator has learned Latin, he would not have translated the work he originally wrote in Latin any differently than the translator has done. But the second, which does not show the author as he himself would have translated but as he, as a German, would have originally written in German, can have no other measure of perfection than if it could be certified that, could all German readers be changed into experts and contemporaries of the author, the original would have meant exactly the same to them as the translation means to them now—that the author has changed himself into a German. This method is obviously meant by all those who use the formula that one should translate an author in such a way as he himself would have written in German. From this opposition it is immediately obvious how different the procedure must be in every detail, and how, if one tried to switch methods in the course of one and the same project, everything would become unintelligible as well as unpalatable. I merely would like to add that there cannot be a third method, with a precisely delimited goal, over and above these two. The two separated parties must either meet at a certain point in the middle, and that will always be the translator, or one must completely join up with the other; and of these two possibilities only the first belongs to the field of translation; the other would be realized if, in our case, the German readers totally mastered Latin, or rather if that language totally mastered them to the extent that it actually transformed them. Whatever is said about translation following the letter and translation following the sense, faithful translation and free translation, and whatever other expressions may have gained currency: Even though there are supposedly various methods, they must be reducible to the two methods mentioned above—though if we want to talk about virtues and mistakes in this context, the faithful translation that follows the sense, or the translation that is too free or too literal will not be the same according to one method as it is according to the other. It is therefore my intention to put aside all problems related to this matter, which have been discussed among specialists, and to observe only the most general features of these two methods in order to show what the peculiar advantages and disadvantages of each are, as well as the limits of their applicability, and in what respect each best attains the goal of translation. After such a general survey, two things would remain to be done to which this essay is the introduction only. A set of rules could be designed for the two methods, taking into consideration the different genres of speech, and the best attempts that have been made according to either point of view could be compared and judged; this would clarify matters even more. But I must leave both tasks to others or at least to another occasion.

The method that tries to give the reader the impression he would obtain as a German from reading the original work in the original language must, of course, first define what kind of understanding of the original language it wants to imitate. For there is one kind it should not imitate and one kind it cannot imitate. The first is a schoollike type of understanding, which laboriously bungles itself through separate parts, possessed by an attitude close to loathing, and which therefore never gains a clear overview of the whole, a living comprehension of its connections. When the more educated part of a nation has, as a whole, no experience of a more intimate penetration into foreign languages, let those who have progressed beyond this be saved by their good genius from trying to produce this kind of translation. For if they wanted to take their own understanding as a measure, they themselves would be little understood and have little impact, but if their translation were to represent common understanding, their ungainly work could not be shoved off the stage fast enough. In such a time, free imitations should first awaken and sharpen the desire for the foreign, and paraphrases prepare a more general understanding, to open the way for future translations. But there is another understanding, which no translator is able to imitate. Let us think of those wonderful people as nature produces every so often, as if to show that it is also capable of destroying the barriers of the common in iso-lated cases: people who feel such a peculiar kinship with a foreign existence that they completely live and think in a foreign language and its products, and while they are totally occupied with a for-eign world, they let their own language and their own world be-come totally foreign. Or let us think of those people who are, as it were, destined to represent the power of language in its totality and for whom all languages that they can attain in any way have the same value; in fact, they dress up in them as if they had been born into them. These people have reached a point at which the value of translation becomes nil, for since there is not even the slightest influence of the mother tongue in their perception of for-eign works, and since they by no means become conscious of their understanding in their mother tongue, but are immediately and totally at home in the original language itself, they also do not feel any incommensurability between their thinking and the language in which they read; it is therefore obvious that no translation can reach or portray their understanding. And just as it would be like pouring water into the sea or even into wine, if one were to trans-late for them, just so they are wont to smile with sympathy from their great height—and rightly so—the attempts made in this field. For if the audience for which translations are made were their equal, then, of course, we would not have to go to all this trouble. Translation, therefore, relates to a state of affairs in between these two extremes, and the translator must therefore take as his aim to give his reader the same image and the same delight that the read-ing of the work in the original language would afford any reader educated in such a way that we call him, in the better sense of the word, the admirer and the expert, the type of reader who is fa-miliar with the foreign language while it yet always remains for-eign to him: He no longer has to think every single part in his mother tongue, as schoolboys do, before he can grasp the whole, but he is still conscious of the difference between that language and his mother tongue, even where he enjoys the beauty of a for-eign work in total peace. Granted, the definition and the opera-tional radius of this type of translation remain unsettled enough, even after we have settled this point. We can only observe this: As the desire to translate can originate only when a certain ability for intercourse with foreign languages is widespread among the educated part of the population, just so the art will develop and the aim be set higher and higher, the more love and knowledge of foreign products of the spirit spread and increase among those elements of the population who have exercised and trained their ears without specializing in the knowledge of languages. But at the same time we cannot hide from ourselves the fact that the more readers are predisposed towards this kind of translation, the higher the difficulties of the enterprise pile up, all the more so if efforts are concentrated on the most characteristic products of a nation's art and scholarship, which are the most important objects for the translator. For as language is a historical fact, there can be no right sense for it without a sense of history. Languages are not invented, and all arbitrary work in them and on them is stupid; but they are gradually discovered, and scholarship and art are the powers through which this discovery is promoted and brought to fulfillment. Every excellent spirit in whom a part of the ideas of a nation shapes itself in a peculiar way in one of those two forms works in language and influences it to that end, and his works must, therefore, also contain part of that language's history. This presents the translator of scholarly work with great, indeed often insurmountable, difficulties, for whoever reads an excellent work of that kind in the original language will not easily overlook its influence on language, provided he is equipped with sufficient knowledge. He notices which words, which combinations, still appear to him in the first splendor of novelty; he observes how they insinuate themselves into the language through the special needs of the author's spirit and his expressive power; and this type of observation very essentially determines the impression he derives. It is therefore the task of translation to transplant that very same impression into its reader; otherwise he loses part of what was intended for him—often a very important part. But how can this be achieved? To start with particulars: How often will a new word in the original best correspond to one that is old and used in our language, so that the translator would have to replace it with a foreign ingredient, and therefore would have to move into the field of imitation if he wanted to reveal the language-shaping aspect of the work? How often, when he can render the new by means of the new, will the word that is closest in etymology and derivation not render the sense most faithfully, and he will nonetheless have to awaken other connotations if he does not want to obscure the immediate connection? He will have to console himself with the thought that he can make good his omissions where the author did use old and well-known words, and that he will therefore achieve in general what he is unable to achieve in every particular case. But if one considers in its totality the word-shaping work produced by a master, his use of related words and roots of words in a great number of interrelated writings: How does the translator propose to find a happy solution here, since the system of concepts and their signs in his language is totally different from that of the original language, and since roots of words do not cover each other in parallel, but rather cut through each other in the most amazing directions? It is therefore impossible for the translator's use of language to be as coherent as that of his author. In this case he will have to be content to achieve in particular what he cannot achieve in general. He will reach an understanding with his readers that they will not think of the other writings as stringently as the readers of the original would, but rather consider each one on its own, and that they should in fact praise him if he manages to salvage similarity with regard to the more important objects in particular writings, or even in parts of them only, so that one single word does not acquire a number of totally different representatives, or that a colorful variety reigns in the translation where the original has strictly related expressions throughout. These difficulties reveal themselves for the most part in the field of scholarship; there are others, and they are by no means smaller in size, in the field of poetry and more artistic prose, in which the musical element of language, which becomes apparent in rhythm and change of tone, also has a specific and higher meaning. Everyone feels that the finest spirit, the highest magic or art in the most perfect products is lost, or even destroyed, when this is not taken into account. Hence, what a sensible reader of the original observes as peculiar in this respect, as intentional, as influencing tone and mood of feeling, as decisive for the imitative and musical accompaniment of speech, that will also have to be translated by our translator. But how often—indeed it is almost a miracle if one does not have to say always—will rhythmical and melodic fidelity not be locked in irreconcilable combat with dialectic and grammatical fidelity! How difficult it is to avoid sacrificing something, now here, now there, while swinging to and fro, and to avoid what is often exactly the wrong result. How difficult it is for the translator even to restore to his author impartially, when he has occasion for it, what he has had to take away from him before, and not even unconsciously to fall into a persistent one-sidedness because his inclination goes out to one artistic element above the others. For if his taste in works of art gravitates more towards ethical subject matter and the way in which it is treated, he will be less inclined to see where he has failed to do justice to the metrical and musical elements of the form, and he will, instead of thinking of replacing them, be satisfied with a translation that is more and more diluted in the easy and the semiparaphrastic. Should the translator on the other hand happen to be a metrician or a musician he will put the logical elements last in order to grasp the musical element completely, and as he sinks deeper and deeper into this one-sidedness his work will become less and less felicitous, and on comparing his translation in general with the original, one will find that he comes closer and closer—without noticing it—to that schoolboyish inadequacy that loses the whole in the parts; a totally different overall impression must be the result if he changes what is light and naturally rendered in one language into heavy and objectionable expressions in the other merely for love of the material similarity of rhythm and tone.

Still other difficulties appear when the translator reflects on his relationship with the language he is writing in and on the relationship of his translation with his other works. If we except those miraculous masters to whom many languages are as one, or to whom a learned language is even more natural than their mother tongue—those for whom one cannot translate, as has been said before—all others retain a sense of the strange, no matter how fluently they read a foreign language. How should the translator transfer this feeling—that they have something foreign before them—to the readers whom he offers a translation in their mother tongue? Of course you will say that the answer to this riddle was given long ago, and that the problem has often been solved more than adequately for our case, for the more closely the translation follows the turns taken by the original, the more foreign it will seem to the reader. That may well be true, though it is easy enough to ridicule this position in general. But if this pleasure is not to be purchased too cheaply, if the most skillful is not to be thrown out in one bath with the worst and the most schoolboyish, it will have to be admitted that an indispensable requirement of this method of translation is a feeling for language that is not only not colloquial, but also causes us to suspect that it has not grown in total freedom but rather has been bent towards a foreign likeness; and it must be admitted that to do this artfully and with moderation, without disadvantage to one's language or oneself, is probably the greatest difficulty our translator has to overcome. The attempt seems to be the strangest form of humiliation a writer who is not a bad writer could impose upon himself. Who would not like to permit his mother tongue to stand forth everywhere in the most universally appealing beauty each genre is capable of? Who would not rather sire children who are their parents' pure image, and not bastards? Who would willingly force himself to appear in movements less light and elegant than those he is capable of, to seem brutal and stiff, at least at times, and to shock the reader as much as is necessary to keep him aware of what he is doing? Who would put up with being considered clumsy by trying to keep as close to the foreign language as his own language allows? Who would suffer being accused, like those parents who abandon their children to acrobats, of bending his mother tongue to foreign and unnatural dislocations instead of skillfully exercising it in its own natural gymnastics? Finally, who would like to be smiled at in pity by the greatest experts and masters who could not understand his laborious and ill-considered German if they did not supplement it with their Greek and Latin. These are the sacrifices every translator must needs take upon himself, these are the dangers he exposes himself to when he does not observe the finest line in his attempts to keep the tone of the language foreign—and he never escapes from them altogether because everyone draws that line a little differently. If he also thinks of the inevitable influence of habit in addition to this, he may fear that much that is raw, that does not really belong, will insinuate itself into his free and original production via translation, and that habit will somewhat blunt in him the tender sense of the natural feeling for language. And should he think of the great host of imitators and of the slowness and mediocrity that reign among his writing audience, he will be horrified at the amount of unlawfulness, of genuine stiffness and clumsiness, of linguistic corruption of all kinds perpetrated by others, and yet he will probably have to answer for it, for no doubt only the best and the worst will not attempt to derive a false advantage from his endeavors. This type of complaint—that such a translation must of necessity be harmful to the purity of language and its peaceful development—has often been heard. Even if we want to put it to one side with the consolation that there will be advantages, too, to counterbalance these disadvantages, and that, since all good is mixed with evil, true wisdom is to acquire as much as possible of the former and to assume the least possible of the latter, some consequences must, in any case, be drawn from this difficult task of representing what is foreign in one's mother tongue. First, this method of translating cannot thrive equally well in all languages, but only in those that are not the captives of too strict a bond of classical expression outside of which all is reprehensible. Such restrained languages should expect a broadening of their sphere when they are spoken by foreigners who need more than their mother tongue; they will be perfectly suited to this. They may incorporate foreign works by means of imitations or even translations of the other type; they must, however, relinquish this type to languages that are freer, in which innovations and deviations are tolerated to a greater extent, in such a way that their accumulation may, under certain circumstances, generate a certain characteristic mode of expression. Another obvious consequence is that this type of translation has no value whatsoever if it is practiced only by chance and in isolated instances in a given language. For that obviously falls short of the aim that a foreign spirit should blow toward the reader; on the contrary, if he is to be given a notion, albeit a very weak one, of the original language and of what the work owes to it, so that his failure to understand that language is somewhat made up for, he must not only be given a very vague impression that what he reads does not sound completely familiar; he must also be made to feel that it sounds like something different yet distinct. But that will only be possible if he is able to make massive comparisons. If he has read something he knows has been translated from other modern languages and something else that has been translated from classical languages, and if they have been translated in the sense described above, he will acquire an ear with which to distinguish between the old and the newer. But he will

have to have read much more if he is to be able to distinguish
between works of Greek and Roman origin or Italian and Spanish.
And yet even this is hardly the highest goal; on the contrary, the
reader of the translation will become the equal of the better reader
of the original only when he is able first to acquire an impression
of the particular spirit of the author as well as that of the language
in the work and by and by to develop a definite grasp of it. He
can do so only through his powers of observation, but a much
greater volume of comparisons is indispensable if he is to be able
to exercise those powers. These comparisons are not available if
only isolated works of masters of isolated genres are sporadically
translated into a language. In this way even the most educated
readers can achieve only a very deficient knowledge of what is
foreign by means of translation, and it is inconceivable that they
would be able to reach any judgment of either the translation or
the original. This method of translation must therefore be applied
extensively, a transplantation of whole literatures into a language,
and it makes sense and is of value only to a nation that has the
definite inclination to appropriate what is foreign. Isolated works
of this type are of value only as precursors of a more generally
evolving and developing willingness to adopt this procedure. If
they fail to arouse this, things will work against them in the language and the spirit of the time; they can then appear only as
mistaken attempts and have little or no success in themselves. But
even if this way should prevail, it should not complacently be expected that a work of this nature, be it ever so excellent, will gather
general approval. Since many factors have to be considered and
many difficulties resolved, it is inevitable that different opinions
should develop as to which parts of the task should be considered
of primary and which of secondary importance. Thus different
schools, so to speak, will arise among the masters, and different
parties among the audience as followers of those schools, and even
though the method is basically the same, different translations of
the same work, undertaken from different points of view, will be
able to exist side by side, and we shall not really be able to say
that one is, as a whole, more or less perfect than another; only
certain parts will be more successful in one version and others in
another, and not until they are all taken together and related to
each other and it becomes clear how one translator attaches par-

ticular value to this approximation to the original and another to that, or how one translator exercises particular forbearance towards what is native, not until then will they completely exhaust their task, for each one in itself will always be of relative and subjective value only.

These are the difficulties that beset this method and the imperfections essentially inherent in it. But once we have conceded them, we must acknowledge the attempt itself and cannot deny its merit. It rests on two conditions: that understanding foreign works should be a thing known and desired and that the native language should be allowed a certain flexibility. Where these conditions are fulfilled, this type of translation becomes a natural phenomenon, influencing the whole evolution of a culture and giving a certain pleasure as it is given a certain value.

But what of the opposite method, which does not expect any labor or exertion on the part of the reader, aspiring to bring the foreign author into his immediate proximity as if by magic and to show the work as it would have been if the author himself had originally written it in the reader's language. This requirement has not seldom been formulated as the one a true translator would have to fulfill and as being of a much higher and more perfect nature when compared to the other; isolated attempts have been made, even masterpieces perhaps, which have clearly taken this for their goal. Let us now find out what they are like, and whether it would perhaps not be a good thing if this procedure, which has without a doubt been more rarely applied up to now, were to be followed more frequently and to supplant the other, which is of a dubious nature and unsatisfactory in many ways.

It is immediately obvious that the translator's language has nothing at all to fear from this method. The first rule he must follow is not to allow himself anything—considering the relationship in which his work stands to a foreign language—which would not also be allowed in an original work of the same genre in his native tongue. Indeed, it is his duty above all to observe at least the same care for the purity and perfection of language, to strive after the same light and natural style for which his author is famous in the original language. It is equally true that, if we want to make clear to our compatriots what an author meant for his language, we cannot think of a better formula than to introduce him speaking in a way such as we imagine he would have spoken in ours, especially when the level of development at which he found his language is similar to the level our language happens to have reached. We can imagine, in a certain sense, how Tacitus would have spoken if he had been a German, or, more accurately, how a German would speak who meant the same to our language as Tacitus to his—and good luck to him who is able to imagine this so vividly that he can actually make him speak. But whether this would happen if he let him say the same things Roman Tacitus said in the Latin language is another question that cannot easily be answered in the affirmative. For it is one thing to grasp correctly the influence a man has exerted on his native language and somehow to show it and quite another to want to know how his thoughts and their expression would have shaped themselves if he had originally been wont to think and express himself in another language. Can anyone who is convinced of the internal and essential identity of thought and expression—and the whole art of all understanding of speech and therefore also of all translation is based on this conviction—can such a person want to sever a man from the language he was born into and think that a man, or even just his train of thought, could be one and the same in two languages? Or if they are, in a certain way, different, can he presume to dissolve speech down to its very core, separate from that the part played by language, and let this core, as if through a new and almost chemical process, combine with the essence and the power of another language? To do this, one would obviously have to separate neatly everything in a man's written work that is influenced by whatever he may have spoken and heard in his mother tongue from childhood on, after which one would have to add, so to speak, to that same man's naked, peculiar way of thought—perceived as directed towards a certain object—whatever would have been the influence of whatever he might have spoken and heard in the foreign language from the beginning of his life onwards, or from his first acquaintance with it, until he had become capable of original thinking and expression in it. This will be possible only when it becomes possible to combine organic products successfully by means of a chemical process. Indeed it might be said that the aim of translating in a way such as the author would have originally written in the language of the translation is not only out of reach, but also null and void in itself, for whoever acknowledges the shaping power of language, as it is one with the peculiar character of a nation, must concede that every most excellent human being has acquired his knowledge, as well as the possibility of expressing it, in and through language, and that no one therefore adheres to his language mechanically as if he were strapped into it, to use a superficial simile, and that no one could change languages in his thinking as he pleases the way one can easily change a span of horses and replace it with another; rather everyone produces original work in his mother tongue only, so that the question cannot even be raised of how he would have written his works in another language. Everyone will of course adduce two cases against this, and they occur often enough.

First, there obviously is such a thing as the ability to write in languages other than one's native tongue, indeed even to philosophize in them and to write poetry in them—not just in isolated exceptions, even though these occur as well, but also in general. Why then should one not, to acquire a more reliable yardstick, confer this ability, in thought, on every author one wants to translate? Because this ability is of such a nature that it is present only in those situations in which the same thing could not have been said at all in the native language, or at least not by the same person. If we go back in time to the point where the Romance languages began to develop, who can say which language was native to people at that moment? And who will choose to deny that Latin was more of a mother tongue than the vernacular for those who were drawn to scholarly aspirations? This goes much deeper for isolated needs and activities of the mind. As long as the mother tongue has not been developed for them, that language from which those directions of the spirit have communicated themselves to an evolving nation remains a partial mother tongue. Grotius and Leibniz could not write philosophy in Dutch or in German, at least not without becoming totally different people. Indeed, even when that root is completely dried out and the shoot has been completely torn off the old trunk, whoever is not at the same time a being who shapes and uproots language will necessarily often adhere to a foreign tongue, either by choice or because he is forced to do so by subordinate causes. Our great king [Frederick II of Prussia] received all his finer and higher thoughts in a foreign language, which he had most intimately appropriated for this field. He was incapable of producing in German the literature and philosophy he produced in French. It is to be deplored that the great preference for England which dominated a part of the family could not have taken the direction of familiarizing him from childhood on with the English language, whose last golden age was then in bloom, and which is so much closer to German. But we may hope that he would have preferred to produce literature and philosophy in Latin, rather than in French, if he had enjoyed a strict scholarly education. Insofar as this is subject to particular conditions, insofar as people do not produce in just any foreign language but only in a definite one, and then only what they were not able to produce in their mother tongue, it does not prove anything in favor of a method of translation that wishes to show how someone would have written in another language what he has, in effect, written in his mother tongue.

But the second case, that of original reading and writing in a foreign language, seems to be more favorable to this method. For who will deny to our courtiers and diplomats that they have immediately thought in the same language whatever sweet nothings they let pass their lips in foreign tongues, without first translating them from poor old German in their mind? And as it is their claim to fame to be able to say these sweet nothings and dainty phrases with the same excellence in many tongues, they must of course think in all these languages with the same ease, and everyone will know how the other would have said in Italian what he has just said in French. But these speeches do not belong in the realm in which thoughts grow forcefully from the deep root of a particular language; they are more like the pepperwort that a man of ingenuity manages to grow on a white cloth, not in any soil. These speeches are neither the sacred seriousness of language nor its beautiful well-measured game; rather, as nations appear to mix in our time to a greater extent than they did before, the marketplace is everywhere and these are conversations of the marketplace, whether they are social or literary or political, and really do not belong in the translator's domain but rather in that of the interpreter. If these conversations are gathered together and put on paper, as sometimes happens, then that type of work that takes place totally in the light and lovely life, without opening up any depth of being or preserving any particular traits of a nation, can be translated according to those rules—but that type of work only, because only that type could just as well have been written in another language. And this rule should not apply beyond that, except possibly to the prefaces or introductions of deeper and more noble works that often belong entirely to the domain of light social life. But the more the special features of a nation and, perhaps even beyond that, the shape of a time long past adhere to the simple thoughts contained in a work and to the relationships between them, the more that rule simply loses its meaning. For as true as it is in many ways that a man is in a certain sense educated and a citizen of the world only through his knowledge of various languages, we must concede that just as we do not consider that type of world citizenship real that supplants love for one's country at critical moments, just so such a general love that desires to equate any language old or new with the national language for both colloquial and higher usage is not a true and really civilizing love in the field of languages. Just as a man must decide to belong to one country, he must adhere to one language, or he will float without any bearings above an unpleasant middle ground. It is right that even now Latin is being written among us as the language of officialdom, to keep alive the consciousness that this was the scholarly and sacred mother tongue of our ancestors; it is good that this should also happen in the field of the common European economy, to make commerce easier; but in that case, too, it will succeed only to the extent that the object is everything for such a representation and that one's own opinion and the way in which one combines objects count for very little. The same holds true for French. Whoever is forced to write such a language for official purposes will be very conscious of the fact that his thoughts are German in their initial origin and that he merely begins to translate them very early, while the embryo is still shaping itself; and whoever subjects himself to this for the sake of scholarship will find himself translating at ease, in an open and natural way, only where he feels himself totally in the power of the object. There is, of course, in addition to this also the writing of Latin or French as a free pastime, and if the object of this exercise were really to produce as well as in a foreign language as in his own and with the same originality, I would not hesitate to declare it to be an evil and magic art, like that of being someone's double, by means of which men not only attempted to ridicule the laws of nature, but also to confuse others. But this is not the case; rather this pastime is merely a refined game of mimicry with which to while away the hours pleasantly in the outer courts of scholarship and art. Production in a foreign language is not original; rather remembrance of a certain writer or even of the style of a certain period, which represents a general person, appears before the soul, so to speak, almost as a living outside image, and the imitation thereof guides production and defines it. This is also the reason why so rarely anything of real value comes into being in this way, except for imitative accuracy, and one can enjoy one's favorite piece all the more harmlessly because the person mimicked can be seen clearly enough everywhere. But if, contrary to nature and morality, someone has formally become a deserter to his mother tongue and given himself to another, it is not artificial and imputed scorn when he asserts that he cannot move in it any more; it is merely a justification he owes himself that his temperament is really a marvel of nature contrary to all rules and order, and a reassurance to others that at least he does not have a double emanation as ghosts do.

But we have dealt with what is strange at too great length, and it must have seemed as if we have been talking about writing in foreign languages instead of translating from them. The case is this: If it is not possible to write something in a foreign language worthy of—and in need of—translation as art, or if this is at least a rare and miraculous exception, we cannot set up as a rule for translation that it should imagine how the writer himself would have written precisely what he has written in the language of the translator, for there is no abundance of examples of bilingual authors from which an analogy could be drawn for the translator to follow; rather he will be left almost totally to his own imagination for all works that do not resemble light entertainment or commercial transactions. Indeed, what can be the objection if a translator were to tell a reader: Here is the book just as the author would have written it if he had written in German, and if the reader were to reply: I am much obliged to you, in the same way as if you had brought me the picture of the author just as he would have looked if his mother had conceived him with another father? For if the writer's particular spirit is the mother of works belonging to scholarship and art in a higher sense, his national language is the father. Artificialities, on the other hand, lay claim to secret insights that nobody has, and only as a game can one enjoy them without inhibition.

That the applicability of this method is severely limited, indeed that it is almost equal to zero in the field of translation, is borne out best when one views the insuperable difficulties that entangle it as far as isolated branches of scholarship and art are concerned. We must admit that there are in colloquial usage only a few words in a language that correspond completely to words in another, so that one might be used in all the cases in which the other is used and that one would produce exactly the same effect as the other in the same configuration; how much more true is this for all concepts, the more a philosophical essence is added to them, and hence it is most true of genuine philosophy. Here more than anywhere else every language, in spite of differing contemporary and successive opinions, contains within it a system of concepts which, precisely because they touch each other in the same language, because they connect and complement each other, are a *whole* whose isolated parts do not correspond to any in the system of other languages, not even if we except God and *is,* the original noun and the original verb. For even what is commonly held to be universal is illuminated and colored by language, though it may lie outside the boundaries of the particular. The wisdom of every individual must be dissolved in this system of language. Everyone partakes of what is there, and everyone helps to bring to light what is not yet there but prefigured. In this way only is the wisdom of the individual alive and can really rule his existence, which he completely summarizes in that language. If, therefore, the translator of a philosophical writer does not want to make the decision to bend the language of the translation as far as possible towards that of the original in order to communicate as far as possible an impression of the system of concepts developed in it, if he would rather make his author speak as if he had originally fashioned thoughts and speech in another language, what choice does he have, in view of the dissimilarity of elements in both languages: He must either paraphrase—in which case he fails to achieve his aim, for a paraphrase can never look like what has originally been produced in the same language—or he must transpose his author's entire knowledge and wisdom into the conceptual system of another language and therefore change all isolated parts, in which case it is hard to see how the wildest arbitrariness might be kept within bounds. Indeed, it should be said that no one who has even the slightest respect for philosophical endeavors can allow himself to be drawn into so loose a game. I leave it to Plato to justify my going on from the philosopher to the writer of comedies. This genre is, from the linguistic point of view, closest to the domain of colloquial conversation. The whole representation is alive in the morals of the people and the time, and those in turn mirror themselves perfectly, in the most lively way, in language. Lightness and naturalness in elegance are its prime virtue, and that is precisely the reason why the difficulties of translating according to the method we have just considered are immense. For any approximation to a foreign language is bound to harm those virtues of diction. If the translation wants to make a playwright speak as if he had originally written in its language, it will not be able to let him show many things because they are not native to its people and therefore also have no symbol in their language. In this case the translator must consequently either cut them out completely, and in so doing destroy the power and form of the whole, or else he must replace them. It is obvious that if the formula is faithfully followed in this field, it will either lead to pure imitation or to an even more clearly repulsive and confusing mixture of translation and imitation that cruelly bounces the reader back and forth like a ball between the foreign world and his own, between the author's wit and imagination and that of the translator; he will not derive any pure pleasure from this, but in the end he will certainly be left with enough dizziness and frustration. On the other hand the translator who follows the other method is not required to undertake such self-willed changes, because his reader must always remember that the author lived in a different world and wrote in a different language. He is bound only by the admittedly difficult art of supplying knowledge of this strange world in the shortest and most efficient way and letting the greater lightness and naturalness of the original shine through everywhere. These two examples taken from opposite extremes of art and scholarship show clearly how little the real aim of all translation, the unadulterated enjoyment of foreign works within the limits of the possible, can be achieved by means of a method that insists on breathing the spirit of a language alien to it into the translated work. Add to this that every language also has its own peculiarities of rhythm, for prose as well as for poetry, and that, once the fiction is to be established that the author could also have written in the translator's language, one would also have to let him appear in the rhythm of that language, which would disfigure his work even more and limit even further the knowledge of its particular character that translation provides.

This fiction, on which alone rests the theory of translation now under discussion, goes far beyond the aim of that activity. As seen from the first point of view, translation is a matter of necessity for a nation in which only a small minority of people are able to acquire sufficient knowledge of foreign languages, whereas a greater minority has a desire to enjoy foreign works. Should the latter be totally subsumed under the former, all translation would be useless, and it would be difficult to have anyone take on that thankless task. Not so from the second point of view. Translation has nothing to do with necessity; rather it is the labor of recklessness and lasciviousness. Let knowledge of foreign languages be as widespread as possible and let access to their noblest works be open to anyone who is competent; it would still be a miraculous endeavor, which would gather around itself more and more increasingly intrigued listeners, if someone were to promise to show us a work by Cicero or Plato in the way these authors would have written it directly in German at the present moment. And if someone were to bring us to the point that we would do this not only in our mother tongue but also in another, foreign language, he would obviously be a master of the difficult and almost impossible art of dissolving the spirits of languages into each other. One can see, however, that this would not be translation, strictly speaking, and that its goal would not be the most precise possible enjoyment of the works themselves; it would become more and more an imitation, and only he could truly enjoy such a work or piece of art who was already immediately and independently familiar with those authors. And the true aim could only be, in particular, to show a similar relationship in difficult languages between many expressions and combinations and certain inner features and, in general, to illuminate language with the particular spirit of a foreign master, but one who is completely separated and cut off from his own language. As the former is only an artificial and elegant game, and as the latter rests on a fiction that is almost impossible to put into practice, it is understandable why this type of translation is only sparingly applied in a few attempts which serve to demonstrate that it cannot be applied more widely. It is also understandable why only excellent masters who may venture the miraculous could work according to this method, only those who have already done their duty by the world and may therefore allow themselves to be drawn into an exciting and somewhat dangerous game are entitled to do so. One understands all the more easily why the masters who feel capable of trying such a thing look down with a certain compassion on the busyness of those other translators. For they believe that they alone are engaged in that beautiful and fine art, and any others seem to be much closer to the interpreter insofar as they, too, serve a need, albeit a slightly nobler one. Such interpreters seem to be all the more deserving of pity since they invest much more labor and art than could possibly be justified in a subordinate and thankless business. Hence the masters are always ready to advise that one should get by with paraphrases as much as possible, the way interpreters do in difficult or dubious cases, and that one should not produce this type of translation.

Well then? Should we share this opinion and follow this advice? The ancients obviously translated little in that most real sense, and most moderns, deterred by the difficulties of true translation, also seem to be satisfied with imitation and paraphrase. Who would want to contend that nothing has ever been translated into French from the classical languages or from the Germanic languages! But even though we Germans are perfectly willing to listen to this advice, we should not follow it. An inner necessity, in which a peculiar calling of our people expresses itself clearly enough, has driven us to translating *en masse;* we cannot go back and we must go on. Just as our soil itself has no doubt become richer and more fertile and our climate milder and more pleasant only after much transplantation of foreign flora, just so we sense that our language, because we exercise it less owing to our Nordic sluggishness, can thrive in all its freshness and completely develop its own power only through the most many-sided contacts with what is foreign. And, coincidentally, our nation may be destined, because of its respect for what is foreign and its nature, which is one of mediation, to carry all the treasures of foreign arts and scholarship, together with its own, in its language, to unite them into a great historical whole, so to speak, which would be preserved in the center and heart of Europe, so that, with the help of our language, whatever beauty the most different times have brought forth can be enjoyed by all people, as purely and perfectly as is possible for a foreigner. This appears indeed to be the real historical aim of translation in general, as we are used to it now. To this end, however, only the method we have discussed first should be followed. Art must learn, as much as possible, to overcome its difficulties, something we have not tried to hide. We have made a good beginning, but the greater part of the work still remains to be done. Many exercises and attempts must be gone through first, in this field as in any other, before a few excellent works come into being, and much shines at the outset that is later supplanted by what is better. The extent to which individual artists have already in part overcome these difficulties and in part skirted them in a felicitous way is evident in many examples. And even if there are those working in the field who are less able, we should not fear great harm to our language from their endeavors. For it must be established at the outset that there is, in a language in which translation is practiced to such an extent, a field proper to translators, and that much should be allowed to them that probably ought not to emerge elsewhere. Whoever further transplants these innovations without authorization will find a few imitators only, or none, and if we want to close the account after not too short a period of time, we can rely on the assimilating process of language to discard again whatever has been accepted only because of a passing need and does not really correspond to its nature. On the other hand, we should not fail to acknowledge that much of what is powerful and beautiful in our language has in part developed through translations or has in part been drawn from obscurity by them. We speak too little and make, proportionately, too much conversation, and it cannot be denied that for quite a while our style had evolved too far in that direction and that translation has contributed more than a little to the reestablishment of a stricter style. If ever the time should come in which we have a public life out of which develops a sociability of greater merit and truer to language and in which free space is gained for the talent of the orator, we shall be less in need of translation for the development of language. If only that time might come before we have rounded with dignity the whole circle of difficulties in translation.

Translated by André Lefevere

School for Aesthetics

Jean Paul Friedrich Richter

Course I. On Poetry in General

1. *Its Definitions*

Nothing can actually be defined except a definition itself; and a false one teaches as much about our subject as a true one. The essence of poetic presentation, like all life, can be represented only by a second poetic presentation; one cannot use *colors* to paint the *light* which itself first brings them into existence. Even mere similes can often express more than literal explanations. Thus, "Poetry is the only *second* world in this world," or, "As singing is to speaking, so poetry is to prose; the singing voice (according to Haller) is higher even at its lowest pitch than the highest tone of speech; as the singing tone itself is music, even without beat, melodic sequence, or harmonic support, so there is poetry even without meter, dramatic or epic sequence, or lyric power." At least images would mirror kindred life better than do dead concepts, though differently for every man. For nothing brings out better the individuality of men than the effect which poetry has on them. Hence, there will be just as many definitions of poetry as readers and listeners.

Only the spirit of a whole book—may heaven grant this book such a spirit—can contain the true definition. If, however, you want a short, literal one, then the old Aristotelian definition, according to which the essence of poetry consists in a beautiful (spiritual) imitation of nature, is negatively the best, because it excludes two extremes: poetic nihilism and materialism. It can become

31

positive, however, only through a closer determination of what *beautiful* or *spiritual* imitation actually is.

2. Poetic Nihilists

It follows from the lawless, capricious spirit of the present age, which would egotistically annihilate the world and the universe in order to clear a space merely for free *play* in the void, and which tears off the *bandage* of its wounds as a *bond,* that this age must speak scornfully of the imitation and study of nature. When the history of an age gradually becomes unimportant to a historian and religion and patriotism are lost, then the arbitrariness of egotism must stumble at last on the hard, sharp commandments of reality. Then egotism prefers to flee into the desert of fantasy, where it finds no law to follow except its own narrower and pettier ones for the construction of rhyme and assonance. In an age when God has set like the sun, soon afterwards the world too passes into darkness. He who scorns the universe respects nothing more than himself and at night fears only his own creations. Is not nature now spoken of as if this creation of a Creator, in which the painter himself is only a dot of color, were hardly fit to be the picture nail or the frame for some small painted creation of a creature? As if what is greatest were not precisely the infinite! Is not history the highest tragedy and comedy? If the scorners of reality would only first bring before our souls the starry skies, the sunsets, the waterfalls, the lofty glaciers, the characters of a Christ, an Epaminondas, the Catos, even with the petty accidents which confuse our sense of reality, as the great poet does through bold details in drawing his characters! Then indeed they would have produced the poem of poems and would have repeated God. The *Universe* is the highest, boldest word of the language and the rarest thought; most people see in the universe only the marketplace of their own narrow life, in the story of eternity only their own town history.

Who has pursued and illuminated reality in its deepest valleys, even down to the tiny worm, more than the twin stars of poetry, Homer and Shakespeare? As sculpture and the graphic arts forever work in the school of nature, so the most fertile poets have always been the most tenacious, the most industrious children in delivering to other children the portrait of mother nature with new resemblances. If anyone wants to conceive of a supreme poet, he should grant some genius a metempsychosis through all nations and all times and conditions and let him sail around all the coasts of the world. What nobler, bolder drawings of its infinite form he would sketch and bring home with him! The poets of the ancients were merchants and warriors before they were singers; great epic poets especially have always had to practice holding the helm strongly against the waves of life before they take pencil in hand to describe the journey.[1] Thus Camoëns, Dante, Milton, and others; Klopstock is the only exception, almost more as proof than as refutation of the rule. How Shakespeare and even more Cervantes had to be harrowed and plowed and furrowed by life before the seed of their poetic flower burst out into growth! The first school for poets which Goethe attended was composed, according to his autobiography, of craftsmen's shops, painters' studios, coronation halls, imperial archives, and everything at Frankfurt fair time. And Novalis, a collateral and elective relative to the poetic nihilists, or at least their liege cousin, presents the most solid character in his novel precisely when he describes for us the miner from Bohemia, because he himself had been one.

With equal talents, even the most slavish copier of nature will give us more (even if only illuminated capital letters) than the arbitrary painter who paints ether upon ether with ether. Genius is distinguished by the fact that it sees nature more richly and more completely, just as man is distinguished from the half-blind and the half-deaf animal; with every genius a new nature is created for us, in that he further unveils the old one. Every poetic representation admired by successive ages is distinguished by some freshly sensuous individuality and manner of perception. All study of reality—astronomy, botany, landscape gardening, and all other sciences—profitable to the poet; in Goethe's poetic landscapes are reflected those he painted. Beneath the clear transparent glass of the poet, the underlay of dark life is necessary before he can mirror the world. Mental offspring resemble the physical children

---

[1] Strangely enough, the heroic poets have had to die far too often in life's storms away from land and harbor; into the lives of Camoëns, Tasso, Milton, Dante, Homer very little sunlight fell. But many *tragic* poets have been the happiest of men—first Sophocles, for example, then Lope de Vega, Shakespeare, Voltaire, and so on.

whom ancient Romans had touch the *earth,* believing that they would thus learn to *speak.*

Because of their inexperience, young people find the imitation of nature a difficult task. Until we can study nature from all sides, we are one-sidedly dominated by the individual parts. The young imitate nature, but only a part, not the whole, not its free spirit with a free spirit. The novelty of their own feelings appears to them as a novelty in the objects, and through the former they think to give you the latter. They therefore throw themselves either into the unknown and unnamed, into foreign lands and times represented without individuality, into Greece and the Orient,[2] or by preference into the lyrical. For here no nature is to be imitated except that which they bring within themselves; here a daub of color draws its own outline. With individuals as with peoples, coloring precedes drawing, *hieroglyphic* precedes *alphabetic* writing. Youths who write poetry, these neighbors of the nihilists, such as Novalis or the writers of novels about art, eagerly seek to portray a poet or painter or other artist as hero. In the broad all-inclusive bosom and capacity of the artist, they can properly deposit everything, their own hearts with each personal opinion and feeling. They would rather give us a poet than a poem.

Now if the flattery of conceit is added to the weakness of youth, and if the vacuous young man can make himself believe that his innate lyricism is a higher form of romanticism, then through neglect of all reality—except the limited one within himself—he will flutter away in a rarefied and flimsy fashion into the wilds of lawlessness; and like the atmosphere, he will lose himself at the greatest height in the impotent and formless void.

Nothing is so disadvantageous to a young poet as to read a powerful poet frequently; the best epic of the latter melts away into a lyric in the former. Indeed, I believe it is healthier for a youth to have a job than to read a book—although in later years the reverse is true. The Ideal blends most easily with any ideal, or one generality with another. The blooming young man draws na-

---

[2] According to Kant, the formation of heavenly bodies is easier to deduce than that of a caterpillar. The same is true for the celebration of them in song; and a particular provincial is harder to represent poetically than a nebulous hero from the Orient; just as, according to Scaliger (*de Subtil. Ad. Card. exerc. 359* Sec. 13), an angel more easily acquires a body than does a mouse (because he needs less).

ture from a poem, instead of the poem out of nature. The consequence is what stares at us out of all the book stores: colored shadows instead of bodies, not even *echoing* but only reechoing images of original images. The cut-up pictures of others are arranged as tesserae for new pictures. Poetic images are now used as icons were used in the Middle Ages, from which one scratched away flakes of color, to be taken in sacramental wine.

3. Poetic Materialists

But is it then all one, whether you imitate *nature* or imitate *according* to nature? Is repetition imitation? Actually, the principle of copying nature faithfully hardly has any meaning. Since it is impossible to exhaust her individuality with any one copy, and since a copy must always choose which traits it leaves out or includes, the question of imitation becomes the new question: Following what law, by the hand of what artist, is nature raised into the realm of poetry?

Even the meanest copier of reality recognizes that universal history is no epic (although quite possibly an epic on a higher level), that even a true, good love letter does not fit well into a novel, and that there is a difference between the landscapes of the poet and the tourist's measurements of meadows and heights. We all easily upon occasion engage in normal conversation with other people; yet nothing is rarer than an author who can write a lifelike dialogue. Why is a real military camp not the equivalent of Wallenstein's camp as described by Schiller, though his lacks the charming completeness of reality?

Hermes' novels have almost everything one could ask for in a poetic *body:* knowledge of the world, truth, imagination, form, delicacy, language. But because the poetic *spirit* is lacking, they are excellent antinovels or antidotes to the incidental poison of novels. You would have to own excellent investments and have much ready cash to laugh at poverty as it is described in his works. But such description is quite unpoetic. Unlike reality, which achieves a distribution of the flowers of prosaic justice through infinite spaces and times, poetry must grant her favors within limitations. She is the only goddess of peace on earth; she is the angel who leads us, if but for a few hours, out of our prisons up to the stars; like Achilles' lance, she must heal every wound she herself

inflicts.[3] Would anything be more dangerous than a poet who en-
closed *our* reality completely in *his own,* and thus put us in a
double prison? Because this novelistic preacher Hermes pursues
moral education with an antipoetic spirit, he misses this goal too,
and even jeopardizes and undermines morality (in the novel *For
Noble Daughters,* for example, and in the torture story of the repulsive moral self-incarcerator, Mr. Kerker).

Yet the false stereotype of reality does provide some pleasure,
partly because it teaches us, partly because people so gladly see
their own condition brought to paper and thus removed from confusing personal proximity to a clarifying objective distance. If one
records one day in a man's life with complete fidelity, without
embellishments, in pen and ink alone, and then lets that man read
the record over, he will approve it and feel soothed as if in a bath
of tepid waves. Even the daily life of another person will win
approval, if presented in a poem. But the poet—even the comic
poet—cannot take any real character from nature without transforming it, as the day of judgment does the living, for hell or for
heaven. If some unworldly, utterly strange character existed, as a
unique person without any symbolic similarity to other men, no
poet could use or describe him.

Even humorous characters of Shakespeare are general and symbolic, though this aspect is hidden beneath the stuffing and con-
volutions of humor.

Allow me a few more examples of unpoetic repeaters, mimick-
ing the great world clock. Brockes's *Earthly Pleasure in God* is
such a faithful *camera obscura* of external nature that a true poet
might use it as a tourist's description of the Alps, as nature itself;
that is to say, he might select among the scattered particles of
color and paint them out into a picture of his own. The thrice-
published *Luciniade* of Lacombe sings the art of midwivery[4] (What
a recalcitrant subject for poetry!); like most didactic poems, which
present us their subject chopped-up limb for limb (though each is
wrapped in poetic tinsel), this work shows how far the prosaic
aping of nature is removed from poetic imitation.

---

[3] For this reason, Klopstock's ode of vengeance against Carrier, "Retribution," allows the mind no poetic peace. The horror is constantly renewed; the cannibalistic
vengeance torments the eye of the spectator in vain; and the poetic barbarity of
the punishment imitates the criminal's prosaic cruelty.

[4] A while ago a prize was even offered for a poem on the fall of Sodom.

The absence of the poetic spirit is most repulsive in the comic, however. In the epic or tragedy, the slightness of the poet can often hide behind the grandeur of the theme, since great objects even when real move the beholder poetically. This explains why young writers like to begin with Italy, Greece, assassinations, heroes, immortality, terrible misery, and the like, as actors do with tyrants. But in the comic, the baseness of the material exposes the whole dwarflike nature of a poet, if such he happens to be.[5] In German comedies—consider the atrocious examples in Eschenburg's *Collection,* even plays by the better poets, Krüger, Gellert and others—the principle of simply aping nature shows the full force of its vulgarity. The question is whether the Germans even yet have a *whole* comedy, and not simply some acts. To us the French seem to be richer in this genre. But this is partly illusory, since *foreign* fools and foreign rabble in themselves, without the effort of any poet, have a deceptive appearance of poetic distinction. The British on the contrary *are* richer, although the same exotic idealization contributes deceptively to this effect. A single book might convince us of this truth; it is by the only man whose spirit of parody mirrors the truth with genius. *Wagstaff's Genteel Conversations* by Swift faithfully depicts England's dignitaries, making them just as vulgar and witless as ours appear in German comedies. Since these bores never appear in English comedies, however, it must be not so much the fools as the comic dramatists across the channel who are wittier than those in Germany. The field of reality is a game board divided into squares on which the author can play either common checkers or the kingly game of chess, depending on whether he has only disks or both figures and skill.

How little poetry is a copy of the book of nature, one can best see in young writers, who speak the language of the emotions worst precisely when emotions dominate and cry within them. Too much water in the poetic mill hinders instead of driving it; the apes of nature believe falsely that poets need only write down what is dictated to them. No hand can hold and steadily guide the poetic, lyric brush in which a fever pulse of emotion throbs. Simple indignation does make verses, but not the best; even satire is sharper

---

[5] The requirement of poetic superiority, and not that of knowing human nature, is what makes comedy so rare and so difficult for the young. Aristophanes could easily have written a comedy at fifteen-and-a-half and Shakespeare one at twenty.

through mildness than through wrath, as vinegar is made sour by sweet grape stalks, but flat by bitter hops.

The poet cannot use the material of nature, and still less its form in a raw state. Imitation of the material supposes a higher principle; to every man a different nature appears, and the question becomes one of who sees the most beautiful nature. Nature is for man in an eternal process of becoming man, even in its shape. For man the sun has a full face, the half-moon a profile, the stars surely eyes. Everything lives for the living, and the universe contains only pseudocorpses, not pseudolife. Here lies the difference between prose and poetry; the question is: *Which* soul animates nature, that of a slave captain or that of a Homer?

As for the form to be imitated, the poetic materialists eternally contradict not only themselves but art and nature; because they *half* ignore what they want, they only half know what they want. They allow the use of meter to express the wildest passion, or any passion at all, thereby establishing a different principle of imitation. In the storm of excitement, they allow the highest degree of euphony and some splendid imagery (how splendid, however, depends on the caprice of the review). They accept contractions of time (though with the reservation of a certain, i.e., uncertain, consideration for the nature to be imitated). They countenance the gods and other marvels of epic and opera—pagan mythology in the middle of the present twilight of the gods (Götterdämmerung).[6] They accept the long funeral sermons of the heroes *before* the killing in Homer, parody, although to the point of nonsense in the comic, an impossible romantic folly in Don Quixote, the bold intrusion of the present into Sterne's monologues, and the introduction of odes into the dialogue and countless other things in Thümmel and others. But isn't it as flagrant an anomaly as *speaking* in the midst of *singing,* to introduce into such poetic liberties the prosaic bondage of mere imitation and to prescribe, as it were, embargoes on fruit and merchandise for the universe? I mean, do you not contradict yourself, your own licenses, and the beautiful, if into this sundrunk realm of wonder, where divine shapes walk erect and blissful, over which no heavy earthly sun shines, where lighter times fly past and other languages rule, where, as in the life

[6] This beautiful and terrible expression in Nordic mythology designates the judgment day, when the supreme god destroys the other gods.

beyond, there is no more real pain—if into this transfigured world the savages of passion should step with the rude cry of exultation and of pain? And what if every flower there should have to grow as slowly and amid as much grass as in the sluggish world, if time should be measured longer instead of shorter by the iron wheels and iron axles of the heavy clock of history and of the centuries instead of by the heavenly flower clock,[7] which but gently swells open and shut and always exudes perfume?

For as the organic realm takes up, transforms, masters, and binds the mechanical realm, so the poetic world governs the real world, and the spiritual kingdom the physical kingdom. Hence in poetry we do not marvel at any marvel; there is none except the commonplace. Assuming equal excellence, the poetic tone is at the same pitch at the beginning of both a genuine comedy and a genuine tragedy, even a tragedy with romantic marvels. Wallenstein's dreams are poetically in no way inferior to the visions of the Maid of Orleans. The highest pain, the highest heaven of passion ought never to be expressed on the stage as it is expressed even in the first, best theater box—that is, *monosyllabically* and poorly. I find that French tragedians always, and the Germans often, call up the squalls of passion to say either, "ô ciel," or "mon dieu," or "ô dieux," or "hélas," or nothing—or with the same effect, someone faints. But this is completely unpoetic! Certainly nothing is closer to nature and to the truth than this very monosyllabic faint. If this could succeed, however, nothing would be more amusing than to portray that which is precisely most difficult; the abyss and the summit of the innermost being would be much more easily and clearly revealed than the stages in between.

Poetry can press close to the lonely soul, which like a broken heart hides itself in dark blood; it can catch the low word with which each soul expresses its infinite weal or woe. Let poetry therefore be a Shakespeare and bring us that word. A man's own voice, which, deafened in the storm of emotion, he himself misunderstands, should escape poetry as little as the most muted sigh escapes a supreme divinity. Are there not messages which can come to us only on poetic wings? Is there not a nature which comes into being when man ceases to be, and which he anticipates? When the

---

[7] As is well known, the sequence of the opening and closing of flowers (according to Linnaeus) can be used to measure the hours.

dying man is already stretched out alone in that dark waste around which the living stand distant on the horizon like lowering clouds or sunken lights, and he lives and dies, solitary in the wilderness, we learn nothing of his last thoughts and visions. But poetry passes like a white ray into the deep desert and we see into the last hour of the solitary man.

4. *Closer Determination of the Beautiful Imitation of Nature*

The view we have expressed has already implied a determination of what *beautiful (spiritual)* imitation of nature is. A dry definition of beauty does not take you very far. Kant's definition: "The beautiful is what pleases universally without concept" implies in the term *pleasing,* as distinguished from *being agreeable,* that which was to be explained. The appositive *without concept* holds true for all feelings, just as all feelings, indeed all mental states secretly claim to be *universal,* although experience often contradicts this. Kant, who arbitrarily enough grants beauty only to design and mere charm to color,[8] always takes his illustrations from the graphic and plastic arts. What then is poetic beauty, which can give an even higher brilliance to a painted or sculpted beauty? The gulf that we have supposed between natural beauty and artistic beauty appears in its entire range only for poetic beauty; beauties of the plastic arts could certainly at times have been created by nature, even if only as rarely as creative geniuses. Furthermore, the explanation of beauty hardly has a high place in a poetics, because this goddess has other gods at her side in poetry: the sublime, the pathetic, the comic, etc. A reviewer of this aesthetics complacently appropriates a sterile, empty definition of the beautiful by Delbrück. (This is a moderate compliment to Delbrück, who should be respected as a delicate, discerning art lover and critic, for instance of Klopstock and Goethe.) The definition runs literally (except for my parentheses) thus: "The beautiful consists in a *purposeful, harmonious* variety of ideas" (Don't both adjectives here assume precisely the concept to be explained, as if you were to say, a variety consonant with beauty?), "which the imag-

---

[8] The description of the beautiful as something universally pleasing without concept applies even better to colors than to outlines, as all children and savages prove, who prefer living red and green to dead black, while the enjoyment of fine design, of course, varies among peoples according to their concepts.

ination calls up in itself" (How indefinite! And with what and from where?), "in order to add to a given concept" (To which concept, or to every one?) "much that is ineffable" (Why precisely *much*? *Ineffable* would have been enough; furthermore, which ineffable?), "and more than on the one hand can be perceived, or on the other hand clearly conceived therein" (*Clearly?* In the ineffable there is already the unclear. But what then is this *more*, which is neither to be seen nor clearly conceived? And what limits does this relative *more* have?); "the pleasure in this beauty is produced through a free, yet regular play of the imagination in accord with the understanding" (The latter was already implied in *regular:* but how indistinct are the expressions *play* and mere *accord*!). The reviewer in the *Supplementary Pages* ties to Delbrück's definition his own shorter one: "Fine art arises as fine art from its manner of presentation by means of aesthetic ideas." Since in *aesthetic* you already have the whole thing to be defined (beauty), a certain truth cannot be denied to this definition, nor to any identical proposition.

Let us look at just one more definition—for who wants to waste his time for reading and writing by examining everything that has been printed? Beauty, says Hemsterhuis, is what yields the greatest number of ideas in the least time, an explanation which borders both on the older "sensuous unity in multiplicity" and on the later "free play of the imagination." We may omit the question of how ideas can be measured by time at all, since time can be measured only by ideas themselves. In fact every idea is only a bolt of lightning, lasting a sixtieth of a second; to hold it fast would be to disassemble it into its parts, limits, and consequences, and thus not in fact to hold it fast any more, but to survey its kinships and its neighborhood. In order to identify beauty with a quantity of ideas in the least time (which, for example, a review of memorized sequences of mathematical or philosophical calculations also provides), you first need some appropriate distinguishing mark. Finally, what if someone were now to define ugliness as the presentation of the greatest number of ideas in the least time? For an oval satisfies and fills my eye, but a zigzag of lines enriches it with a numbing multiplicity of ideas flying back and forth, because the object is at the same time to be grasped, fought, fled and resolved. One could perhaps rephrase Hemsterhuis's definition thus: Beauty is a circle of the imagination, just as there is a circle of logic, because the circle is the richest, simplest, most inexhaustible, most easily grasped figure; but the real circle is of course itself beautiful, and thus the definition would become (as every definition unfortunately does) a logical circle.

We return to the principle of poetic imitation. If in poetic imitation the copy contains more than the original or even produces its opposite—pleasure from poetic sorrow, for example—this occurs because a double nature is being imitated: an outer and an inner one, each the mirror of the other. This may be called, following one astute critic, "The presentation of ideas through imitation of nature." More detailed discussion belongs in our section on genius. External nature becomes something different in every inner nature, and this transubstantiation into the divine gives the spiritual poetic matter, which, if it is genuinely poetic, builds its own body (the form) like an *anima Stahlii,* and does not receive it already measured and ready-made. The matter is missing for the nihilist, and therefore the living form; the life of the matter is missing for the materialist, and therefore again the form; in short, the two kinds of work intersect in the region of nonpoetry. The materialist has the clod of earth but can breathe no living soul into it, because it is only a clod, not a body; the nihilist would like to breathe life, but doesn't even have the clod. The true poet in his marriage of art and nature will imitate the English landscape gardener, who knows how to join his artificial garden to the natural surroundings, as if they were limitless continuations. But the poet does this at a higher level and surrounds limited nature with the infinity of the idea, letting the one disappear into the other as if on an ascent to heaven.

5. Use of the Marvelous

All that is truly marvelous is poetic in itself. But the two false principles and the true principle of poetry are revealed most clearly in their different ways of shedding this moonlight on an artistic structure. The first or material method is to change the moonlight after a few volumes into everyday daylight, that is, to break the spell of the marvelous through Wiegleb's magic and to dissolve it into prose. Then, of course, a second reading discovers a paper form instead of an organic one, shabby confinement instead of poetic infinity; and Icarus lies without wax, his dried quills on the ground. One would gladly have spared Goethe from unlocking his cabinet of machinery and digging up the pipes which spouted the transparent, many-colored waterworks. A magician is no poet, and even a magician is only worthy and poetic as long as he does not destroy his marvels by resolving them; no man will look at tricks that have been explained.

Other poets avoid the mistake of explaining their marvels but commit a second error in merely inventing them. This certainly is quite easy, and therefore wrong per se; the poet must distrust and renounce whatever is facile without inspiration, for this is the facility of prose. A continual marvel is by its very nature none at all, but rather a more ethereal, second nature in which, because of its arbitrariness, no beautiful violation of a rule can occur. Actually, such poetry is a self-contradictory acknowledgment of opposed conditions, the confusion of the materially marvelous with the ideal, like the combination one sees on old cups, half word, half picture.

But the best is a third method. Here the poet neither destroys the marvel, as does an exegetical theologian, nor imprisons it unnaturally in the physical world, as does a magician, but rather locates it in the soul, the only place where it can dwell next to God. Let the marvelous fly neither as a bird of the day nor as one of the night, but as a twilight butterfly. *Meister*'s wondrous nature lies not in the wooden wheelworks—they could be more polished and steely—but in Mignon's and the Harp player's splendid spiritual profundity, which luckily is so great that the genealogical ladders let down afterwards fall much too short. A fear of ghosts is better than an apparition, a ghost seer better than one hundred ghost stories.[9] Not the common physical marvel, but the belief in it is what paints the nocturne of the spirit world. The self is the alien spirit before which it shudders, the abyss on whose brink it believes it stands; and on seeing the stage sink into the realm of the underworld, the spectator also sinks.

If, however, a poet has once made the significant midnight hour strike in a spirit, then he may also set into motion a mechanical wheelwork of conjurer's marvels which can be taken apart; for

[9] Although many marvels in *Titan* are turned by the mechanic, the Baldhead, into mere tricks, the deceiver himself is a marvel, and while he is deceiving others, new phenomena are introduced which deceive and shock *him*.

through the spirit the body receives the power of miming and each earthly event becomes otherworldly.

Indeed, there are beautiful inner marvels whose life the poet may not dissect with the psychological anatomical knife, even if he could. In Schlegel's (too little known) *Florentin,* a pregnant woman constantly sees a beautiful wonder child, who opens its eyes with her and silently runs toward her at night, but who disappears forever at the time of her delivery.

An explanation was at hand; but it was correctly omitted for poetic reasons. In general, inner marvels have the advantage that they outlive their explanation. For the great indestructible marvel is the faith of men in marvels, and the greatest spiritual apparition is that of our fear of spirits in a wooden life full of the mechanical. Hence the heavenly suns of characters will dim and shrink to small clumps of earth, if the poet leads us out of their full light and shows us their cradle scenes. At times it is the duty of the novelist to suppress the future history as well as the past history of a wonderful character, and the author of *Titan* will hardly, if he is enough of an aesthetician, paint the past of Schoppe or the future of Linda after her disappearance. I almost wish I did not know who Mignon and the Harp player had really been from birth on. In Werner's *Sons of the Valley* one attends the awesomely splendid initiation into the order of Templars; voices of the night promise to solve the immense riddle of the world, and in the profound distance mountaintops are unveiled by passing mists, summits from which a man can look far into the desired other or second world (which actually remains our first and last). Finally, the poet brings us and the story to these mountain peaks, and a master of the lodge informs us what the order demands and promotes: good moral conduct. And there the old sphinx lies dead before us on all stony fours, carved out by a stonemason. In order not to be unfair to the tragic poet, perhaps it would be best to take it all for a joke on most masters of the Templar and Sacristan orders, who are conspicuous more for enciphering than for deciphering, and for doing so in the presence of the excluded than in that of the elect.

We are now coming closer to the *spirit* of poetry, whose mere external *nourishing matter* in imitated nature is far removed from its *internal* matter.

If the nihilist transparently dissolves the particular into the general and the materialist petrifies and ossifies the general into the particular, living poetry must comprehend and achieve a union of the two in which every individual can find himself and in whose generality (since individuals exclude one another) each will find only his own particularity. In short, poetry should become like the moon, which by night follows one wanderer in the woods from peak to peak and at the same time another from wave to wave and thus attends each, while it simply describes its great arc across heaven and yet ultimately draws it around the earth and around the wanderers also.

Course V. On Romantic Poetry

21. The Relationship between the Greeks and the Moderns
No age is satisfied with itself; young men think of the future as more ideal than the present, old men the past. We adopt both attitudes toward literature. Since man seeks the same unity in his love as in his reason, he is prejudiced either in favor of or against peoples as long as he does not know how to resolve their differences in a higher unity. So in England and even more so in France, the comparison between the ancients and the moderns is always partial, either pro or con. The German, especially in the nineteenth century, is in a position to be impartial toward all nations except for his own misunderstood nation.

Let us therefore supplement our picture of the Greeks as follows: First, the mountain of their muses bloomed on its eastern side; the most beautiful and the simplest human relationships and involvements of courage, love, sacrifice, good luck, and bad luck were appropriated by these fortunate people. To later poets they left only the possibilities of repeating these or awkwardly representing more artificial relationships.

Second, exalted by death, they appear to us holy and transfigured. They must affect us more strongly than they affected themselves, for we are charmed not only by the poem, but by the poet. The beautiful rich simplicity of the child will enchant not another child, but a person who has lost that simplicity. The withered scatter of leaves in the heat of culture enables us to see the fullness pressed together in the Greek buds more than could the

Greeks themselves. Indeed, the charm extends to such definite details that Olympus and Helicon and the Vale of Tempe and every temple have a poetic luster for us even outside poetry, because we do not see them too close at hand, immediately before our own windows. In the same way, honey, milk, and other Arcadian terms attract us more as images than the originals do. The material detail of Greek poems, from the history of gods and men down to the smallest coin and article of dress, lies before us like a poetic diamond, even without the illumination and setting provided by poetic form.

Third, we seem to confound the Greek maximum of sculpture with the maximum of poetry. The physical figure and physical beauty have limits of perfection which no time can extend. Limited also are the eye and the externally shaping imagination. On the contrary, the centuries heap up the external as well as the internal matter of poetry ever more richly, and the mental power which forces such matter into the forms of poetry is exercised ever more vigorously with the lapse of time. Therefore, it is more correct to say, "This Apollo is the most beautiful figure," than it is to say, "This poem is the most beautiful poem." Painting, like poetry, is much closer than sculpture to romantic infinity and in landscapes often dissolves into it completely.

Finally, it is an old mistake of men witnessing the eternal spectacle of time to call for repetitions of the beautiful (*ancora*), as if anything in superabundant nature could return. Not even the worst can. The duplication of a whole people would be a greater wonder than a fantastic sky of clouds completely matching some former sky. Not even in Greece could antiquity be resurrected. Indeed it is idle for one people to call another to account about intellectual riches, as when the French ask us, "Where are your Voltaires, Rousseaus, Diderots, Buffons?" "We have none," we say "but where are your Lessings, Winckelmanns, Herders, Goethes, et al.?" Not even wretched authors have matching apes abroad. In all England and France, among all novelists, the famous ——— (in ———) has no twin; and, of course, these countries are lucky.

We have praised the power of Greek myths about gods and heroes. But we should not take any single member in the many-limbed life of a people and make it into the soul. Nor should we cause nourishing seeds and eggs straightway to sprout and hatch.

Did not the divine host pass from Egypt's sad labyrinths over Greece's bright mountains to Rome's seven hills? But where did it set up its poetic heaven except upon Helicon, upon Parnassus, and at the springs of both these mountains? The same is true of the heroic age, which shone also over the Egyptians, over the Peruvians, and over almost all other peoples, without ever leaving behind such a poetic reflection among any of these as among the Greeks.

If not even the Romans, who were related to the Greeks in time and religion, learned by imitation to write poetry like the Greeks, then our distance and our lack of success in imitation are the more natural. The Romans were poetic only as practical dramatists and as actors on the stage of the earth, more as a people than as individuals, more in deeds than in words, and more therefore as historians than as poets. For us the Greek gods are only flat images and empty dress for our feelings, not living beings. Indeed, whereas then there were hardly any false gods on earth and every people could be a guest in the temple of another, now we know hardly any but false gods. This cold age throws, as it were, a whole universe between man and his god. Northern life is not especially serene, no more cheerful than the heaven above it. In the middle of our brightest winter noon, long evening shadows are thrown, morally and physically. The sons of Phoebus are the first to perceive that their father, the sun, does not favor a land without light, wood, roof, food, and fur. In fair lands the ships fly singing along the shore and one harbor lies next to another. As for our own heroic age, it stands before us—unlike the Greek, which was adorned with the signs of divinity—either dressed in a bear skin or driven back by religion into the oak groves, so that we fancy ourselves much more akin to Adam and Noah than to Hermann, and we pray to Jupiter more than to the god Thor.

Ever since the arrival of Klopstock, we degrade ourselves more for not elevating ourselves enough and insist more self-consciously on more self-consciousness. To name finally the evil genius of art, poetry was the object of the people among the Greeks, as the people were the object of poetry; today we sing from one study across the hall to another about what is most interesting in each. Nothing need be added for a partisan portrait. But how much is lacking yet for a complete picture of the truth! How pointless to take a people, even more so its era, and above all, the ever-changing play of color of its geniuses, in other words, to take a great various life, ever flowering in a different form, and nail it to a pair of broad generalities (like *plastic* and *romantic* poetry, or *objective* and *subjective*) as if to two crossed boards. Certainly the distinction is valid; as valid as the similar one which divides all nature into straight and crooked lines (the crooked as the infinite is romantic poetry), or as the division into quantity and quality; as valid as the division of all music into two kinds depending on whether harmony or melody predominates, or, more briefly, into the preponderance of simultaneity and that of succession; as valid as the polarizing, empty classifications by aestheticians of the school of Schelling. But what can dynamic life gain from this atomistic sterility? Schiller's division of poetry into *naive* [10] (for which *objective* would be clearer) and *sentimental* (whereby only one aspect of "modern" subjectivity is expressed) is no more helpful for denoting or differentiating the various romanticisms of a Shakespeare, a Petrarch, an Ariosto, or a Cervantes than it is for the various objectivities of a Homer, a Sophocles, a Job, or a Caesar.

Every single people with its age is a climatic organ of poetry, and it is very difficult to disentangle the intricate wealth of the

[10] See volume 2 of his *Works*. "Because the highest harmony exists between thought and feeling in the Greek condition, the most complete imitation of reality possible constitutes the naive poet, while the sentimental poet is the first to raise reality to the ideal"; "he therefore reflects first about the impression of the objects on himself" and "treats reality as limit, the idea as the infinite." Meanwhile, however, "All poetry must have an infinite content. It may be infinite in form, in that it presents the object with all its limits; this is the absolute presentation by the naive poet. Or it may be infinite in material, when it removes all limits; this is the presentation of the absolute by the sentimental poet." But, "Not the *real*, but *true* nature" is "the subject of naive poetry, and that seldom exists." And thereby the whole distinction is canceled out. For *true* nature is separated from the *real* and presupposed by it only in the idea and the ideal; neither of the two natures as such is consequently ever the original of the poetic copy, but the idea is; not even a complete imitation of reality by itself nor any absolute representation of it can be decisive. Either the whole resolution of the question is secretly assumed and surreptitiously obtained in the phrase *"true"* nature, or after all, no *external* subject and matter as such is essential to the distinction between the two kinds of poetry. And so too with the other expression. If true nature "seldom" exists, Greek poetry is hardly explained. All nature becomes poetic only through the poet (otherwise the poet would be made not the poem, and every poet for every poem). Even sculptors had to idealize the "true" nature of the Greeks. In differentiating naive and sentimental poetry, therefore, no difference in objects can be admitted (as if modern times had lost all worthy ones).

organization into a system without dropping as many parts of life as are included.

This, however, cannot delete the great distinction between Greek and romantic poetry, any more than the chain of being that connects animals can annul their classification by species.

22. The Character of Romantic Poetry, and Differences between Southern and Northern Forms

"The origin and character of all modern poetry can be derived from Christianity so easily that romantic poetry might as well be called Christian poetry." With this assertion, the author began the present paragraph several years ago, but the refutation and instruction by more than one worthy critic obliges him now to alter part of that and even to remove part, like a suburb, in order to protect the whole city or the inner fortress. The first question is: How is romantic style[11] distinguished from the Greek? Greek images, charms, motives, feelings, characters, even technical forms, can easily be transplanted into a romantic poem without destroying its cosmopolitan spirit; on the contrary, transplanted romantic graces would find no comfortable place in a Greek work of art, with the possible exception of the sublime, which connects ancient and romantic like a border god. Even the so-called modern irregularity of the Italian opera or of the Spanish comedy could be filled with and moved by the spirit of antiquity. Mere technique cannot bisect the spiritual world of poetry into an ancient and a modern or American hemisphere. This is beautifully confirmed by Bouterwek's remark that despite its poverty of ideas, Italian poetry follows and approaches the model of the Greek through clarity, simplicity, and grace more closely than any other modern poetry. Yet Italian forms clash with the Greek more than do German and English forms. And with this truth, Bouterwek contradicts his other opinion, that the romantic consists largely in an un-Greek blending of the comic, the serious, and even the tragic. That mixture is not a necessary characteristic of romanticism, where it is often lacking, nor is its opposite a characteristic of antiquity, for Aristophanes harshly and abruptly mixes the sublime choruses with

---

[11] Schiller calls it the *modern,* as if everything written after the Greeks were modern and new, whether one or two thousand years old; he also calls it the *sentimental,* a term which the romancers Ariosto and Cervantes would not take too seriously.

the debasement of the gods themselves, as if he would arouse an emotion with its comic relief.

Let us rather ask our feelings why we can find even a landscape romantic. A statue excludes romanticism with its narrow and precise contour; painting approaches it in human groupings and reaches it in landscapes without men, like those of Claude Lorrain. A Dutch garden seems the very opposite of romanticism, but an English garden which extends into an undefined landscape can surround us playfully with a romantic region, that is, with the background of an imagination left free to wander in the beautiful. What is it, furthermore, that imparts the romantic stamp to the following poetic examples? In Cervantes's tragedy *Numancia* all the inhabitants of the city swore to die a common death in order not to be subjugated by hunger and by the Romans. When the oath had been carried out and nothing was left in the city but corpses and funeral pyres, then Fama stepped up on the wall and proclaimed to their enemies the suicide of the city and Spain's future glory. Or in the middle of Homer there is that romantic passage where Jupiter looks down from Olympus over the martial tumult on the plains of Troy and then over the distant Arcadian meadows full of quiet men, both lit by the same sun. Or there is the brilliant, although weaker, passage in Schiller's *William Tell* where the poet's eye sweeps down from the towering mountain chains into the long, laughing grainfields of the German plain. In all these examples it is not the sublime *height* which, as we have said, blends so easily into the romantic, but the *breadth* which is characteristic. The romantic is beauty without limit, or *beautiful* infinity, just as there is a *sublime* infinity. Thus in the example cited above, Homer is romantic, whereas he is simply sublime when Ajax begs the gods during the battle fought under an eclipse, for nothing more than light. It is more than an analogy to call the romantic the undulant hum of a vibrating string or bell whose sound wave fades away into ever-greater distances and finally is lost in ourselves and, although outwardly already quiet, yet sounds within. In the same way, moonlight is both image and instance of the romantic. The uncertain light of the romantic was so distant and foreign to the sharply delimiting mind of the Greeks that even Plato, so much a poet and so close to Christian exaltation, uses merely the confined and sharply outlined allegory of a cave, in which we chained prisoners see only the shadows of real beings passing behind us, to express the truly romantic infinite idea of the relationship between our poor finitude and the splendid palace room and starry heaven of infinity.

If poetry is prophecy, then romantic poetry is presentiment of a greater future than finds room here below; the romantic blossoms swim around us, just as unknown varieties of seeds in the past swam to Norway's shore through the all-uniting sea from the yet undiscovered new world.

Who is the mother of this romanticism? Certainly not in every land and century the Christian religion. Every other religion, however, is related to this mother of god. Two romantic species outside Christianity, strangers to one another in culture as in climate, are that of *India* and that of the *Edda.* The *Old Norse,* bordering more on the sublime, found in the shadowy realm of its dark and awesome natural climate, in its nights and on its mountains, a limitless world of spirits for its spectral Orcus into which the narrow material world dissolved and sank away. Ossian[12] belongs there with his evening and night pieces, in which the heavenly nebulae of the past hover and gleam over the thick cloudy night of the present. Only in the past does Ossian find future and eternity.

Everything in his poem is music, but distant and thereby doubled and absorbed into the infinite, like an echo which charms not by a raw fidelity of reproduced tones but by an ever fainter mellowing of them.

Indian romanticism is active within an all-animating religion which breaks down the barriers of the world of sense by breathing a spirit into it. This world becomes as great as the world of spirits, and full, not of scolding poltergeists, but of flattering spirits; earth and heaven sink into each other as the horizon sinks into the sea. For the Indian the flower is more alive than is a man for the Norseman. Now add to this the Indian climate, this luxuriant bridal night of nature, and imagine the Indian like a bee resting in the honeyed chalice of a tulip, cradled by zephyrs and lulled by its sweet swaying. For just that reason, Indian romanticism has had

[12]Much as Ahlwardt's translation recommends itself by giving us a more correct text, it still seems to me that the lightness, fidelity, and harmony of Jung's translation have not nearly received just praise.

to dissolve further into the magic of the senses; and if moonlight and fading cadences are signs and emblems of other kinds of romanticism, then a dark perfume may characterize the Indian, particularly since perfume so often plays a role in their lives as well as in their poems.

Oriental poetry is less akin to Greek than to romantic poetry because of its predilection for the sublime and the lyric, its impotence in drama and characterization, and most of all, the Oriental mode of thinking and feeling. A feeling, that is, of the earthly nothingness of the swarming shadows that inhabit the night of our existence, shadows cast not by a sun but by moon and stars whose weak light resembles shadows. A feeling as if the day of life were spent under a total eclipse of the sun, full of awe and of evening sentiments, like those eclipses when the moon swallows the entire sun and stands before it with a brilliant ring. This way of thinking and feeling which Herder, the greatest depicter of the Orient, described so exactly for his Northern audience, had to approach romantic poetry along the same path its kindred Christianity took in reaching and developing it completely.

We have now arrived at *Christian* romanticism. First we should show why it assumed and created other forms in the South (in Italy and in Spain particularly) than in the North, where, as we have said, the very soil made the pagan parvis into the Christian, romantic Holy of Holies. The South is manifestly so very different from the North by nature and in its manifold historical complications, that any remarks deriving romanticism from sources other than Christian must be weighed carefully and verified.

Bouterwek assigns the following parentage to the Southern and earliest romanticism: a higher respect for women transmitted by the old Germans, and hence a more spiritual style of love.

Romantic love first dwelled, however, not in the old German forests, but in Christian temples; a non-Christian Petrarch would be impossible. The peerless Mary endows all women with romantic nobility; a Venus is merely beautiful, but a madonna is romantic. This higher love was or is the very blossom and flower of Christianity, which with its ardent zeal in opposing the earthly dissolves the beautiful body into the beautiful soul in order to love the body in the soul, the beautiful in the infinite. The name "Platonic love" is known to have been borrowed from another love, a

pure unblemished friendship between youths, which was so innocent that Greek lawmakers even counted it among the civic duties
and so enthusiastic that the lover was punished for the errors of
his beloved. Here then a deifying love, except of a different sex,
identical to that of the old Germans, kept by nature farthest from
pollution, would appear, but not that love sanctified by Christianity which invested its object with the glamor of romance.

The *spirit of chivalry,* which embroidered love and religion, a
lady and Our Lady, side by side on its banners, and the Crusades,
which were considered secondly as the progenitors of romanticism, are children of the Christian era. To go to the *Promised*
Land, which two religions at once and the greatest personage on
earth had exalted into a twilit realm of holy presentiment and into
an isthmus between the first and second worlds for the imagination, signified the romantic transfiguration of a man, and a sub-
jugation of the low earthly powers, both prosaically and poetically, by the two powers of courage and religion. What equivalent
of this could the heroic ages and the Argonauts' expeditions produce?

The passing centuries must also be counted as servants and mute
squires of romanticism, for outwardly they bring all peoples into
ever closer relationships, rounding off their sharp divisions; time,
like Christianity, increasingly dissolves from within the solid physical world by the increasing sunlight of abstraction. All this makes
one bold to predict that the future of poetry will become ever
more romantic and poorer or richer in laws, and its distance from
Greece ever greater. Its Pegasus will grow so many more wings
that through their very excess it will experience great difficulty in
flying straight, unless it uses some of its wings as veils, like the
six-winged figure in Ezekiel. What, however, does time or eternity
matter to aestheticians and their preparatory schools? Shall only
creeping philosophy make progress, and flying poetry rust into
lameness? After three or four thousand years and as many million
horae, shall no other division of poetry appear than the weak division into sentimental and naive made by Schiller in his *Horen?*
One might maintain that every century is differently romantic, just
as one might suppose, both in jest and in earnest, on every planet
a different poetry. Poetry, like everything divine in man, is chained
to time and place and must always become a carpenter's son and

a Jew. But in another time the scene of humiliation can begin on Mount Tabor and the transfiguration can occur upon a sun and dazzle us.

For the rest, it follows that Christianity, although the common father of the romantic children, must beget different ones in the South and in the North. The Southern romanticism of Italy, which is related to Greece in its climate, must assume a gayer mood in Ariosto and fly or flee less away from the ancient form than does the Northern in a Shakespeare, and the same Southern romanticism must take on still another, more orientally bold form in ardent Spain. Northern poetry and romanticism is an aeolian harp through which the storm of reality strums melodies, releasing howls as musical tones. But melancholy trembles on the strings, indeed, at times a cry of pain rips through.

We can thus begin the following eighth paragraph on Northern romanticism just as we did the seventh.

23. *The Source of Romantic Poetry*

The origin and character of all modern poetry can so easily be deduced from Christianity that romantic poetry could just as well be called Christian. Christianity, like a day of judgment, destroyed the entire material world with all its charms, crushed it into a grave mound, made it into a ladder leading to heaven, and replaced it with a new spiritual world. Demonology became the real mythology [13] of the physical world and seductive devils entered into men and into statues of the gods. All present time on earth evaporated into the future of heaven. What was left for the poetic spirit after this collapse of the external world? That into which it plunges: the *inner* world. The spirit descended into itself and its night and saw other spirits. But since the finite clings only to bodies and in spirits everything is unending or not yet ended, the realm of the infinite flowered in poetry over the cinders of the finite. Angels, devils, saints, souls of the blessed, and the Infinite One had no bodily forms [14] or divine bodies; so the monstrous and

[13] We know that according to the Manicheans the entire corporeal world belonged to the evil angels and that the Orthodox extended the curse of original sin to all creatures, etc.

[14] Or the supernatural attached itself to inartistic embodiments, to relics, crosses, crucifixes, holy wafers, monks, bells, icons, which all spoke more as letters and signs than as physical substances. Even actions tried to dispense with the physical,

immense opened up their depths. In place of serene Greek joy there appeared either infinite longing or ineffable bliss—perdition without limit in time or space—the fear of ghosts which dreads itself—enthusiastic, introspective love—unlimited monastic renunciation—Platonic and Neoplatonic philosophy.

In the vast night of infinity man was more often afraid than hopeful. Fear as such is stronger and richer than hope (just as in the sky a white cloud lifts a black one, not the black the white), because the imagination finds many more images for fear than for hope; the images in turn are provided by the organ for pain, the physical sense of touch, which can become the source of an infernal flux at any point of the skin, while the senses allot so meager and narrow a ground for joy. Hell was painted with flames, heaven designated at most by music,[15] which itself produces indefinite longing. Astrology had many dangerous powers. Superstition was more often threatening than promising. As mezzotints of this darker coloring we should also add the confusion of peoples, the wars, the plagues, the enforced baptisms, and the dark polar mythology united to an orientally ardent language.

24. *The Poetry of Superstition*

So-called superstition, a fruit and nourishment of the romantic spirit, deserves separate attention. When we read that the augurs in Cicero's time explained the twelve vultures seen by Romulus as a sign that his work and kingdom would last twelve centuries, and when we compare the actual fall of the Western empire in its twelfth century with this prophecy, our first thought is of some power higher[16] than the combinations of chance we later calculate. Let each man remember from his childhood—if his was po-

i.e., with the present: the Crusades sought to bind a holy past with a holy future. The same is true of the legends of miracles, and of the expectation of Doomsday.
[15] Is it not possible that the indefinite, romantic character of music was conducive to the appearance of great composers much earlier in the misty Netherlands than in cheerful, sunny Italy, where the distinctness of painting was preferred? For the same reasons, the Dutch may have idealized more in indefinite landscapes, and the Italians more in the definite human form.
[16] Even a Leibniz finds it worth noting, for example, that Christ was born in the sign of the Virgin. *Otium Hanover,* 187. Hence a passing allusion may be forgiven: space was kept empty in the imperial picture gallery at Frankfurt for years for a single picture of a German emperor; then fate filled and closed the line with the picture of the last emperor.

etic enough—the sense of mystery with which the twelve holy
nights were mentioned, especially Christmas Eve, when earth and
heaven like children and adults seemed to open their doors to each
other for the common celebration of the greatest birth, while the
evil spirits withdrew into the distance and were afraid. Or let him
think of the awe with which he heard of the comet whose naked
fiery sword was brandished up and across heaven above the un-
easy world as if stretched out by an angel of death, to reveal and
point towards the dawn of a bloody future. Or let him think of
some man's deathbed, where one could for the most part see figures busily running with lights behind the long black curtain hid-
ing the spirit world; there, for the sinner, one caught sight of open
claws, hot, hungry demons' eyes, and restless motion. But for the
pious man on his deathbed, there appeared flowery tokens, a lily
or a rose in his pew, strange music, or his double. Even the signs
of good fortune inspired dread: the signs just cited, a blessed white
shadow floating by, or the proverbial angels playing with a child
when it smiles in its sleep. How lovely! The present author for one
is glad that he was born several decades ago and spent his youth
in a village, so that he was brought up with some superstition. In
this memory, he now tries to find comfort when playing angels are
replaced in explanations by theories of stomach acids.[17] If he had
been educated and refined in a French school and in this century,
he would have to experience first through the poet many romantic
feelings which he himself now supplies for the poet. In France
there has always been the least superstition and the least poetry;
the Spaniard has more of both; the serene Italian resembles Romans and Greeks, whose superstition referred not to our realm of
spirits but to earthly fortune, mostly announced by physically de-
finable beings. The gay, cruel, wanton groups on the old urns and
sarcophagi of the Greeks, and even of the somber Etruscans, would
never have been painted on German coffins.

Nordic superstition, which saw a bloody index finger pointing
to stormy slaughter among nations in the fighting of crows or in
the war games of children, was more romantically sublime, the
smaller and less significant the prophetic images were. Thus the
witches in Shakespeare's *Macbeth* seem more frightful, the more

[17] As is well known, the smile of sleeping children comes from acids in the stomach,
but in adults this is not betrayed noticeably by either smiles or angels.

they crawl and shrivel into their ugliness; but in Schiller's *Macbeth* the cothurni on which he elevated them are the witches' slippers of a Pater Fulgentius, which break their charm. The disproportion between a figure and vast power opens an immeasurable range of fear for the imagination; hence our disproportionate fear of small animals. It must be a brave general who can keep his place as calmly and impassively before the close persistent hum of a maddened hornet as before the hum of a cannon. In dreams one shudders more before mysterious dwarfs than before the clearly visible, upright figure of a giant.

What then is true in sham or superstitious belief? Not the special object and its personal meaning—for both change with nations and the times—but the principle, the feeling, first the teacher of superstition and then the student, evoked and transfigured by the romantic poet: the immense, almost helpless feeling with which the mute spirit stands as if stunned and alone in the wild, gigantic mill of the universe. He sees countless unconquerable world wheels circling behind one another in the strange mill and hears the roar of an eternally driving stream. Around him it thunders and the ground trembles. Now here, now there a brief tinkle sounds in the storm, here things are ground up, there swept forward and gathered up, and so he finds himself abandoned in the omnipotent, blind, solitary machine which roars about him mechanically and does not address him with any living tone. But his spirit looks fearfully about for the giants who have set up and adapted the marvelous machine to certain goals, and whom he must suppose to be, as spirits of such a complexly constructed body, much greater than their work. Thus fear becomes not so much the creator as the creation of the gods; but since actually what differs from the world machine and wanders mightily about and above it begins in ourselves, it follows that the inner night is indeed the mother of the gods, herself a goddess. Every material or universal realm becomes finite and narrow and nothing, as soon as a realm of spirits is thought to be its supporting earth and sea. But that a will— consequently something infinite or indefinite—reaches through what is mechanically determined, we are told not only by our will but by the inscriptions on the two gates leading *in* and *out* of life. For *before* and *after* earthly life, there is life, although not an earthly one. It is announced also by dreaming, a special, *freer,* voluntary union of the spiritual world with the heavy one, a condition where the gates around the whole horizon of reality stay open the entire night without one's knowing what strange figures fly in through them. The dreams of others are never revealed to us without producing a certain shudder.[18]

Indeed, we may say that once one supposes even a single human spirit with a human body, one implies the whole spiritual realm, the background of nature, with all its powers of contact; a strange ether drifts then, before which the gutstrings of the earth tremble and harmonize. Once harmony between body and soul, earth and spirits is granted, then the spiritual lawgiver, whether with or without physical laws, must manifest himself in the universe, just as the body expresses both the soul and itself at the same time. The error of superstition consists only in our first thinking we understand completely this spiritual mimicry of the universe, as a child thinks it understands that of its parents, and, secondly, wanting to relate it wholly to ourselves alone. Actually every event is a prophecy and manifestation of spirit, not for us alone, however, but for the universe; therefore we cannot explain it.[19]

25. Examples of Romanticism
Isolated rays of romantic light fall already in Greek poetry: in Oedipus's disappearance as presented by Sophocles, in the fearful Demogorgon, in Fate, for example. But the true magician and master of the romantic spiritual realm remains Shakespeare, although he is also king of many Greek islands. This beautiful man, who would have invented belief in the spiritual realm, if he had not found it, like all romanticism finds his image in the plains of Baku. The night is warm, a blue fire which neither injures nor ignites runs over the whole plain, and all the flowers are burning, but the mountains loom dark in the heavens.

---

[18] We hear the dreams of others with a romantic feeling; but we experience our own without such a feeling. This difference between you and me extends through all the moral relationships of man and deserves and receives consideration elsewhere.

[19] Probably for just this reason Karl Philipp Moritz, more a visionary than a creator of spirits, mentioned dreams, apparitions, premonitions, etc., in his *Empirical Psychology* so much more often than he explained them. Behind the screen of the collector and interpreter, he thus hid his spiritualism from the materialism of Berlin.

Now Schiller should be named. If philosophy is sunlight, and romanticism moonlight, this poet sheds daylight over the center of the world in his reflective poetry, while he casts his poetic light over the two ends of life and death into the two eternities, the world before us and the world behind us—in brief, over the *immovable* poles of the movable world—as the sun alternately at either pole dawns without setting all day long like a moon. Hence the moon glimmer of his astrology, of his *Maid of Orleans*,[20] and of his "Song of the Bell." The latter is romantic already in its choice of the romantic superstition that hostile spirits usually struggle over the casting of bells, since these holiest of all instruments call only from this world into the other and in this world always speak to us on Hercules' crossroads.

Herder's splendid *Legends* have not yet found an audience to interpret them as Christian romanticism. The Mooress Zorayda looks down from the romantic starry heaven of *Don Quixote* as a nearer star. Although too much absorbed in the romantic and German past to assume and present the present, Tieck has presented in *Sternbald* an almost Shakespearean humorous fantasy about the imagination.

Gozzi gleams with a warm Italian enchanted night next to Goldoni, whose cold and pure snow falls over Rome. Hebel's *Alemannic Poems* are deliciously romantic.

A strange feeling like that in an unheard dream runs through Goethe's romantic *Meister* as if a dangerous spirit ruled over the accidents therein, as if he would step any minute from his storm cloud, as if one looked down from a mountain at the gay bustle of men, in short as if a natural catastrophe were at hand. Among Goethe's fairy tales, the one in the *Horen,* and among the dramas his *Faust* will gleam as romantic Gemini above posterity.

The following are examples of the romantic, with the limitation that I pronounce as romantic and poetic only the works, not their authors. Let this be my excuse when I cite as romantic the love of the page Fanno and the princess Rose in Klinger's *Golden Cock,* or his *Bambino,* and assert correctly that he first shed romantic rose and lily light on court life in that work; for in his poetic

---

[20] Except that, as often happens in the theater, an opening stage door sometimes lets in external light on the latter, and so cancels the poetic illumination through a worldly one.

youth the poetic and civic worlds contended with one another until the latter finally carried off the victory, as his newest work (*Observations,* etc.) proves by the judgments which it passes and which have been passed on it. I ask every reviewer of novels or even of aesthetic literature in supplements to general literary journals, whether he must not—as long as he is more mature than his judgment—admit and realize that Klinger's poems only widen the gap between reality and the ideal instead of closing it, and that each of his novels, like a village fiddle piece, resolves the dissonances into a last shrill dissonance. At times in *Giafar* and other works a faint, brief, hopeful peace or an eye-sigh closes the well-motivated battle between fortune and merit. But a primeval mountain chain of rare manliness running through his works as through his life compensates for our vain desire for a happier, more colorful play. Romantic too is Friedrich Schlegel's sonnet "The Sphinx" in the *Athenäum.* An awesome superstition is turned to romantic purposes in both Schlegel's *Alarcos* and the old Spanish romance *Del Conde Alarcos* by the first interpreter of the legend: The villain dies in three days if his dying victim summons him before the divine tribunal. The construction passes gracefully into a romantic twilit evening. Though too briefly developed, it is a sublime and true idea that a dying woman should lose her earthly love for her murderer in the cold moment of departure, when the second sterner world is already beginning, and that like a tribunal of the dead she insists on justice. Romantic is the love story running from the 185th to the 210th night of the *Arabian Nights* and the poetry of "The Seasons" in Mnioch's *Analects* (I, 67), but so much the more unpoetic his poetry about the inner being. Klopstock is far more romantic and very seldom Greek; like Haydn, who paints with music in *The Creation,* he conversely often only sings in his verbal painting. One should not confuse every kind of simplicity (often it is only philosophical) with the Greek spirit.[21]

Nothing is rarer than the flower of romanticism. If, as for the Greeks, the fine arts are a kind of music, romanticism is the music

[21] The ancients unconsciously expressed themselves with brevity and simplicity and wanted to communicate in a simple fashion only the effect of the object which moved them. The moderns tailor for themselves a coquettish brevity from a self-conscious pretentious complexity, and thereby hope to win the prizes of both simplicity and wealth.

of the spheres. It demands the whole of a man in the most delicate development, the blossoms of the finest, highest twigs; in a poem it wants to hover above the whole, like an invisible but intense perfume. A well-known author close to us all sometimes makes his romantic perfume too visible and too dense, like frost. The Germans, whose poetic character Herder found to consist in honesty and common sense, are too heavy for romantic poetry and almost more skilled at the plastic. The great Lessing, who had almost every spirit but the romantic, could pass as characteristic spokesman and representative of the German spirit, although he was romantic (if the bold expression may be allowed), not indeed in poetry but in philosophy. Voss's plastic idylls rank far above his odes, which lack not poetic body, but often the ideal spirit. The same inadequacy is even more true of his comic poems. Just as rare as romantic talent is romantic taste. Since the romantic spirit, this poetic mysticism, is never to be grasped and retained in detail, the most beautiful romantic blossoms are exposed to brutal handling and trampling by the crowd who judge writers for readers. Hence the awful fate of the good Tieck and even more so of genuine fairy tales. Change makes the repetition of a rule more difficult here, for the plastic sun gives uniform light, like waking; the romantic moon glimmers changeably, like dreaming.

When the kinds of poetry are animated by the romantic spirit, the lyric becomes sentimental; the epic becomes fantastic, as in the fairy tale, the dream, and the novel; the drama becomes both, because it is actually the union of these two kinds of poetry.

Translated by Margaret R. Hale

Aphorisms and Fragments
Novalis

On Anacreon and His Poetic Form

If there is a poetic form that characterizes gentle pleasure and charming grace, then it is certainly the delicate Anacreontic. How pleasing are his poetic works! How gay his descriptions! How delightful and lively his images! When I read him, I do not view him as a poet—no! He is the most sensual, agreeable, seductive of Greeks. I join him at the table, I follow him and his beloved into a bower dedicated to love, I follow him in his sweet dallying, and he makes me as happy, as drunk with bliss as he is himself; I feel what he feels. This delightful naiveté and truth and nature are the greatest charms of Anacreon's lyrical pieces, and it is on account of this that they are still interesting and agreeable to us after so many centuries and such changes in customs and manners. Yet there are many proud ones today, contemptuous of the deathless works of the ancients, who show no respect even for this delightful painter of nature, this dear favorite of the graces, and often treat him slightingly. I have noticed that recent poets often prefer the odes of Anacreon, his most charming pieces. And why? Because they have found them wittier than the works of those ancients, as if wit were of greater worth than a deep feeling for nature. Our lyrics are never translated and yet are so popular in France, far more than the songs of Anacreon, which all the nations love to read. Why is this? Because the French are far more frivolous than delicate, favoring wit more than gentle feeling. And for the same reason our songs possess less inner feeling and more ingenuity, less simplicity and nature and more wit. I exclude those

62

that were composed by us in the olden times. For these have simplicity, nature, and feeling in abundance, but too little taste. Every
step that we now take removes us more from nature; its hues do
not appear lively enough to us and we seek cosmetics. Soon we
shall find Corneille cold, Racine dull, and Quinaut flat. These verses
of Fontenelle:

> You must not love
> if your heart is too tender

are certainly preferred to those of Quinaut, which say the same
thing but in a different manner:

> If I ever loved in vain
> Then I'd know my heart full well
> Were soft, 't would be too tender.

These verses of Quinaut are delicately turned, yet they will be considered ordinary and those of Fontenelle charming, even in the
mouth of a shepherdess. Anacreon, who was very naive and sensitive, thought like Quinaut and would have expressed himself
likewise. But Coulange and Vadé, surely unknown to foreigners,
are preferred to Quinaut, whose poetry we now find very flat and
common. La Motte Oudart [Houdar], a fine wit, as *galant* (we
have no German word, at least I know none, that expressed the
idea of *galant*) as Fontenelle, but like him neither a poet nor a
lover, has already said it in his lecture on the ode, though he has
by no means proved it: An Anacreontic song is the product of an
instant, not of cool reflection. It is an impromptu.

Apology for Friedrich Schiller

Almost everywhere there has been loud lamenting over that excellent poem of the Honorable Councillor Schiller, "The Gods of
Greece" [*Die Götter Griechenlands*], and people have called him
an atheist and I know not what and, in their holy zeal, have very
nearly shipped him off to hell. Wiser and unbiased heads have, for
the most part, judged more properly, but no one except Wieland,

who gave a hint in the *Deutsche Merkur,* has openly declared himself or made a move to shame the zealots and other enthusiasts, who were perhaps only swept up by some holy enthusiasm. While I do not put myself among the wise ones, I nonetheless flatter myself to be at least unbiased in that I neither know the poet nor account myself an atheist, naturalist, deist, neologist, or strict orthodox, nor an adherent of any sect whatever. Thus, for those few who have read my piece, I think I am justified in providing another viewpoint of a man whom Germany ranks among its leading lights, a viewpoint which, I am firmly convinced, reflects what he deserves. Even Count Stollberg, a man for whom I have the greatest respect both on account of his poetic genius and his exalted character, seems to me to have understood the poem from a false perspective; so also Herr von Kleist in the *Deutsche Merkur,* though I am fully prepared for both of these gentlemen to render full justice to their works as poetic achievements.

From **Pollen**

*Friends, the soil is poor; we must scatter seeds abundantly
even to get only moderate harvests.*

25. Whoever describes nothing but his own experiences, his favorite objects, and cannot bring himself patiently to examine and depict even a totally unknown and uninteresting object, will never achieve anything preeminent as an artist. The artist must be able and willing to describe everything. This is the basis of the great manner of description that is so justly admired in Goethe.

27. One of Goethe's singular talents consists in his manner of connecting small, insignificant incidents with more important occurrences. He seems to have no other intention in this than to stimulate the imagination poetically with a mysterious game. Here too this remarkable man has penetrated the heart of nature and possessed himself of one of its clever strategies. Ordinary life is full of such coincidences. They are a game which, like all games, consists fundamentally of surprise and dissimulation.

Many common sayings derive from an insight into this contrary relationship—thus, for example, bad dreams signify luck; declaration of death, long life; a hare crossing the path, misfortune. Virtually all the superstition of common people is based on interpretations of this game.

29. Humor is a manner assumed arbitrarily. Its arbitrariness is what makes it a stimulant. It is the result of a free mingling of the conditioned and the unconditioned. It is through humor that what is specifically conditioned becomes generally interesting and achieves objective value. Wit arises where imagination and judgment come into contact; humor, where reason and the will are coupled. Raillery belongs to humor but is a degree lower. It is no longer purely artistic and much more limited. What Friedrich Schlegel characterizes so sharply as irony is actually, as I see it, the result of and akin to true reflection—the veritable presence of the spirit. Schlegel's irony seems to me true humor. Many names are advantageous for an idea.

53. The task of the critic of the arts is to devise formulations for artistic entities that will allow them truly to be understood. Such work prepares the history of art.

56. The true letter is by its nature poetic.

68. A translation is either grammatical or transforming or mythic. Mythic translations are translations in the supreme sense. They set forth the pure, ultimate character of the individual work of art. They give us not the actual work but its ideal. There does not yet exist, I believe, a fully realized model of this. But one finds luminous traces of it in the spirit of certain works of criticism and descriptions of works of art. This calls for a brain fully possessed by the poetical and the philosophic spirit. Greek mythology is in part such a translation of a national religion. The modern madonna is also such a myth.

Grammatical translations are translations in the ordinary sense. They require a great amount of learning but only discursive capacities.

The transforming translations, if they are to be genuine, call for the highest poetical spirit. They lapse easily into travesties, like

Bürger's Homer in iambics, Pope's Homer, and the French translations altogether. The true translator of this sort must in fact be the artist, capable at will of presenting the idea of the whole this way or that. He must be the poet of the poet, capable of speaking at once according to his own and to the poet's idea. The innate genius of mankind stands in a similar relation to every individual man.

Not books alone but everything may be translated in these three ways.

70. Our language is either mechanical, atomistic, or dynamic. True poetic language should, however, be organic and vital. How often one feels the poverty of words that cannot hit off many ideas in a single stroke.

71. In the beginning, poets and priests were one; it was only in later times that they became separated. The true poet, however, has always remained a priest, just as the true priest has remained a poet. And will not the future restore this former state of affairs?

101. The lore of tales contains the history of the original ideal world; it encompasses the distant past, the present, and the future.

102. Every true book is a Bible when the spirit gives its blessing. But a book is written only rarely for the sake of the Book; and though the spirit may be like a precious metal, most books are Ephraimites. Of course, every useful book must, at the least, be strongly alloyed. Precious metal is not to be used in pure form for exchange or mixing. Many true books suffer the same fate as those gold nuggets in Ireland. For many a year they serve simply as weights.

103. Many books are longer than they seem. They have veritably no ending. The boredom that they induce is truly absolute and endless. Exemplary in this sense are works by Messrs. Heydenreich, Jacob, Abicht, and Pölitz. Here is a staff that everyone may augment with appropriate acquaintances known to him.

104. Many antirevolutionary books have been written for revolution. But Burke wrote a revolutionary book against revolution.

106. Isn't it excellent to be the contemporary of a truly great man! Most cultivated Germans today are not of this opinion. They are so delicate as to reject everything that is great and practice the leveling method. If the Copernican system were not so firmly established, they would be quite content to make the sun and stars into jack-o'-lanterns once more and the earth into the universe. Thus Goethe, at present the true custodian of the poetic spirit on earth, will be viewed with contempt and treated as meanly as possible, if his behavior does not conform to the standards of ordinary intercourse, and he even momentarily puts them into question. The reception that the general public has given to *Hermann und Dorothea* represents an interesting symptom of this weakness of soul.

107. The geognosts believe that the physical center of gravity lies under Fez and Morocco. Goethe as an anthropognostic considers, in *Meister,* that the intellectual center of gravity is to be located within the German nation.

109. Nothing is more poetical than recollection and intimation, or the imagining of the future. To imagine early times draws us to death, to evaporation. To imagine the future incites us to stimulation, to summation, to assimilative action. Thus all recollection is melancholy, all intimation joyful. The former moderates an excessive liveliness, the latter heightens a deficient life-force. Ordinary experience of the present connects past and future through contraction and limitation. This results in contiguity, a kind of crystallization brought about through reflection. But there is a kind of spiritual sense of the present that identifies the two by means of dissolution, and this mixture is the element, the atmosphere of the poet.

114. The art of writing books has not yet been invented. But it is on the point of being invented. Fragments of this sort are literary seeds. There may indeed be barren grain among them: yet if only some sprout!

From **Miscellaneous Notations**

112. In a great many books the *raisonnement* of the author, that is to say, that element onto which the data and experiences are attached, consists of a collection of the strangest psychic phenomena—extraordinarily instructive for the anthropognostic—full of traces of asthenic tendencies and indirect sparks of stimulation.

125. The true reader must be an extended form of the author. He is the higher authority who receives the object in a preliminary form from a lower one. The feeling with which the author has sorted out the materials of his work is set into motion once more in the reading in order to separate what is rough from what is polished in the book. And if the reader will work over the book according to his idea, then a second reader will clarify it yet further, and thus, in consequence of the fact that the formed material is repeatedly put into freshly fashioned containers, the whole mass finally becomes a significant entity, an element of the vital, active spirit.

The author can often himself clarify his book by *impartial* rereading. The uniqueness of a work is often lost with strangers, for it is such a rare gift to be able fully to enter into an alien idea. Often even for the author. To correctly censure a book is no sign of greater intellect or higher powers. A greater acuity and discrimination is quite natural with new impressions.

From **Logological Fragments**

Poetry

32. The poet, just as he has begun the procession, brings it to a close. If the philosopher puts all in order, sets it up, the poet dissolves all ties. His words are not general signs—they are tones—terms of enchantment that put comely groups into motion around them. Just as the clothes of saints still contain wondrous powers, so is many a word blessed on account of a marvelous remembrance and becomes almost a poem in itself. For the poet language

is never too poor but always too general. He often requires commonplace, used-up words. His world is simple, as is his instrument—but just as inexhaustible in melodies.

34. The poetry of primitive people is a narrative without beginning, middle, or end. The pleasure that it gives them is merely pathological—simply pastime, mere dynamic activation of the power of imagination.

Epic poetry is the ennobled form of primitive poetry. In essence, altogether the same.

The novel already stands much higher. The former continues, the latter grows. In the former there is a rhythmic progression, in the novel, geometric.

35. Whoever cannot make poems will only judge them in a negative manner. True criticism must possess the capacity to bring forth the product it would criticize. Taste alone judges only negatively.

36. Poetry is creation. Every poetic work must be a living individual.

42. Poetry is the great art of the construction of transcendental well-being. Thus the poet is the transcendental physician.

Poetry works its ends by means of hurt and titillation, pleasure and pain, error and truth, health and sickness. It mixes all in its great goal of goals—*the raising of mankind above itself.*

43. Just as the philosophical systems up to the present relate to logology, so do the past poetic achievements to the poetry that is to come.

Those poetic creations usually achieved their ends dynamically; the forthcoming, transcendental poetry may be called organic. Once it has been invented, one will realize that all true poets hitherto have created organically *without knowing it,* but that the lack of awareness of what they did exercised a significant influence on the whole of their work, so that they were for the most part really poetic only in isolated instances, but on the whole merely unpoetic. Logology will necessarily bring about this revolution.

44. The content of the drama is a coming into being and a vanishing. It shows the emergence of an organic form out of a fluid medium, a well-structured action out of chance. It shows the dissolution, the collapse of an organic form into chance. It may show both of these, and this makes it into a perfect drama. It's easy to see that its content must involve a transformation, a process of refinement and reduction. *Oedipus at Colonus* is a fine example of this, so also *Philoctetes*.

45. Goethe's *Fairy Tale* is a narrated opera.

46. Poetry dissolves alien existence into one's own.

47. Transcendental poetry is a mixture of philosophy and poetry. Fundamentally, it includes all transcendental functions, and in fact contains the transcendental in itself. The transcendental poet is the transcendental man himself.

48. The working out of a transcendental poetry should result in a system of tropes, a tropology, which would encompass the rules of the *symbolic construction* of the transcendental world.

49. Genius in itself is poetical. Where genius has been at work, it has worked poetically. The true moral individual is the poet.

50. The true origin is Nature Poetry. The end is the second beginning—and it is Art Poetry.

51. It would be a nice question to determine whether the lyric poem is actually poetry, that is, plus poetry, or prose, that is, minus poetry. Just as the novel has been taken for prose, so the lyric poem has been taken for poetry, and in both cases mistakenly. The highest, truest prose is the lyric poem.

So-called prose has come about through a restriction of absolute extremes. It exists only ad interim and plays a subordinate, temporal role. A time will come when it will no longer exist. Then a breakthrough will have come out of the restriction. A true life will have come into being, and prose and poetry will thus be intimately united and put into mutual exchange.

Poeticisms

52. Lessing's prose often lacks a hieroglyphic component.

53. Lessing saw too keenly and consequently lost the sense of the indistinct whole, the magical perception of objects together in manifold illumination and obscurity.

54. Just as the epic, lyric, and dramatic ages followed one another in the history of Greek literature, a period of antiquity, modernity, and a combination of the two succeed one another in universal history. Most interesting is the matter of minus literature.
The core of that combination seems to have begun with Goethe. Whoever can guess how it came about will provide the basis of a complete history of literature.

55. For the ancients, religion was already to a certain extent what it should become for us—practical poetry.

56. Voltaire is one of the greatest minus poets who ever lived. His *Candide* is his *Odyssey*. Too bad that his world was a Parisian boudoir. With less personal and national vanity he would have become much more.

57. Klopstock's works appear for the most part to be free translations and adaptations of an unknown poet by a very talented but unpoetic philologian.

58. Every representation of the past is a tragic drama in the veritable sense; every representation of what is to come, the future, a comic drama. The tragic drama is appropriate to the highest level of existence of a people, as the comic drama to a weak level. Tragic dramas would now be fitting for England and France, and comic dramas for Germany.

59. One should never look at works of the plastic arts without music, and correspondingly one should listen to musical works only in beautifully decorated chambers.
Further, works of poetry should never be enjoyed without both. This is why poetry has such an extraordinary effect in beautiful

theaters or in tasteful churches. In every good social gathering, one should periodically listen to music. Visiting rooms have been instituted as a result of the realization that architectural and sculptural decorations are essential for true sociability. Select food, social games, elegance in dress, dancing, and even a more discriminating, freer, more general manner of conversation grew out of this sense of a higher type of existence in society and the new ways of combining beauty with lively manners.

60. The lyric poem is the chorus in the drama of life—of the world. The lyric poet is the sweetly mixed chorus fashioned of youth and age, joy, sympathy, and wisdom.

158. Fine poetic Hogarthisms, for example, love. Hogarth's sheets are novels. Hogarth's works are pictured wit, true Roman satires for the eye. Thus a true musical fantasy should be a satire for the ear. Hogarth is first of the satiric poets; Shakespeare of his type as well.

159. The lyric poem is for heroes, it produces heroes. The epic poem is for humans. Heroes are lyric, humans epic, genius is dramatic. Man lyric, woman epic, marriage dramatic.

174. Mankind: metaphor.

Anecdotes

206. Witty, significant, sentimental, moral, scholarly, political, historical, characteristic, individual, facetious or amusing, artistic, humorous, romantic, tragic, poetic anecdotes.

History is an immense anecdote. An anecdote is a historical element, a historical molecule or epigram. A history in anecdotes— Voltaire has produced something like that—is a most interesting work of art. History in its usual form is something that has been welded together, or an interlocking series of anecdotes that has run together into a continuum.

What is to be preferred, the continuum or the discretum? A vast individuality or a mass of smaller individualities? The former endless, the latter defined, finite, oriented, determined?

A master of anecdotes must be able to transform everything into anecdotes. Schlegel is right, the true novel must be a satire.

Something like Lichtenberg's commentary on Hogarth remains to be written about *Wilhelm Meister*. Up to now, a review has been understood as the sum and substance of what could be written and said of a book—and it must even be methodic and systematic. We are far from that yet. What if it could first be a satire. Let us divide this task first into various components. A book brings about, like everything, thousands of sensations and functions— determinate, defined, and free.

207. A major class of anecdotes consists of those that display a human characteristic in an unusual, striking manner, for example, cunning, generosity, courage, inconstancy, eccentricity, cruelty, wit, fantasy, affability, propriety, love, friendship, sagacity, modesty, etc. In short, this is a gallery of manifold human actions, a characterization of mankind. These anecdotes belong to the science of man and are thus didactic. Another major class constitutes those that are intended to produce an effect, to occupy our imagination in an agreeable way. These are perhaps to be called poetic anecdotes, though only the fewest of them may be authentic (absolute) poetry.

Thus we would have two principal classes, characteristic and poetic anecdotes. The former affect our cognition, the latter our faculty of desiring—*sit venia verbis*. The two may be mixed, and they should be to a certain extent. The more poetical the characteristic anecdotes, the better. Inversely, all poetic anecdotes, insofar as they are artistic and possess poetic content, are characteristic with respect to poetics or the study of the nature of poetry. Goethe's travels with Kraus represent an interesting contribution to the art of poeticizing ordinary life.

The art of anecdoting. A true anecdote is already in itself poetic. It takes hold of the imagination. Isn't the imagination, or the higher organ, the poetic sense itself? Yet when the imagination is stimulated for the sake of reason or of the understanding, we do not have pure poetry. The witty anecdote consists of arousing the attention, a sense of suspense, and then stimulation or a lack thereof. Deceptive anecdotes belong to this last class. (Laughter, paroxysms, fascination, disinterest.) (Suppressing someone.)

The narrative often involves ordinary occurrences, but it is entertaining. It maintains the imagination in suspension or in a state of alternation, puts it in an induced, feverish condition, and then, on completion, releases it with renewed well-being. (Continuing fever, alternating fever.)

All poetry interrupts the ordinary state of existence, almost like slumber, in order to renew us—and thus to keep our sense of life fresh.

To a certain extent, illnesses, accidents, extraordinary occurrences, journeys, social gatherings have a similar effect. Unfortunately, the whole existence of mankind up to now has demonstrated the effects of irregular, imperfect poetry.

What we call faith in reconciliation is nothing but the trust of a perfected poetic intelligence in the destiny of our life.

We shall make ourselves into our own poetic Fato by mastering the tuning hammer of our higher organ—thereby poeticizing our lives and letting them be poeticized as we desire.

My anecdotes should be witty, humorous, fantastic, peculiar, philosophical, dramatic (poetic) anecdotes.

A dialogue is actually an anecdote when it possesses absolutely brevity.

Characteristic anecdotes refer to an interesting subject and arouse interest only from the outside. The purely poetic anecdote refers to itself and arouses interest for its own sake.

Mathematical anecdote on chess. Transformation of an anecdote into an indefinite task.

237. The work of books is in fact only a caricature of the real world. Both derive from the same source. The former, however, appears in a freer, more mobile medium—thus all its colors are harsher, less mezzotint; the movements are more lively, the outlines thus more striking, and the expression hyperbolic. The former appears only *fragmentary,* the latter *complete.* Therefore the former is more poetic, spiritual, interesting, picturesque, but also less true, less philosophical, less moral. Most men, including most scholars, possess only a bookish perspective—a fragmentary view of the real world—and so it suffers from the same discrepancies but also enjoys the same advantages as the world of books. Many books are also nothing but depictions of such isolated, fragmen-

tary views of the real world. More on the relation of the world of books (world of literature) to the real world.

238. . . . Writers are as one-sided as all artists of a given medium, and even more stubborn. Among professional writers, there are surprisingly few liberal individuals, particularly when they have no other means of subsistence than their writing. To live on one's writings is a most risky undertaking, even for someone who possesses true intellect and a free spirit.

296. The true poet is *all-knowing*—he is a real world in miniature.

Teplitz Fragments

445. Goethe is altogether a practical poet. He is, with respect to his works—like the English with respect to their manufacture—preeminently simple, neat, convenient, and durable. He has accomplished in German literature what Wedgwood did in the world of the English arts. Like the English, he possesses a taste that is economical by nature and discriminating through the intellect. The two are very well integrated and have a close relationship, in the *chemical* sense. In his studies on natural philosophy it becomes clear that his tendency is rather to bring to completion something insignificant—to give it the highest polish and most useful shape—than to open up a world and undertake something about which one knows in advance that he cannot fully realize it, that it will certainly remain imperfect, and that he can never attain the skill of a master therein. Even in this field, he chooses a romantic or an otherwise deeply involuted subject. His investigations of light, of the metamorphosis of plants and insects represent a confirmation, and at the same time the most convincing proof, of the fact that even the perfectly realized didactic lecture belongs in the sphere of the artist. One could also in a certain sense maintain justly that Goethe is the foremost physicist of his age—and in fact that he marks an epoch in the history of physics. It's not a question of the extent of his knowledge, just as little as one could say that discoveries determine the rank of the scientific investigator. The issue here is whether one views nature as the artist does antiquity—for

what is nature but a living antiquity? Nature and insight into nature originate at the same time, just as antiquity and the knowledge of antiquity; for it is a great error to think that there exist multiple antiquities. Antiquity is only now beginning. It comes to be under the eyes and the soul of the artist. The remains of early ages are only the specific stimuli for the formation of antiquity. Antiquity is not fashioned by hands. The intellect brings it forth by way of the eye—and the chiseled stone is nothing but the body that gains significance through it and comes to be its manifest form. Just as Goethe the physicist stands in relation to the other physicists, so the poet to the other poets. He is now and then surpassed in range, variety, and profundity, but who could be his equal in formative power? With him everything is act—as with others it is only tendency. He makes something real, whereas others make something only possible—or necessary. We are all creators by way of necessity or possibility—but how little by way of reality. The academic philosopher might perhaps call this active empiricism. We will content ourselves with a consideration of Goethe's artistic talent together with a glance at his intellect. With him one may come to learn the capacity of abstracting in a new light. He abstracts with a rare precision but never without at the same time constructing the object to which the abstraction corresponds. This is nothing but applied philosophy—and so we discover at the end, to our not inconsiderable astonishment, that he is an applied, practical philosopher, as in fact every true artist has ever been. Even the *pure* philosopher will be practical, though the applied philosopher need not occupy himself with pure philosophy, for this is an art in itself [Goethe's *Meister*]. The seat of art in its true form is solely in the intellect, and it does its work of construction in accord with its own, singular notions. Fantasy, wit, and judgment are only requisitioned by it. Thus *Wilhelm Meister* is altogether an artistic product, a work of the intellect. From this point of view, one would find a number of very ordinary works admitted into the precincts of art, whereas most of the writings that are held in high esteem would be excluded. One finds artistic talent far more often among the Italians and Spaniards than with us. Even the French are not lacking in it—the English have far less and resemble us in this, who are also very rarely endowed with *artistic talent,* although we may be the most richly endowed among all nations in those capacities that the intellect, in its operation, employs. Of course, this excess in the requisites of art is what makes the few artists among us so unique—and so outstanding; and we may be assured that the most remarkable works of art will be created among us, for no nation can match us in vital universality. If I have understood the most recent friends of the literature of antiquity well, their call to imitate the classical authors signifies nothing else than to make us into artists, to awaken the artistic talent in us. No modern nation has ever had the artistic intellect in so high a degree as the ancients. With them everything is a work of art—but perhaps one would not go too far in assuming that this is, or could be, so only for us. Classical literature has the same status as antiquity; it is actually not given to us, not existent, but must first be brought forth by us. A classical literature—one that the ancients themselves did not possess—comes into being for us as a result of assiduous and resourceful study of the ancients. The ancients would have had to undertake an inverse task—for the mere artist is a one-sided, narrow individual. Goethe probably stands behind the ancients in respect to discipline, but he surpasses them in content, though this accomplishment is not his own. His *Meister* comes close enough to them, for how much is it a novel pure and simple, without qualification—and how much this means in our time!

Goethe will and must be transcended, but only as the ancients may be transcended, in content and power, in variety and depth—as artist actually not, or only to a small degree, for his accuracy and discipline are already perhaps more exemplary than they seem.

Dialogues

I.

A: The new catalogue of the book fair?
B: Just hot off the press.
A: What a load of letters—what an unbelievable output of time—
B: You seem to belong to the Omarists—if one may name you after the most consistent of all of you.

A: You surely don't want to make yourself into the panegyrist of this epidemic of books.

B: Why the panegyrist? But I am in truth delighted over the yearly increase in this commodity, which brings in only honor when exported, but solid profit when imported. There are, after all, more true, substantial ideas passing in exchange among us than among all our neighbors put together. The discovery of these immense mines in Germany—which are greater than those of Potosi and Brazil, and which in truth have produced and will continue to produce a more important revolution than the discovery of America—comes in the middle of the present century. And how much have we gained since in scholarly expertise, efficiency, and brilliant and useful arrangements of all sorts. At present we gather everywhere the crude ore or the lovely forms—melt down the former and become adept in imitating and surpassing the latter.

And would you have us pour it all back and return to the crude poverty of our fathers! Is this not at least a spur to activity? And is not every form of activity praiseworthy?

A: If we proceeded in this fashion, there would be nothing to object, but let us now reflect on great art and precious metal somewhat more closely.

B: I will not admit arguments against the whole, which are based on the weakness and deficiencies of a part. Something like this must be considered as a whole.

A: A whole made up of wretched elements is itself wretched, or rather, it is no single whole. Of course, if there were a *planned, regulated progress*—if every book filled a gap somewhere—would every book fair then become a systematic unit in the train of culture? Then every such fair would be a necessary episode, and a perfected path to an ideal cultural formation would finally come into being from such orderly progression—such a systematic catalogue—how much smaller in volume and how much greater in weight!

B: You and many others do as the Jews. They await the Messiah endlessly, and he is already long since here. Do you think, then, that human destiny or, if you will, the nature of mankind needs first to frequent our lecture halls in order to learn what a system is? It seems to me that our system makers would do well to attend to its teaching. Accidents constitute the specific data—the combining of accidents, their coming together, is not another accident but a law, the consequence of the most deeply considered, orderly wisdom. There is not a book in the fair's catalogue that has not produced its fruit, even if it were only to fertilize the soil in which it grew. We fancy that there are many tautologies there. But in the place where they arose, they provided an excellent stimulus for this or that idea. Only for the whole, for us, are they tautologies; the poorest novel has at least given some pleasure to the author's friends. Paltry sermons and moralizing tracts have their public, their adherents and, by virtue of their typographical armor, exercise a tenfold impact on their auditors and readers—and so in everything.

A: You seem totally to forget the negative consequences of reading and the enormous expense of this modern luxury commodity.

B: My dear friend, isn't the purpose of money to activate? And why shouldn't it also serve this need of our nature, to inspire and satisfy the faculty of thinking? In regard to the negative consequences, let me ask you to please give this a moment's serious consideration, for such an objection on your part comes close to upsetting me.

A: I know what you're driving at, and I certainly don't wish to adopt outright philistine strictures as my own, but haven't you yourself often complained about your reading of books? Haven't you often enough spoken of the deadly addiction to nature in print?

B: It may be that my complaints of that sort could give rise to misunderstandings—but aside from the fact that they are usually only an expression of momentary low spirits when one's ideas are not general but subject to the passing affect and mood, I have usually in such cases denounced the unavoidable weakness of our nature, its tendency to submit to habit and comfort, and have not basically meant the domain of signs. This cannot be held responsible for the fact that we finally see only books and not things and that we have as much as lost our five bodily senses. Why do we cling so devotedly, like some wretched moss, to the printer's bar?

A: But if things continue in this fashion, it will be impossible in the end to study the whole of a discipline—the mass of writing grows so enormously.

B: Don't you believe it. Practice makes perfect, and so also with the reading of books. You'll soon learn to know your man—often you don't have to get beyond two pages of an author to know whom you have before you. The title often provides a sufficient physiognomic reading. The preface too is a subtle measure of a book. Thus the wiser ones now usually omit this traitorous index of the contents, and the slackers do so because a good preface is more difficult than the book—for, as the young, revolutionary Lessing put it, the preface is at once the root and square of the book, and I add to that, it is thus nothing but its authentic review.

Those citations and formulas of commentary of the older philologians, what were they but children of want—in books and their surfeit—in literary spirit.

A: I really don't know—I find an overabundance even of excellent books. How much time do I give to a single good book, or rather, every good book becomes the vehicle of a lifelong occupation—the object of an inexhaustible pleasure. Why then do you restrict yourself to only a few good men of wit and intelligence? Isn't it for the same reason? Aren't we after all so limited that we are capable of wholly enjoying only a few things? And isn't it better in the end thoroughly to possess a single lovely object than to glance past hundreds, to sip everywhere, and thus to dull one's senses prematurely with many, often antagonistic partial pleasures, without having thereby gained anything for good?

B: You speak like a religious brother. Unfortunately, you find a pantheist in me for whom the immeasurable world is just large enough. I restrict myself to a few good men of wit and intelligence—because I must. Where would I find more? So also with books. The making of books is still by far not vast enough for me. If I had the good fortune to be a father, I could not have enough of children—not merely ten or twelve—at least a hundred.

A: And women, too, greedy one?

B: No, only a *single* one, in all seriousness.

A: What a bizarre inconsistency.

B: Not more bizarre nor more inconsistent than to have only *one spirit* in me, and not a hundred. But just as my spirit may transform itself into hundreds and millions of spirits, so my wife into all the women there are. Every man is endlessly variable. Just as with the children, so with the books. I would like to have a whole collection of books before me, comprising all the arts and sciences, as the work of my spirit. And so with everything. *Wilhelm Meis-*

ters Lehrjahre is all we have now. We should possess as many *Lehrjahre* ["Years of Apprenticeship"], written in the same spirit, as possible—*Lehrjahre* of this sort for all the people who have ever lived—

A: Stop now— I am getting dizzy. More tomorrow. Then I will again be fit to drink a few glasses of your favorite wine with you.

II.

A: Are you in the mood today to tell me more of your ideas about authorship and such matters—I hope that I shall be able to bear a lively, paradoxical thrust—and if you set me going, I shall perhaps help you out. You know that when the laggard is set into motion, he is all the more daring and irrepressible.

B: Naturally, the more intensely an object expends force, the more force it is capable of taking on—and with this remark we stand before German literature, which strikingly confirms the truth thereof. Its capacity is immense. There would surely be no reproach in saying that it does not lend itself readily to filigree work. Still, there is no denying the fact that in its mass it is very much like the old warrior horde of its nation—which would certainly have defeated ten Roman armies in man-to-man combat—but as a mass was easy enough to overthrow by means of total impact, discipline, well-coordinated rapid movement, and command of the opportune situation.

A: Do you think that its momentum and force are still in the ascendance, or at least still in a period of uniformly accelerating movement?

B: In the ascendance certainly—and in fact in such a manner that its core separates and cleanses itself more and more from the loose matter that surrounded it and impeded its movement. In the case of a substance like literature, the force that provided the initial thrust, the originating force, augments in relation to its acceleration, and its capacity is thus multiplied to the same extent. You realize that what is projected here is an infinite measure. There are two variable factors that stand in augmenting interrelation to one another and whose product advances hyperbolically. But to make this image clearer, we must bear in mind that we are dealing not with movement and expansion in a quantitative fashion but with an ennobling *variation* (differentiation and separation) of qualities we call nature. Let us call one of these changeable factors the capacity of sense—the organic—the vitalizing force—wherein variability is also to be included. Let the other be energy, order, and multiplicity of the originating potencies. Think of the two in ongoing mutual augmentation and then conclude what will be the series of products. Wealth grows with simplicity, resonance with harmony, the identity and autonomy of the part with that of the whole, inner unification with outward differentiation.

A: As accurate and flattering this image of the history of our writing may be, it is nonetheless a bit too scholarly. I understand it only superficially—but perhaps that's just as well—and in place of an inexplicable explanation, I ask you to leave behind the eternal snow line and to speak as plainly as possible with me about certain phenomena at the foot of the mountain and amid the vegetative zone. Here you would not be so close to the gods and I would not have to fear an oracular tongue.

Monologue

Actually, it is a peculiar affair, speaking and writing: Real discourse is nothing but wordplay. One can't help but be astonished at the absurd, wholly erroneous assumption people make—that their talk is about things. No one knows what is most distinctive about language, namely, that it is concerned solely with itself. This is why it is such a marvelous and fertile mystery—that when someone speaks just in order to speak, he pronounces the most magnificent and original truths. But if he wants to speak about something specific, the capricious nature of language will cause him to say the most ridiculous and mistaken things. This is also why a number of serious people hate language. They note its mischievousness but don't perceive that worthless chatter constitutes the infinitely serious aspect of language. If one could only make clear to them that it is with language as with mathematical formulas—they constitute a world by themselves, they play only among themselves, express nothing but their own marvelous nature, and for that very reason they are so expressive and mirror the singular interplay of things. It is only through their freedom that they are parts of nature, and only in their free movement does the world soul express itself and make them into a delicate measure and abstract plan of things. So it is too with language—whoever is sensitive to its touch, its tempo, its musical spirit, whoever hearkens to the gentle workings of its inner nature and moves his tongue or hand accordingly, will be a prophet; however, whoever knows it well enough but possesses neither ear nor understanding for it will write truths like these but be taken in by language and mocked by men, like Cassandra by the Trojans. If I have thought here to have explained the nature and function of poetry as clearly as possible, I well know that no man can understand it and that I have spoken nonsense; for I have wanted to say this and no poetry has come into being. But what if I had been forced to speak and this compulsion to speak were the sign of the inspiration of language, of a vitality of language within me? And what if my will also wished only what I were compelled to do? Then might not this, after all, without my knowledge and conviction, be poetry and elucidate a mystery of language? And might I not then be called to be a writer—for what is a writer but one who is inspired by language?

Translated by Alexander Gelley

Dialogue on Poetry

Friedrich Schlegel

Epochs of Literature

Wherever living spirit appears captured in a formed letter, there is art, there is division, material to be overcome, and tools to be used; there are plans and laws of execution. This is why we see the masters of poetry striving so vigorously to form it in the most manifold way. Poetry is an art, and when it still was not, it had to become so. And when it becomes art, it excites in those who truly love it a strong desire to know it, to comprehend the intention of the master, to grasp the nature of the work, the origin of the school, and to discover the process of its development. Art is based on knowledge, and the discipline of art is its history.

It is an essential quality of all art to follow closely what has already been formed. Therefore, history goes back from generation to generation, from phase to phase, always farther back into antiquity, to its original source.

For the modern generation, for Europe, this source resides in Greece, and for the Greeks and their poetry it was Homer and the old school of the Homerids. This was the inexhaustible source of the poetry that in every respect was capable of being formed, a mighty stream of representation in which waves of life rush against one another, a peaceful ocean where the fullness of the earth and the splendor of the heavens are amiably reflected. Just as the sages sought the beginning of nature in water, so does the oldest poetry manifest itself in fluid form.

The body of legends and songs grouped itself around two different focal points. On the one hand, there is a great, common

84

undertaking, an onrush of power and discord, the glory of the bravest; and on the other hand, the abundance of the sensuous, the new, strange, and charming, the happiness of a family, a paragon of most versatile ingenuity, the way he succeeds in returning home in spite of difficulties. This original division prepared and shaped what we call the *Iliad* and *Odyssey* and whatever else in this grouping found a firm foothold and thus was preserved for posterity, rather than other songs of the same time.

In the growth of Homeric poetry, we see analogically the development of all poetry. But the roots of it are concealed from our eyes, and the flower and branches of the plant arise with incomprehensible beauty from the night of antiquity. This enticingly formed chaos is the seed from which the world of ancient poetry was organized.

The epic form declined rapidly. In its place there arose, even among the Ionians, the art of the iambics, which in both theme and treatment was the direct opposite of mythic poetry. For this reason, the iambics became the second focal point of Greek poetry, and along with it the elegy, whose changes and transformations are almost as manifold as those of the epic.

What the poetry of Archilochos was, we must guess not only from the fragments, information, and imitation in Horace's *Epodes,* but also from the analogy with the comedy of Aristophanes, and even the more distant analogy with Roman satire. We have no other material to fill the largest gap in the history of art. Yet everyone willing to reflect does realize that it is a permanent feature of the highest poetry to burst out in holy wrath and express its full power even in the strangest material, that is, everyday reality.

There are the sources of Greek poetry, its basis and beginning. The most beautiful flower includes the lyrical, choral, tragic, and comic works of the Dorians, Aeolians, and Athenians from Alcman and Sappho to Aristophanes. What remained from this truly golden age in the best genres of poetry bears the mark of a more or less beautiful or great style, the mark of the lively power of enthusiasm, and the formation of art in divine harmony.

The whole rests on the firm foundation of ancient poetry, one and indivisible by virtue of the joyously solemn life of free men and the holy power of the ancient gods.

First lyric poetry with its music of beautiful emotions joined iambic poetry, which reflects the violence of passion, and the elegiac, where the changing moods in the play of life appear so alive that they can be taken for love and hate; emotions which moved the peaceful chaos of Homeric poetry to new forms and creations. The choral songs, on the other hand, gravitated more toward the heroic spirit of the epic, and like it were differentiated so naturally according to the prevalence either of moral seriousness or of sacred freedom in the disposition and mood of the people. What Eros inspired in Sappho breathed music. And just as Pindar's dignity is mellowed by the merry charm of gymnastic games, so did the dithyrambs, we assume, imitate exuberantly the most daring beauties of orchestration.

The founders of the art of tragedy found their material and their prototypes in the epic. Just as the epic developed parody within itself, so did the same masters who invented tragedy delight in the invention of satirical plays.

Simultaneously with sculpture, there originated a new genre similar to it in the power of form and the laws of structure.

From the union of parody and the old iambic poetry there arose, in contrast to tragedy, comedy, which abounds in the highest kind of mimicry that is possible through words alone.

Whereas in tragedy actions and events, characteristic features, and passion were harmoniously ordered and formed out of a given legend into a beautiful system; here, a lavish abundance of ingenuity was boldly cast as a rhapsody, with deep understanding in seeming incoherence.

Both kinds of Attic drama intruded most effectively into life through their relationship to the ideal of both great forms, in which the highest and only life appears, the life of man among men. Enthusiasm for the Republic is found in the works of Aeschylus and Aristophanes, and a lofty prototype of a beautiful family in the heroic conditions of ancient times is at the basis of Sophocles' art.

Whereas Aeschylus is the eternal prototype of austere greatness and unrefined enthusiasm and Sophocles is a model of harmonious perfection, Euripides already shows that unfathomable delicacy possible only in a decadent artist, and his poetry is often only the most ingenious recitation.

This original body of Greek poetry—the old epic, iambic poetry, the elegy, festive songs and plays—is poetry itself. Everything that follows up to our own times is remnant, echo, isolated presentiment, approximation, and return to that highest Olympus of poetry.

For the sake of completeness, I must mention that the first sources and prototypes of the didactic poem—the interrelationship of poetry and philosophy—are also to be looked for in this period when the old forms flourished: in the nature-inspired hymns of the mysteries, in the ingenious teachings of the gnomes of social morality, in the universal poems of Empedocles and other poet-philosophers, and perhaps in the symposia where philosophical dialogue and its presentation are entirely transformed into poetry.

Such singularly great minds as Sappho, Pindar, Aeschylus, Sophocles, and Aristophanes have never reappeared. There were still, however, ingenious virtuosi of genius like Philoxenos who characterize the state of disintegration and fermentation, which is the transition from the great poetry of ideas to the precious, learned poetry of the Greeks. The center of this latter poetry was Alexandria. Yet not only here did there flourish a classical Pleiades of tragic poets; on the Attic stage, too, there shone a score of virtuosi. Yet even though the poets were making numerous attempts in all genres to imitate and transform each ancient form, this occurred primarily in the dramatic genre, where what remained of this period's inventive spirit expressed itself through a rich abundance of the most ingenious and often peculiar new combinations and compounds, partly in seriousness, partly in parody. However, this genre did not go beyond the ornamental, the witty, and the artificial, as was also true of the other genres, among which we mention only the idyll as a peculiar form of the period, a form, however, whose distinctiveness resides almost exclusively in its formlessness. In the rhythm, in many a turn of its language and the manner of presentation, it follows to some extent the epic style. The plot and dialogue follow the Doric single-scene mimes taken from social life with its local color, and in the antistrophic songs the idyll follows the artless songs of the shepherds. Its erotic spirit is like that of the elegy and the epigram of that time, when this spirit invaded even the epic works. Many of those, to be sure, were epic in form only, and the artist wanted to show in the didactic genre that his art could successfully deal with even the most difficult and driest material. On the other hand, some wrote on mythological themes to prove that they knew even the rarest and could regenerate and refine even the oldest and best developed forms. Or they simply played in ornate parodies with only seemingly real objects. In general, the poetry of that age spent itself either in the artificiality of the form, or in the sensuous charm of the material that was current even in the new Attic comedy; but the most sensual of those were lost.

But even when the possibilities of imitation were exhausted, they were satisfied with making new wreaths of old flowers; thus anthologies close the period of Greek poetry.

The Romans had only a short outburst of poetry, during which they energetically struggled and strove to appropriate the art of their models. They received these models first from the Alexandrians; therefore, the erotic and learned elements dominate in their works and, where art is concerned, these elements must remain the vantage point from which their art is to be appreciated. For the man of sense lets every production remain in its own sphere and judges it only according to its own ideal. To be sure, Horace appears interesting in any form, and we would look in vain for a man of this Roman's stature among the later Greeks. But this general interest in him is more a romantic one than a judgment of his art, which can rank him high only in satire. It is a splendid phenomenon when Roman vigor and Greek art become one to the point of coalescence. Thus Propertius created a great universe by means of the most learned art; the stream of fervent love flowed powerfully from his sincere heart. He can console us for the loss of the Greek elegiac poets, as Lucretius does for the loss of Empedocles.

For the course of a few generations, everybody in Rome wanted to write poetry and everybody believed he had to court the Muses and help them along. And this the Romans called their Golden Age of poetry. It was like a barren flower in the making of that nation. The moderns have followed them; what occurred under Augustus and Maecenas prefigured Italy's cinquecentists. Louis XIV tried to force the same spiritual renaissance in France; the English, too, agreed to consider the taste during Queen Anne's reign as best. Henceforth, no nation wanted to remain without its Golden

Age; each following age was even emptier and worse than the one before and what the Germans finally imagine to be their Golden Age the dignity of this presentation prohibits from a more accurate description.

I am returning to the Romans. They had, as was said, only one attack of poetry, which in fact was always alien to them. Only the poetry of urbanity was natural to them, and only with satire did they enrich the realm of art. Under each master, their satire assumed a new form, now by emulating the grand old style of Roman social life and wit, now by imitating the classical daring of Archilochos and of ancient comedy. Or it shaped the carefree lightness of an improviser into the clean elegance of a correct Greek, or it returned in the stoical manner and the purest style to the great old way of the nation, or again it gave way to the fervor of hate. Through satire there appears in new splendor what survives of the urbanity of eternal Rome in Catullus and Martial and otherwise remains isolated and scattered. The satire affords us a Roman vantage point for the achievements of the Roman spirit.

After the force of poetry had subsided as quickly as it had come, man's spirit took a new direction: Art disappeared in the clash of the old world and the new, and more than a millenium had passed before a great poet arose in the Occident again. He who among the Romans had rhetorical talent devoted himself to legal matters, and if he was a Greek he gave popular lectures about various kinds of philosophy. The Romans were satisfied with merely preserving old treasures of any kind, collecting and mixing them, abridging and spoiling them. As in the other branches of education, also in poetry there was only rarely a trace of originality, isolated and without emphasis. Nowhere was there an artist, no classical work in such a long time. On the other hand, religious invention and inspiration was all the more lively: In the creation of a new religion, in the attempts at transforming the old, in mystical philosophy must we seek the energy of that time, which in this respect was great: It was a border area of culture, a fertile chaos leading to a new order of things, the true Middle Ages.

A pure fountainhead of new heroic poetry flowed across Europe with the appearance of the Teutons. And when the wild energy of Gothic poetry merged through the influence of the Arabs with the echoes of the charming fairy tales of the Orient, there flourished on the southern coast of the Mediterranean a merry trade of inventors of lovely songs and unusual stories, which also spread, now in this form, now in that, along with the Latin saints' legends, worldly romances, praising love and arms.

Catholic hierarchy had meanwhile come of age; jurisprudence and theology allowed a certain return to antiquity. The great Dante, sacred founder and father of modern poetry, took this path, uniting religion and poetry. From the ancestors of the nation, he learned to condense the most peculiar and unusual, the most sacred and the sweetest in the vernacular into classical dignity and power, thus ennobling the Provençal art of rhyming. And since he was not fortunate enough to go back to the very sources, the Romans indirectly could stimulate the general idea of a great work of ordered structure. Powerfully he seized upon this idea and concentrated in *one* center the energy of his inventive spirit and in *one* immense poem embraced in his strong arms his nation and his age, the church and the empire, wisdom and revelation, nature and God's kingdom. The poem was a selection of the finest and the most infamous he had seen, of the greatest and the most peculiar he could invent; it was the most candid presentation of himself and his friends, the most glorious glorification of his beloved; everything was true to fact and truthful in the realm of the visible and full of secret meaning and relation to the invisible.

Petrarch gave the canzone and the sonnet perfection and beauty. His songs are the essence of his life, and a spirit animates and forms them into one indivisible work: Eternal Rome on earth and the Madonna in heaven as reflection of the only Laura of his heart symbolize and capture in beautiful freedom the spiritual unity of his entire poetry. His feeling, as it were, created the language of love and even after centuries is valued by all men of nobility. In the same way, Boccaccio's mind established for the poets of every nation an inexhaustible source of peculiar, mostly true, and very thoroughly elaborated stories, which through their power of expression and the excellent structure of his periods raised the narrative language of conversation to a solid foundation for the prose of the novel. As strict as Petrarch is in purity of love, just so earthly is the talent of Boccaccio, who preferred to console all charming women rather than to worship one. Through joyful grace and sociable jest, Boccaccio succeeded in being original in the canzone even after Petrarch, more than the latter did in his attempt to approximate the great Dante's vision and terzinas.

These three are the pillars of the old style of modern art; the connoisseur should appreciate their value; to the sensibility of the amateur, however, it is precisely the best and most original in them which remains difficult or at least foreign.

Having sprung from such sources, the stream of poetry in the fortunate Italian nation could not run dry again. These founders, to be sure, left behind no school but merely imitators; quite soon, however, there originated a new species. The form and manner of the creation of poetry, which now again had become art, were applied to the themes of adventure in the books of chivalry, and in this way came into being the Italian Romance, originally meant for public reading, changing either blatantly or subtly with a touch of sociable wit and intellectual spice the miraculous stories of old into the grotesque. But this grotesque is, even in Ariosto, only isolated and not to be found in the whole of his work, which scarcely deserves the name; like Boiardo, he embellished the romance with novellas and, according to the spirit of his age, with beautiful devices derived from the ancients, achieved a great deal of grace in the art of the stanza. Through this excellence and his clear understanding, he surpasses his predecessor; the abundance of clear images and a felicitous mixture of jest and seriousness make him a master and prototype in facile narrative and sensuous fantasies. The attempt to elevate the romance through a weighty subject and classical language to the dignity of the ancient epic—which was envisaged as the masterpiece of masterpieces for the nation and, because of its allegorical meaning, especially for the scholars—no matter how often undertaken, remained only an attempt that missed the mark. In an entirely new way, but applicable only once, Guarini succeeded in *Il Pastor Fido*—the greatest, indeed the only, masterpiece of the Italians after those great ones—to fuse the romantic spirit and classical form in most beautiful harmony and thus gave the sonnet new vigor and charm.

The art history of the Spaniards, who were most intimately familiar with the poetry of the Italians, and of the English, who had at that time a very receptive sense for the romantic elements, which might have come their way even second hand, culminated in the art of two men, Cervantes and Shakespeare, who were so great that everything else in comparison with them appears as merely preparatory, explicatory, and complementary circumstance. The fullness of their works and the gradual ascent of their boundless spirit would alone be material for a story of its own. We merely wish to point to the thread of the story, to discern the chief divisions of the entire work, and at least to see some definite points and the general course of development.

When Cervantes took up the pen after he could no longer wield the sword, he composed *La Galatea,* a wonderfully great composition of undying music of the imagination and love: the most delicate and lovely of all novels. In addition, he also composed many works that dominated the stage and were as worthy as the divine *Numancia* of the old tragic style. This was the first great period of his poetry; its characteristic was sublime beauty, serious but lovely.

The chief work in his second manner is the first part of *Don Quixote,* where fantastic wit and lavish abundance of daring ideas prevail. In the same spirit and around the same time, he also composed many of his novellas, especially the comic ones. In the last years of his life, he gave in to the prevailing taste in drama, and for this reason treated it with negligence. Also, in the second part of *Don Quixote* he took into consideration critical judgment. However, it was up to him to please himself and with unfathomed understanding to fashion the material of the second part—which everywhere bears the stamp of the first and thus constitutes one work consisting of two separate and fused parts—an opus which, as it were, contemplates itself. He wrote the great *Pérsiles* with thoughtful art in an earnest, dark manner, according to his own idea of the novel of Heliodorus. The other things he wanted to create—presumably in the genre of the books of chivalry and of the dramatized novel—as well as the completion of the second part of *La Galatea* were prevented by his death.

Spanish prose in the books of chivalry before Cervantes was antiquated in a beautiful manner, flourishing in the pastoral novel and in the romantic drama imitating artless life sharply and exactly in the language of everyday. The most lovely forms for tender songs, full of music and thoughtful dallying, and the romance, devised to tell with nobility and simplicity, seriously and with truth, a noble and moving old story, were at home in that country for ages. For Shakespeare the way was prepared to a lesser degree, almost exclusively through the colorful variety of the English theater. Now scholars, now actors, noblemen, and court fools worked for the theater, where mystery plays from the childhood of drama or old English farces alternated with patriotic histories and other subjects in every form and manner, but there was nothing that we would call art. Yet it was a fortunate circumstance for both the effectiveness and even the thoroughness of the theater that the actors had to work early for a stage that was not designed for exterior appearance, and that in the historical drama the monotony of theme directed the writer's and the viewer's attention to the form.

Shakespeare's earliest works[1] must be seen in the same light in which the connoisseur admires the antiquities of Italian painting. They are without perspective and other perfections, but they are thorough, great, and show good sense, and in their genre only the works in the best manner by the same master are superior to them. We include here *Locrinus,* whose tragic pathos in the Gothic dialect is glaringly fused with robust old English gaiety, and the divine *Pericles,* and other works of art by that only master which were denied authenticity against all history because of the madness of shallow critics or their own stupidity. We assume that these productions are earlier than *Adonis* and the sonnets since there is no trace in them of that sweet and lovely form, nor of the lofty spirit that breathes more or less in all the later plays of the poet, especially in those of the greatest perfection. Love, friendship, and noble company, according to his own account, brought about a beautiful revolution in his spirit. His knowledge of the delicate poems of Spenser, the favorite of the elegant set, gave sustenance to his new romantic *élan,* and he might have induced Shakespeare to read the novellas which now, more often than before, he transformed, reconstructed, and dramatized in a fantastically charming manner with a profound understanding of the stage. This development extended also to the historical plays, giving them more fullness, grace, and wit, and inspired all his plays with the romantic spirit which most properly characterizes them along with pro-

---

[1] Concerning the so-called non-authentic plays of Shakespeare and the evidence for their authenticity, we can promise the friends of the poet an extensive study by Tieck, whose erudition and original views directed the attention of this writer to that interesting critical problem.

found thoroughness, and establishes them as a romantic basis for the modern drama, which is durable enough for ages to come.

Of the novellas first to be dramatized, we mention only *Romeo* and *Love's Labour's Lost* as the loftiest points of his youthful imagination, being closest to *Adonis* and the sonnets. In the three plays about Henry VI and Richard III, we discern a steady transition from the older and not yet romanticized manner to a great one. To this group, Shakespeare added the histories of Richard II through Henry V, and this work is the peak of his power. In *Macbeth* and in *Lear* we witness the signposts of his manly maturity, and *Hamlet* vacillates insolubly in the transition between the novella and what these tragedies are. In the last period, we mention the *Tempest, Othello,* and the Roman plays; there is an infinite amount of understanding in them, but already something of the coldness of age.

After the death of those great men, beautiful imagination vanished in their countries. Strangely enough, philosophy—hitherto unpolished—developed into an art and excited and monopolized the enthusiasm of brilliant men. In poetry, on the other hand, there were, to be sure, from Lope de Vega to Gozzi, some appreciable virtuosi, but no poets, and even those only for the stage. Moreover, the multitude of wrong tendencies was increasing in all learned and popular genres and forms all the time. Out of superficial abstractions and rationalizations, out of misunderstood antiquity and mediocre talent, there arose in France a comprehensive and coherent system of false poetry that rested on an equally false theory of literature; and from there this sickly mental malady of so-called good taste spread over all the countries of Europe. The French and English established their various golden ages and carefully selected, as worthy representatives of their nations in the pantheon of fame, a number of classics from among the writers who, all of them, do not deserve mention in a history of art.

Meanwhile, even here there remained a tradition whose contention was to return to the ancients and to nature, and this spark caught fire with the Germans after they had gone through almost all their models. Winckelmann taught that antiquity was to be viewed as a whole and was the first to demonstrate how to establish an art through the history of its genesis. Goethe's universality gently reflected the poetry of almost all nations and ages, an inexhaustibly instructive set of works, studies, sketches, fragments, and experiments in every genre and in the most varied forms. Philosophy arrived in a few daring steps to the point where it could comprehend itself and the spirit of man, in whose depths it was bound to discover the primordial source of the imagination and the ideal of beauty and thus was compelled to recognize poetry, whose essence and existence it had not even suspected. Philosophy and poetry, the two most sublime powers in man, which even in Athens in the period of their highest fruition were effective only in isolation, now intermingle in perpetual interaction in order to stimulate and develop each other. Translation of poets and imitation of their rhythms have become an art, and criticism a discipline that annihilated old errors and opened new vistas in the knowledge of antiquity, whose background reveals a perfect history of poetry.

Nothing further is required but that the Germans continue using these methods, that they follow the example set by Goethe, explore the forms of art back to their sources in order to be able to revive or combine them, and that they go back to the origins of their own language and poetry and release the old power, the sublime spirit, which lies dormant, unrecognized, in the documents of the fatherland's prehistory, from the song of the Nibelungs to Fleming and Weckherlin. Thus, poetry—which in no nation was so excellent and originally developed—beginning as a heroic legend, then becoming a pastime of the knights, and finally, a trade of the citizens—will be and will remain in this nation a basic discipline of true scholars and an effective art of ingenious poets.

Talk on Mythology

Considering your serious reverence for art, I wish to challenge you, my friends, to ask yourselves this question: Should the force of inspiration also in poetry continue to split up and, when it has exhausted itself by struggling against the hostile element, end up in lonely silence? Are the most sacred things always to remain nameless and formless and be left in darkness to chance? Is love indeed invincible, and is there an art worthy of the name if it does not have the power to bind the spirit of love with its magic word, to make the spirit of love follow and obey it, and to inspire its beautiful creations in accordance with its necessary freedom?

You above all others must know what I mean. You yourselves have written poetry, and while doing so you must often have felt the absence of a firm basis for your activity, a matrix, a sky, a living atmosphere.

The modern poet must create all these things from within himself, and many have done it splendidly; up to now, however, each poet separately and each work from its very beginning, like a new creation out of nothing.

I will go right to the point. Our poetry, I maintain, lacks a focal point, such as mythology was for the ancients; and one could summarize all the essentials in which modern poetry is inferior to the ancient in these words: We have no mythology. But, I add, we are close to obtaining one or, rather, it is time that we earnestly work together to create one.

For it will come to us by an entirely opposite way than that of previous ages, which was everywhere the first flower of youthful imagination, directly joining and imitating what was most immediate and vital in the sensuous world. The new mythology, in contrast, must be forged from the deepest depths of the spirit; it must be the most artful of all works of art, for it must encompass all the others; a new bed and vessel for the ancient, eternal fountainhead of poetry, and even the infinite poem concealing the seeds of all other poems.

You may well smile at this mystical poem and the disorder that might originate from the abundance of poetic creations. But the highest beauty, indeed the highest order, is yet only that of chaos, namely, of such a one that waits only for the touch of love to unfold as a harmonious world, of such a chaos as the ancient mythology and poetry were. For mythology and poetry are one and inseparable. All poems of antiquity join one to the other, till from ever-increasing masses and members the whole is formed. Everything interpenetrates everything else, and everywhere there is one and the same spirit, only expressed differently. And thus it is truly no empty image to say: Ancient poetry is a single, indivisible, and perfect poem. Why should what has once been not come alive again? In a different way, to be sure. And why not in a more beautiful, a greater way?

I plead with you only not to give in to disbelief in the possibility of a new mythology. Doubts from all sides and in all directions would be welcome, so that the investigation may become that much more free and rich. And now lend my conjectures an attentive ear. More than conjectures, considering the situation of the matter, I cannot hope to offer. But I hope that these conjectures through you yourselves will become truths. For if you want to employ them in such a way, they are to a certain extent suggestions for experiments.

If a new mythology can emerge only from the innermost depths of the spirit and develop only from itself, then we find a very significant hint and a noteworthy confirmation of what we are searching for in that great phenomenon of our age, in idealism. Idealism originated in just this way, from nothing as it were, and now it has constituted itself in the spiritual sphere as a firm point from which the creative energy of man can safely expand, developing in all directions, without losing itself or the possibility of return. All disciplines and all arts will be seized by the great revolution. You can see it already at work in physics, where idealism erupted of its own before it was touched by the magic wand of philosophy. And this wonderful, great fact can at the same time be a hint for you of the secret correspondence and inner unity of the age. Idealism—from a practical view nothing other than the spirit of that revolution—and its great maxims, which we are to practice and propagate from our own energy and freedom; this idealism, considered theoretically, as great as it manifests itself at this point, is yet only a part, a branch, a mode of expression of the phenomenon of all phenomena: that mankind struggles with all its power to find its own center. It must, as things are, either perish or be rejuvenated. What is more probable, and what does one not hope for from such an age of rejuvenation? Remote antiquity will become alive again, and the remotest future of culture will announce itself in auguries. Yet this is not what matters to me at this point, for I do not want to pass over anything but to lead you step by step to the certainty of the most sacred mysteries. Just as it is the nature of spirit to determine itself and in perennial alternation to expand and return to itself, and as every thought is nothing but the result of such an activity, so is the same process generally discernible in every form of idealism, which itself is but a recognition of this very law. The new life, intensified by this recognition, manifests its secret energy in the most splendid manner through the infinite abundance of new ideas, general comprehensibility, and lively efficacy. Naturally, this phenomenon assumes a different form in each individual; this is why success must often fall short of expectation. But our expectations cannot be disappointed in what the necessary laws allow us to expect for the development as a whole. Idealism in any form must transcend itself in one way or another, in order to be able to return to itself and remain what it is. Therefore, there must and will arise from the matrix of idealism a new and equally infinite realism, and idealism will not only by analogy of its genesis be an example of the new mythology, it will indirectly become its very source. Traces of a similar tendency you can now observe almost everywhere, especially in physics, where nothing is more needed than a mythological view of nature.

I, too, have long borne in me the ideal of such a realism, and if it has not yet found expression, it was merely because I am still searching for an organ for communicating it. And yet I know that I can find it only in poetry, for in the form of philosophy, and especially of systematic philosophy, realism can never again appear. But even considering a general tradition, it is to be expected that this new realism, since it must be of idealistic origin and must hover, as it were, over an idealistic ground, will emerge as poetry that indeed is to be based on the harmony of the ideal and real.

Spinoza, it seems to me, meets the same fate as the good old Saturn of the fable. The new gods pulled down the sublime one from the lofty throne of knowledge. He faded back into the solemn obscurity of the imagination; there he lives and now dwells with the other Titans in dignified exile. Keep him here! Let his memories of the old mastery melt away in the song of the Muses into a soft longing. Let him put away the militant attire of systematic philosophy and share the dwelling in the temple of new poetry with Homer and Dante, joining the household gods and friends of every god-inspired poet.

Indeed, I barely comprehend how one can be a poet without admiring Spinoza, loving him, and becoming entirely his. In the invention of details, your own imagination is rich enough; to stimulate it, to excite it to activity, and to provide it with nourishment there is nothing better than the creations of other artists. In Spinoza, however, you will find the beginning and end of all imagination, the general basis on which all individual creation rests; and especially the separation of the original, the eternal aspect of imagination from the individual and the typical must be very welcome to you. Seize the opportunity and observe. You are granted a profound view into the innermost workshop of poetry. Spinoza's feeling is of the same kind as his imagination. It is not a sensitivity to this or that nor a passion that smolders and dies again, but a clear fragrance that hovers invisibly visible over the whole; everywhere eternal longing finds an accord from the depths of the simple work, which in calm greatness breathes the spirit of original love.

And is not this soft reflection of the godhead in man the actual soul, the kindling spark of all poetry? Mere representation of man, passions, and actions does not truly amount to anything, as little as using artificial forms does, even if you shuffle and turn over the old stuff together millions of times. That is only the visible, the external body, for when the soul has been extinguished, what is left is only the lifeless corpse of poetry. When that spark of inspiration breaks out in works, however, a new phenomenon stands before us, alive and in the beautiful glory of light and love.

And what else is any wonderful mythology but hieroglyphic expression of surrounding nature in this transfigured form of imagination and love?

Mythology has one great advantage. What usually escapes our consciousness can here be perceived and held fast through the senses and spirit like the soul in the body surrounding it, through which it shines into our eye and speaks to our ear.

This is the crucial point: that in regard to the sublime, we do not entirely depend on our emotions. To be sure, he whose emotions have run dry, in him they will nowhere spring forth; this is a well-known truth that I am not in the least inclined to oppose. But we should take part everywhere in what is already formed. We should develop, kindle, and nourish the sublime through contact with the same in kind, the similar, or if of equal stature the hostile; in a word, give it form. If the sublime, however, is incapable of being intentionally created, then let us give up any claims to a free art of ideas, for it would be an empty name.

Mythology is such a work of art created by nature. In its texture, the sublime is really formed; everything is relation and metamorphosis, conformed and transformed, and this conformation and transformation is its peculiar process, its inner life and method, if I may say so.

Here I find a great similarity with the marvelous wit of romantic poetry, which does not manifest itself in individual conceptions but in the structure of the whole, and which was so often pointed out by our friend for the works of Cervantes and Shakespeare. Indeed, this artfully ordered confusion, this charming symmetry of contradictions, this wonderfully perennial alternation of enthusiasm and irony, which lives even in the smallest parts of the whole, seem to me to be an indirect mythology themselves. The organization is the same, and certainly the arabesque is the oldest and most original form of human imagination. Neither this wit nor a mythology can exist without something original and inimitable that is absolutely irreducible, and in which after all the transformations its original character and creative energy are still dimly visible, where the naive profundity permits the semblance of the absurd and of madness, of simplicity and foolishness, to shimmer through. For this is the beginning of all poetry, to cancel the progression and laws of rationally thinking reason, and to transplant us once again into the beautiful confusion of imagination, into the original chaos of human nature, for which I know as yet no more beautiful symbol than the motley throng of the ancient gods.

Why won't you arise and revive those splendid forms of great antiquity? Try for once to see the old mythology, steeped in Spinoza and in those views that present-day physics must excite in every thinking person, and everything will appear to you in new splendor and vitality.

But to accelerate the genesis of the new mythology, the other mythologies must also be reawakened according to the measure of their profundity, their beauty, and their form. If only the treasures of the Orient were as accessible to us as those of antiquity. What new source of poetry could then flow from India, if a few German artists with their catholicity and profundity of mind, with the genius for translation that is their own, had the opportunity that a nation growing ever more dull and brutal barely knows how to use. In the Orient, we must look for the most sublime form of the

Romantic, and only when we can draw from the source, will the semblance of Southern passion that we find so charming in Spanish poetry perhaps appear to us Occidental and sparse.

In general, one must be able to press toward the goal by more than one way. Let each pursue his own in joyful confidence, in the most individual manner; for nowhere has the right of individuality more validity—provided individuality is what this word defines: indivisible unity and an inner and vital coherence—than here where the sublime is at issue. From this standpoint, I would not hesitate to say that the true value, indeed the virtue of man, is his originality.

And if I place so much emphasis on Spinoza, it is indeed not from any subjective preference (I have expressly omitted the objects of such a preference) or to establish him as master of a new autocracy, but because I could demonstrate by this example in a most striking and illuminating way my ideas about the value and dignity of mysticism and its relation to poetry. Because of his objectivity in this respect, I chose him as a representative of all the others. This is the way I reason. Just as the *Theory of Knowledge,* in the view of those who have not noticed the infinitude and eternal abundance of idealism, remains a perfect form, a general system for all knowledge, so, too, is Spinoza in a similar way the general basis and support for every individual kind of mysticism. And this, in my opinion, even those who have no special understanding of either mysticism or of Spinoza will readily acknowledge.

I cannot conclude without urging once more the study of physics, from whose dynamic paradoxes the most sacred revelations of nature are now bursting forth in all directions.

And thus let us, by light and life, hesitate no longer, but accelerate, each according to his own mind, that great development to which we were called. Be worthy of the greatness of the age and the fog will vanish from your eyes; and there will be light before you. All thinking is a divining, but man is only now beginning to realize his divining power. What immense expansion will this power experience, and especially now! It seems to me that he who could understand the age—that is, those great principles of general rejuvenation and of eternal revolution—would be able to succeed in grasping the poles of mankind, to recognize and to know the activity of the first men as well as the nature of the Golden Age that is to come. Then the empty chatter would stop and man would become conscious of what he is: He would understand the earth and the sun.

This is what I mean by the new mythology.

Letter About the Novel

I must retract, my dear lady, what I seemed to say yesterday in your defense, and say that you are almost completely wrong. You yourself admitted as much at the end of the argument, having become involved so deeply, because it is against female dignity to come down in tone, as you so aptly put it, from the innate element of gay jest and eternal poetry to the thorough or heavy-handed earnestness of the men. I agree with you against yourself that you are wrong. Indeed, I maintain that it is not enough to recognize the wrong; one must make amends for it, and, as it seems to me, proper amends for having degraded yourself with your criticism would now be that you force yourself to the necessary patience and read this critical epistle about the subject of yesterday's conversation.

What I want to say I could have said yesterday; or rather, I could not have because of my mood and the circumstances. What kind of opponent are you dealing with, Amalia? Certainly he understands quite well what it is all about, as it could not otherwise be with a clever virtuoso. He could have talked about it as well as anyone else, provided he could talk at all. This the gods have denied him; he is, as I have already said, a virtuoso and that's it; the Graces, unfortunately, stayed away. Since he was not quite certain what you meant in the deepest sense, and externally the right was so completely on your side, I made it my business to argue for you with all my might to prevent the convivial balance from being destroyed. And besides, it is more natural for men, if it really has to be done, to give written instructions rather than oral, which I feel violate the dignity of conversation.

Our conversation began when you asserted that Friedrich Richter's novels are not novels but a colorful hodgepodge of sickly wit; that the meager story is too badly presented to be considered a story; one simply had to guess it. If, however, one wanted to put it all together and just tell it, it would at best amount to a confession. The individuality of the man is much too visible, and such a personality at that.

I disregard this last point because it is only a question of individuality. I admit the colorful hodgepodge of sickly wit; but I shall defend it and emphatically maintain that such grotesques and confessions are the only romantic productions of our unromantic age.

On this occasion, let me get something off my mind that I have been thinking about for a long time.

With astonishment and inner anger, I have often seen your servant carry piles of volumes in to you. How can you touch with your hands those dirty volumes? And how can you allow the confused and crude phrases to enter through your eye to the sanctuary of your soul? To yield your imagination for hours to people with whom, face to face, you would be ashamed to exchange even a few words? It serves no purpose but to kill time and to spoil your imagination. You have read almost all the bad books from Fielding to La Fontaine. Ask yourself what you profited by it. Your memory scorns this vulgar stuff that has become a necessity through an unfortunate habit of your youth; what has to be acquired so laboriously is entirely forgotten.

But then perhaps you remember that there was a time when you loved Sterne and enjoyed assuming his manner, partially to imitate, partially to ridicule him. I still have a few jocular letters of this kind from you which I will carefully save. Sterne's humor did make a definite impression on you. Even though it was no ideally perfect form, yet it was a form, and a witty one, that captivated your imagination. And an impression that is so definite that we make use of it and cultivate it in seriousness and jest is not lost. And what can have a more fundamental value than those things which in some way stimulate or nourish the play of our inner makeup.

You feel yourself that your delight in Sterne's humor was pure and of an entirely different nature than the suspense that can often be forced upon us by a thoroughly bad book at the very time that we find it bad. Now ask yourself if your enjoyment was not related to what we often experience while viewing the witty paintings called arabesques. In case you cannot deny some sympathy with Sterne's sensibility, I am sending you a book, but I have to warn you about it so that you will be careful with regard to strangers, for it has the fortune or misfortune to be somewhat notorious. It is Diderot's *The Fatalist*. I think you will like it and will find in it an abundance of wit, quite free of sentimental admixtures. It is designed with understanding and executed with a firm hand. Without exaggerating, I can call it a work of art. To be sure, it is not a work of high rank, but only an arabesque. But for that reason it has no small merit in my eyes; for I consider the arabesque a very definite and essential form or mode of expression of poetry.

This is how I think of the matter. Poetry is so deeply rooted in man that at times, even under the most unfavorable circumstances, it grows without cultivation. Just as we find in almost every nation songs and stories in circulation and, even though crude, some kind of plays in use, so in our unfantastic age, in the actual estate of prose, and I mean the so-called educated and cultured people, we will find a few individuals who, sensing in themselves a certain originality of the imagination, express it, even though they are still far removed from true art. The humor of a Swift, a Sterne is, I believe, natural poetry of the higher classes of our age.

I am far from putting them next to the great ones; but you will admit that whoever has a sense for these, for Diderot, has a better start on the way to learning to appreciate the divine wit, the imagination of an Ariosto, Cervantes, Shakespeare, than one who did not even rise to that point. We simply must not make exaggerated demands on the people of our times; what has grown in such a sickly environment naturally cannot be anything else but sickly. I consider this circumstance, however, rather an advantage, as long as the arabesque is not a work of art but a natural product, and therefore place Richter over Sterne because his imagination is far more sickly, therefore far more eccentric and fantastic. Just go ahead and read Sterne again. It has been a long time since you read him, and I think you will find him different. Then compare our German with him. He really does have more wit, at least for one who takes him wittily, for he could easily do himself an injustice. And this advantage raises his sentimentality in appearance over the sphere of English sensibility.

There is another external reason why we should cultivate in ourselves this sense for the grotesque and remain in this mood. It is impossible in this age of books not to have to leaf through very many bad books, indeed, read them. Some of them always—one can depend on it—are fortunately of a silly kind, and thus it is really up to us to find them entertaining by looking at them as witty products of nature. Laputa is everywhere or nowhere, my dear friend; it is only a matter of freedom and imagination and we are in the midst of it. When stupidity reaches a certain height, which we often see now when everything is more severely differentiated, it equals foolishness even in the external appearance. And foolishness, you will admit, is the loveliest thing that man can imagine and the actual and ultimate principle of all amusement. In such a mood, I can often break out in almost incessant laughter over books that seem in no way meant to provoke it. And it is only fair that nature gave me this substitute, since I cannot laugh at all at many a thing nowadays called anecdote and satire. For me, on the other hand, learned journals, for example, become a farce, and the one called *Die Allgemeine Zeitung* I subscribe to very obstinately, just as the Viennese keep their Jack Pudding. Seen from my point of view, it is not only the most versatile of them all but in every way the most incomparable: Having sunk from nullity to a certain triviality and from there to a kind of stupidity, now by way of stupidity it has finally fallen into that foolish silliness.

This in general is too learned a pleasure for you. If, however, you are going to carry on what unfortunately you cannot stop doing, then I will no longer scorn your servant when he brings you the stacks of books from the loan library. Indeed, I offer myself as your porter for this purpose and promise to send you any number of the most beautiful comedies from all areas of literature.

I now take up the thread again: For I am determined to spare you nothing but to follow up your statements step by step.

You also criticized Jean Paul, in an almost cavalier manner, for being sentimental.

May the gods grant it was in the sense in which I understand the word and as I feel I must understand it according to its origin and nature. For according to my point of view and my usage, that is romantic which presents a sentimental theme in a fantastic form.

Forget for a moment the usual notorious meaning of the sentimental, by which one understands almost everything that, in a shallow way, is maudlin and lachrymose and full of those familiar noble feelings of which awareness makes people without character feel so unspeakably happy and great.

Think rather of Petrarch or Tasso, whose poetry in comparison to the more fantastic Romanzo of Ariosto can well be called sentimental; I cannot recall offhand an example where the contrast is so clear and the superiority so decisive as here.

Tasso is more musical, and the picturesque in Ariosto is certainly not the worst. Painting is no longer as fantastic, if I can trust my feeling, as it was prior to its best period: in numerous masters of the Venetian school, also in Correggio, and perhaps not only in the arabesque of Raphael. Modern music, on the other hand, as far as the prevailing power of man in it is concerned, has remained true on the whole to its character, so that I would dare to call it without reservation a sentimental art.

What then is this sentimental? It is that which appeals to us where feeling prevails and, to be sure, not a sensual but a spiritual feeling. The source and soul of all these emotions is love, and the spirit of love must hover everywhere invisibly visible in romantic poetry. This is what is meant by that definition. As Diderot so comically explains in *The Fatalist,* the gallant passions, which one cannot escape in the works of the moderns from the epigram to tragedy, are the least essential, or better, they are not even the external letter of that spirit; on occasion they are simply nothing or something very unlovely and loveless. No, it is the sacred breath that moves us in the tones of music. It cannot be grasped forcibly and comprehended mechanically, but it can be amiably lured by mortal beauty and veiled in it. The magic words of poetry can be infused with, and inspired by, its power. But in a poem in which it is neither everywhere present nor could be everywhere, it certainly does not exist at all. It is an infinite being and by no means does it cling and attach its interest only to persons, events, situations, and individual inclinations; for the true poet all this—no matter how intensely it embraces his soul—is only a hint of something higher, the infinite, a hieroglyph of the one eternal love and the sacred fullness of a life of creative nature.

Only the imagination can grasp the mystery of this love and present it as a mystery; and this mysterious quality is the source of the fantastic in the form of all poetic representation. The imagination strives with all its might to express itself, but the divine can communicate and express itself only indirectly in the sphere of nature. Therefore, of that which originally was imagination there remains in the world of appearances only what we call wit.

One more thing resides in the meaning of the sentimental that concerns precisely the peculiar tendency of romantic poetry in contrast with ancient. No consideration is taken in it of the difference between appearance and truth, play and seriousness. Therein resides the great difference. Ancient poetry adheres throughout to mythology and avoids the specifically historical themes. Even ancient tragedy is play, and the poet who presented a true event of serious concern for the entire nation was punished. Romantic poetry, on the other hand, is based entirely on a historical foundation, far more than we know and believe. Any play you might see, any story you read—if it has a witty plot—you can be almost sure has a true story at its source, even if variously reshaped. Boccaccio is almost entirely true history, just as all the other sources are from which all romantic ideas originate.

I have set up a definite characteristic of the contrast between the antique and the romantic. Meanwhile, please do not immediately assume that the romantic and the modern are entirely identical for me. I consider them approximately as different as the paintings of Raphael and Correggio are from the etchings that are fashionable now. If you wish to realize the difference clearly, read only *Emilia Galotti,* which is so extremely modern and yet not in the least romantic, and then think of Shakespeare, in whom I would like to fix the actual center, the core of the romantic imagination. This is where I look for and find the romantic—in the older moderns, in Shakespeare, Cervantes, in Italian poetry, in that age of knights, love, and fairy tales in which the thing itself and the word for it originated. This, up to now, is the only thing which can be considered as a worthy contrast to the classical productions of antiquity; only these eternally fresh flowers of the imagination are worthy of adorning the images of the ancient gods. Certainly all that is best in modern poetry tends toward antiquity in spirit and even in kind, as if there were to be a return to it. Just as our literature began with the novel, so the Greek began with the epic and dissolved in it.

The difference is, however, that the romantic is not so much a literary genre as an element of poetry that may be more or less dominant or recessive, but never entirely absent. It must be clear to you why, according to my views, I postulate that all poetry should be romantic and why I detest the novel as far as it claims to be a separate genre.

Yesterday when the argument became most heated, you demanded a definition of the novel; you said it as if you already knew that you would not receive a satisfactory answer. I do not consider this problem insolvable. A novel is a romantic book. You will pass that off as a meaningless tautology. But I want to draw your attention to the fact that when one thinks of a book, one thinks of a work, an existing whole. There is then a very important contrast to drama, which is meant to be viewed; the novel, on the other hand, was from the oldest times for reading, and from this fact we can deduce almost all the differences in the manner of presentation of both forms. The drama should also be romantic, like all literature; but a novel is that only under certain limitations, an applied novel. On the contrary, the dramatic context of the story does not make the novel a whole, a work, if the entire composition is not related to a higher unity than that of the letter, which it often does and should disregard; but it becomes a work through the bond of ideas, through a spiritual central point.

Having made this allowance, there is otherwise so little contrast between the drama and the novel that it is rather the drama, treated thoroughly and historically, as for instance by Shakespeare, which is the true foundation of the novel. You claimed, to be sure, that the novel is most closely related to the narrative, the epic genre. On the other hand, I want to admonish you that a song can as well be romantic as a story. Indeed, I can scarcely visualize a novel but as a mixture of storytelling, song, and other forms. Cervantes always composed in this manner, and even the otherwise so prosaic Boccaccio adorns his collections of stories by framing them with songs. If there is a novel in which this does not or cannot occur, it is only due to the individuality of the work and not the character of the genre; on the contrary, it is already an exception. But this is only by the way. My actual objection is as follows. Nothing is more contrary to the epic style than when the influence of the subjective mood becomes in the least visible; not to speak of one's ability to give himself up to his humor and play with it, as often happens in the most excellent novels.

Afterwards, you forgot your thesis or gave it up, and decided to claim that all those divisions lead to nothing; that there is *one* poetry, and what counts is whether something is beautiful, and only a pedant would bother with titles and headings. You know what I think of the classifications in current use. And yet I realize that it is quite necessary for each virtuoso to limit himself to a well-defined goal. In my historical research, I came upon several fundamental forms that are not further reducible. Thus, in the sphere of romantic poetry, for instance, novellas and fairy tales seem to me, if I may say so, infinitely contrasted. I only wish that an artist would rejuvenate each of these genres by restoring them to their original character.

If such examples became known, then I would have the courage for a *theory of the novel,* which would be a theory in the original sense of the word: a spiritual viewing of the subject with calm and serene feeling, as it is proper to view in solemn joy the meaningful play of divine images. Such a theory of the novel would have to be itself a novel that would reflect imaginatively every eternal tone of the imagination and would again confound the chaos of the world of knights. The things of the past would live in it in new forms; Dante's sacred shadow would arise from the lower world, Laura would hover heavenly before us, Shakespeare would converse intimately with Cervantes, and there Sancho would jest with Don Quixote again.

These would be true arabesques that, together with confessions, as I claimed at the outset of my letter, are the only romantic products of nature in our age.

It will no longer appear strange to you that I include confessions here, when you have admitted that true story is the foundation of all romantic poetry; and you will—if you wish to reflect on it— easily remember and be convinced that what is best in the best of novels is nothing but a more or less veiled confession of the author, the profit of his experience, the quintessence of his originality.

Yet I appreciate all the so-called novels to which my idea of romantic form is altogether inapplicable, by virtue of the amount of self-reflection and represented life they contain. And in this respect even the followers of Richardson, however much they are on the wrong track, are welcome. From a novel like *Cecilia Beverley,* we at least learn how they lived there in London in boredom, since it was the fashion, and also how a British lady for all her daintiness finally tumbles to the ground and knocks herself bloody. The cursing, the squires, and the like in Fielding are as if stolen from life, and *Wakefield* grants us a deep insight into the world view of a country preacher; yes, this novel would perhaps—if Olivia regained her lost innocence at the end—be the best among all the English novels.

But how sparingly and only drop by drop even the small amount of the real in all those books is handed out. Which travelogue, which collection of letters, which autobiography would not be a better novel for one who reads them in the romantic sense than the best of these?

Confessions, especially, mainly by way of the naive, develop by themselves into arabesques. But at best those novels rise to the arabesque only at the end, when the bankrupt merchants regain their money and credit, all the poor devils get to eat, the likable scoundrels become honest, and the fallen women become virtuous again.

The *Confessions* of Rousseau is in my opinion a most excellent novel, *Héloïse* only a very mediocre one.

I will send you the autobiography of a famous man that, as far as I know, you are not acquainted with: Gibbon's *Memoirs*. It is an infinitely civilized and infinitely funny book. It will meet you halfway, and really the comic novel contained in it is almost complete. You will see before your eyes, as clearly as you could wish, the Englishman, the gentleman, the virtuoso, the scholar, the bachelor, the well-bred dandy in all his affected absurdity, through the dignity of the historic periods. One can go through many bad books and many insignificant men before finding so much to laugh about gathered in one place.

Selected Aphorisms from the Lyceum (1797)

1. One mentions many artists who are actually art works of nature.

3. Whenever Diderot in his *Jacob* has done something rather ingenious, he usually comes right out himself and rejoices at how ingenious it has become.

4. There is so much poetry, and yet nothing is more rare than a poetic work. This is what the masses make out of poetical sketches, studies, aphorisms, trends, ruins, and raw material.

7. My essay on the study of Greek poetry is a stylized hymn in prose on the objective aspect of poetry. The worst part of it seems to me to be the complete absence of indispensable irony, and the best, the confident assumption that poetry is of infinite value, as though it were a matter of fact.

8. A good preface must be the root and the square of the book at the same time.

9. Wit is absolutely sociable spirit or aphoristic genius.

10. One must drill the board where it is the thickest.

11. Nothing truly convincing—which would possess thoroughness, vigor, and skill—has been written against the ancients as yet; especially not against their poetry.

14. In poetry, too, all that is whole might be only half-done, and yet all half-done might actually be a whole.

16. Genius is, to be sure, not a matter of arbitrariness, but rather of freedom, just as wit, love, and faith, which once shall become arts and disciplines. We should demand genius from everybody, without, however, expecting it. A Kantian would call this the categorical imperative of genius.

18. Novels tend to end as the Paternoster begins: with the kingdom of God on earth.

20. A classical work doesn't ever have to be understood entirely. But those who are educated and who are still educating themselves must desire to learn more and more from it.

21. Just as a child is really a thing that wants to become a man, so is the poem an object of nature that wants to become an object of art.

23. In every good poem, everything must be both deliberate and instinctive. That is how the poem becomes ideal.

24. The meanest authors have at least this similarity with the great author of heaven and earth, that they usually say after a completed day of work: "And behold, what he had done was good."

25. The two basic maxims of the so-called historical criticism are the postulate of the common and the axiom of the ordinary. Postulate of the common: Everything really great, good, and beautiful is improbable, since it is extraordinary and therefore at least suspect. Axiom of the ordinary: Our conditions and environment must have existed everywhere, for they are really so natural.

26. Novels are the Socratic dialogues of our time. Practical wisdom fled from school wisdom into this liberal form.

27. A critic is a reader who ruminates. Thus, he should have more than one stomach.

28. Sense (for a particular art, science, human being, and so forth) is divided spirit; self-restraint is consequently the result of self-creation and self-destruction.

29. Gracefulness is a correct life: sensuality that contemplates and forms itself.

30. God the Father and, even more often, the Devil himself, appear at times in the place of fate in the modern tragedy. Why is it

that this has not induced any scholar to develop a theory of the diabolical genre?

31. The division of the works of art into naive and sentimental ones could perhaps be applied quite profitably also to criticism. There are sentimental critiques that lack nothing but a vignette and a motto to be also perfectly naive. As vignette, a postilion blowing a horn; as motto, a phrase of the old Thomasius at the conclusion of an academic address: *Nunc vero musicabunt cum paucis et trompetis.*

33. One of these two is almost always a prevailing tendency of every author: It is either not to say some things that certainly should be said, or to say many things that did not need to be said. The first is the original sin of synthetic, the latter, of analytical natures.

34. A witty inspiration is a dissolution of spiritual substances that consequently, before the sudden separation, must have been most intimately intermingled. Imagination must first be filled to the point of saturation with life of every kind before the moment arrives when the friction of free sociability electrifies it to such an extent that the most gentle stimulus of friendly or hostile contact elicits from it lightning sparks, luminous flashes, or shattering blows.

35. Some speak of the public as if it were someone with whom they have had dinner at the Leipzig Fair in the Hotel de Saxe. Who is this public? The public is not a thing, but rather an idea, a postulate, like the Church.

36. Whoever has not arrived at the clear insight that there might exist greatness entirely outside his own sphere for which he has no understanding, whoever does not have at least a dim inkling in which area of the human spirit this greatness might be situated: He is within his own sphere either without genius, or he has not educated himself up to the point of the classical attitude.

37. In order to be able to write well upon a subject, one must have ceased to be interested in it; the thought which is to be soberly expressed must already be entirely past and no longer be one's

actual concern. As long as the artist invents and is inspired, he remains in a constrained state of mind, at least for the purpose of communication. He then wants to say everything, which is the wrong tendency of young geniuses or the right prejudice of old bunglers. Thus, he fails to recognize the value and dignity of self-restraint, which is indeed for both the artist and the man the first and the last, the most necessary and the highest goal. The most necessary: For wherever we do not restrain ourselves, the world will restrain us; and thus we will become its slave. The highest: For we can restrain ourselves only in those points and aspects where we have infinite power, in self-creation and self-destruction. Even a friendly conversation that cannot at any given moment be broken off voluntarily with complete arbitrariness has something illiberal about it. An artist, however, who is able and wants to express himself completely, who keeps nothing to himself and would wish to say everything he knows, is very much to be pitied. There are only three mistakes one has to be on guard against. What appears to be and ought to appear as unlimited arbitrariness and, consequently, unreason or superreason must in reality be absolutely necessary and reasonable; otherwise caprice will turn into self-destruction. Second: One should not hasten too much toward self-restraint, but allow self-creation, that is, invention and enthusiasm, to develop until it has matured. Third: Self-restraint must not be exaggerated.

38. There is nothing wrong with the prototype of German characteristics set up by a few great patriotic inventors except its wrong position. These German characteristics do not lie behind us, but ahead of us.

39. The history of imitation of the older literature, particularly abroad, has among others also the advantage that the important concepts of unintentional parody and passive wit can be deduced from it most easily and comprehensively.

40. The meaning of the word *aesthetic,* invented in Germany and current there, does betray—as is well known—an equally absolute ignorance of the designated matter, as well as of the designating language. Why is the word still retained?

42. Philosophy is the true home of irony, which might be defined as logical beauty: For wherever men are philosophizing in spoken or written dialogues, and provided they are not entirely systematical, irony ought to be produced and postulated; even the Stoics regarded urbanity as a virtue. It is true, there is also a rhetorical irony that, if sparingly used, performs a very excellent function, especially in polemics, but compared to the lofty urbanity of the Socratic muse, rhetorical irony is like the splendor of the most brilliant oratory compared to ancient high tragedy. In this respect, poetry alone can rise to the height of philosophy, since it is not, as oratory, based upon ironic passages. There are ancient and modern poems that breathe, in their entirety and in every detail, the divine breath of irony. In such poems there lives a real transcendental buffoonery. Their interior is permeated by the mood, which surveys everything and rises infinitely above everything limited, even above the poet's own art, virtue, and genius; and their exterior form by the histrionic style of an ordinary good Italian buffo.

44. We should never invoke the spirit of antiquity as our authority. Spirits are peculiar things; they cannot be grasped with the hands and be held up before others. Spirits reveal themselves only to spirits. The most direct and concise method would be, in this case as well, to prove the possession of the only redeeming faith by good works.

48. Irony is the form of paradox. Paradox is what is good and great at the same time.

51. Wit as an instrument of revenge is as infamous as art is as a means of sensual titillation.

52. In many a poetic work, one gets, here and there, instead of representation merely a title indicating that this or that was supposed to be represented here, that the artist has been prevented from doing it and most humbly asks to be kindly excused.

54. There are writers in Germany who drink the absolute like water; and there are books in which even the dogs make references to the infinite.

55. A genuinely free and educated man should be able to tune himself, as one tunes a musical instrument, absolutely arbitrarily, at his convenience at any time and to any degree, philosophically or philologically, critically or poetically, historically or rhetorically, in ancient or modern form.

57. If the mystical lovers of the arts, who consider all criticism dissection and all dissection destruction of enjoyment, thought logically, an exclamation like "Goodness alive!" would be the best criticism of the most deserving work of art. There are critiques which say nothing but that, only they do so more extensively.

60. All the classical genres are now ridiculous in their rigorous purity.

61. Strictly speaking, the idea of a scientific poem is probably as nonsensical as that of a poetic science.

62. We already have so many theories of the genres. Why don't we have any concept of genre? Perhaps then we would have to get along with a single theory of the genres.

63. Not art and works of art make an artist, but sense and enthusiasm and instinct.

67. In England, wit is at least a profession, if not an art. Everything becomes professional there, and even the rogues of that island are pedants. So are the "wits" there too. They introduce into reality absolute freedom the reflection of which lends a romantic and piquant air to wit, and thus they live wittily; hence, their talent for madness. They die for their principles.

68. How many authors are there among writers? Author means originator.

72. They actually like it if a work of literature is a little wicked, especially in the middle; only the sense of propriety must not be offended outright, and finally, everything must have a happy ending.

73. What is lost in the usual good or excellent translation is precisely the best.

78. Many an excellent novel is a compendium, an encyclopedia of the entire spiritual life of an individual genius; works of this kind, even if they are composed, like *Nathan the Wise,* in a completely different form, thus obtain a tinge of the novel. Also, every man who is educated and is educating himself contains within himself a novel. It is not necessary for him, however, to communicate it or to write it down.

79. German writings attain popularity through a great name, or through personalities, or through good connections, or through effort, or through moderate immorality, or through accomplished incomprehensibility, or through harmonious platitude, or through versatile boredom, or through constant striving after the absolute.

80. Reluctantly do I miss in Kant's genealogical tree of rudimentary concepts the category "nearly," which surely was as effective in the world and in literature and has done as much harm as any other category. In the spirit of natural skeptics, this category tinges all the other concepts and views.

81. To polemicize against individuals shows the pettiness of a retailer. If the artist does not want to use polemics wholesale, he should at least choose individuals who are classics and of lasting value. If, as in the sad case of self-defense, that is not possible, the individuals attacked should by means of polemic fiction be idealized as much as possible to represent objective dullness and objective foolishness: For even they, like everything objective, are infinitely interesting, such as dignified subjects of higher polemics ought to be.

84. From what the moderns want, we must learn what poetry should become; from that which the ancients did, what poetry must be.

87. Since poetry is infinitely valuable, I do not understand why it should be more valuable than this or that which is also infinitely

valuable. There are artists who perhaps do not think art to be too great, for this is impossible, and yet they are not free enough to be able to rise above their own best accomplishments.

88. Nothing is more piquant than when a man of genius possesses mannerisms; to be sure, when he possesses them, but not at all, if they possess him; this leads to spiritual petrification.

89. Is it not superfluous to write more than *one* novel if the writer has not become, say, a new man? Obviously, all the novels of an author not infrequently belong together and are to a certain degree only one novel.

90. Wit is an explosion of the compound spirit.

91. The ancients are neither the Jews, nor the Christians, nor the Englishmen of poetry. They are not an arbitrarily chosen artistic people of God; nor do they possess the only redeeming religion of beauty, nor do they possess a monopoly on poetry.

93. In the ancients, one sees the accomplished letter of entire poetry; in the moderns, one has the presentiment of the spirit in becoming.

94. Mediocre authors who announce a little book as if they were about to let us see a great giant should be forced by the literary police to label their product with the motto: *This is the greatest elephant in the world, except himself.*

98. The following are the universally fundamental laws of literary communication: 1. One has to have something to communicate; 2. One has to have someone to whom one should want to communicate it; 3. One must really communicate it, to be able to commune with him, not only express it for oneself alone; otherwise it would be more to the point to remain silent.

100. The poetry of this one is called philosophical; of the other, philological; of the third, rhetorical, and so on. Which is then the poetic poetry?

104. What one usually calls reason is only one kind of the same, namely, the thin and watered-down kind. There is also a thick, fiery reason that makes wit truly wit and lends to the terse style buoyancy and magnetism.

106. Nothing is more miserable in its origin and more awful in its effect than the fear of being ridiculous. Therefore, for example, the servility of women and many other cancerous afflictions of mankind.

108. Socratic irony is the only entirely involuntary and nevertheless completely conscious dissimulation. It is equally impossible to attain it artificially or to betray it. For him who does not possess it, it will remain an enigma even after the frankest avowal. It will deceive only those who consider it an illusion, who either enjoy its delightful archness of mocking at everybody or who become angry when they suspect that they too are meant. In it, everything must be jest and yet seriousness, artless openness and yet deep dissimulation. It originates in the union of a sense of an art of living and a scientific intellect, in the meeting of accomplished natural philosophy and accomplished philosophy of art. It contains and incites a feeling of the insoluble conflict of the absolute and the relative, of the impossibility and necessity of total communication. It is the freest of all liberties, for it enables us to rise above our own selves, and still the most legitimate, for it is absolutely necessary. It is a good sign if the harmonious dullards fail to understand this constant self-parody, if over and over again they believe and disbelieve until they become giddy and consider jest to be seriousness, and seriousness to be jest. Lessing's irony is instinct; in the case of Hemsterhuis it is classical study; Huelsen's irony is derived from the philosophy of philosophy and could far surpass those others.

112. The analytical writer observes the reader as he is; accordingly, he makes his calculation, sets his machine to make the appropriate effect on him. The synthetic writer constructs and creates his own reader; he does not imagine him as resting and dead, but lively and advancing toward him. He makes that which he had invented gradually take shape before the reader's eyes, or he tempts

him to do the inventing for himself. He does not want to make a particular effect on him, but rather enters into a solemn relationship of innermost *sym*philosophy or *sym*poetry.

115. The whole history of modern poetry is a continuous commentary to the short text of philosophy: Every art should become science, and every science should become art; poetry and philosophy should be unified.

117. Poetry can be criticized only through poetry. A critique that itself is not a work of art, either in content as representation of the necessary impression in the process of creation, or through its beautiful form and in the liberal tone in the spirit of the old Roman satire, has no right of citizenship in the realm of art.

120. Whoever could properly characterize Goethe's *Meister* would have actually expressed the timely trend in literature. He would be able, as far as literary criticism is concerned, to rest.

123. It is a thoughtless and immodest presumption to want to learn anything about art from philosophy. Some do begin as if they hoped to learn something new here; since philosophy cannot and should not do anything further than develop the given art experiences and the existing art concepts into a science, improve the views of art, and promote them with the help of a thoroughly scholarly art history and produce that logical mood about these subjects, too, which unites absolute liberalism with absolute rigorosity.

Selected Aphorisms from the Athenaeum (1798)

1. About no subject is there less philosophizing than about philosophy.

3. Kant introduced the concept of the negative into philosophy. Would it not also be worthwhile to try to introduce the concept of the positive into philosophy?

5. What is called good society is usually nothing but a mosaic of polished caricatures.

10. Duty is for Kant the One and All. Out of the duty of gratitude, he claims, one has to defend and esteem the ancients; and only out of duty has he become a great man.

16. If the essence of cynicism consists in preferring nature to art, virtue to beauty and science; in not bothering about the letter—to which the Stoic strictly adheres—but in looking up to the spirit of things; in absolute contempt of all economic values and political splendor; and in courageous defense of the rights of independent freedom; then Christianity would be nothing but universal cynicism.

19. The surest method of being incomprehensible or, moreover, being misunderstood is to use words in their original sense, especially words from the ancient languages.

22. A project is the subjective germ of a developing object. A perfect project should simultaneously be entirely subjective and entirely objective—an indivisible and living individual. As to its origin, it should be entirely subjective, original, and possible only in this mind; as to its character, entirely objective, physical, and morally necessary. The sense for projects—which could be called aphorisms of the future—differs from the sense for aphorisms of the past only in direction, progressive in the former and regressive in the latter. The essential thing is the ability to idealize and realize matters immediately and simultaneously, to complete them and carry them out partly within oneself. Since the word *transcendental* refers precisely to the unification and separation of the ideal and the real, one could easily say that the sense for aphorisms and projects is the transcendental part of the historical spirit.

24. Many works of the ancients have become fragments. Many works of the moderns are fragments at the time of their origin.

25. The German national character is a favorite subject of character experts, probably because the less mature a nation, the more she is an object of criticism and not of history.

27. Like Leibniz's possible worlds, most men are only equally entitled pretenders to existence. There are few existences.

29. Witty inspirations are the proverbs of the educated.

31. Prudishness is pretense of innocence without innocence. Women have to remain prudish as long as men are sentimental, dense, and evil enough to demand of them eternal innocence and lack of education. For innocence is the only thing that can ennoble lack of education.

32. One should have wit, but not wish to have it; otherwise there will be witticism, the Alexandrian style of wit.

34. Almost all marriages are only concubinages, liaisons, or rather provisional attempts, remote approximations of real marriage. The true nature of marriage does not conform to the paradoxes of this or that system, but rather is in accord with all canonical and secular laws that more than one person should become only one. This ought to warrant the least possible infringement of free will, which certainly has a right to be consulted when the question at issue is whether one is to be an individual or only the integral part of a common personality; it is even hard to see what legitimate argument can be raised against a *marriage à quatre* But if the state must insist on holding together those attempts at marriage that have failed, it is actually obstructing marriage, for its cause would be advanced by new and possibly more successful attempts.

37. Many a witty inspiration is like the surprising reunion of befriended thoughts after a long separation.

39. Most thoughts are only profiles of thoughts. They must be inverted and synthesized with their antipodes. In this way, many philosophical writings become very interesting that would not have been so otherwise.

42. Good drama must be drastic.

43. Philosophy still moves too much straight ahead and is not yet cyclical enough.

44. Every philosophical review ought to be a philosophy of reviews at the same time.

49. Women are treated as unjustly in poetry as in life. The feminine ones are not idealistic, and the idealistic, not feminine.

50. True love should be, according to its origin, entirely arbitrary and entirely accidental at the same time; it should seem both necessary and free; in keeping with its nature, however, it should be both destiny and virtue and appear as a mystery and a miracle.

51. The naive is what is or appears to be natural, individual, or classical to the point of irony or to the point of continuous alternation of self-creation and self-destruction. If it is only instinct, then it is childlike, childish, or silly; if it is only intention, it becomes affectation. The naive, which is simultaneously beautiful, poetic, and idealistic, must be both intention and instinct. The essence of intention, in this sense, is freedom. Consciousness is far from intention. There is a certain enamoured contemplation of one's own naturalness or silliness that itself is unspeakably silly. Intention does not necessarily require a profound calculation or plan. Even Homeric naiveté is not merely instinct; there is at least as much intention in it as in the gracefulness of loving children or innocent girls. Even if Homer did not have particular intentions, his poetry and the actual authoress of his poetry, nature, does have intention.

53. It is equally deadly for a mind to have a system or to have none. Therefore it will have to decide to combine both.

54. One can only become a philosopher, but not be one. As soon as one believes he is a philosopher, he stops being one.

56. Since philosophy now criticizes everything it comes across, a critique of philosophy would be nothing more than a just reprisal.

61. The few existing writings against Kantian philosophy are the most important documents in the case history of sound common sense.

62. Publication is to thinking as confinement is to the first kiss.

63. Every uneducated person is a caricature of himself.

64. The obsession with moderation is the spirit of castrated narrowmindedness.

66. When the author has no idea as to what to reply to the critic, he then likes to say: You cannot do it better anyway. This is the same as if a dogmatic philosopher were to reproach a skeptic for not being able to devise a system.

74. In the corrupt linguistic usage, verisimilitude means as much as "nearly true" or "somewhat true," or something that once could become true. But by its very composition, the word cannot mean all this. What appears to be true does not have to be true even in the smallest degree, and yet it must appear positive. Verisimilitude is the object of intelligence, of the ability to distinguish among the possible consequences of free actions the real ones, and it is something entirely subjective. That which some logicians have called and tried to calculate as verisimilitude is possibility.

77. A dialogue is a chain or a wreath of aphorisms. A correspondence is a dialogue on an enlarged scale, and memorabilia are a system of aphorisms. As yet there is nothing that is aphoristic in matter and form, altogether subjective and individual, simultaneously completely objective, and a necessary part in the system of all sciences.

80. The historian is a prophet looking backward.

82. Philosophical demonstrations are demonstrations in the sense of military language. Philosophical deductions are no better than those of politics: In the sciences, too, one first takes possession of an area and demonstrates one's claim to it later on. We can apply to definitions what Chamfort said about the friends we have in the world. There are three kinds of explanations in science: explanations that throw a light upon, or give a hint at, a matter; explanations that do not explain anything; and explanations that obscure everything. Good definitions cannot be made offhand, but ought to occur to us spontaneously. A definition that is not witty is worth nothing, and for every individual there is an infinite number of real definitions. The necessary formalities of this artificial

philosophy degenerate into protocol and luxury. Their aim and value consist in proving virtuosity to be legitimate, like the bravura arias of singers and the Latin writing of the philologists. It must be admitted, however, that their rhetorical effect is not bad. The main thing, however, is to know something and to say it. The attempt to prove or even to explain it is quite superfluous in most cases. The categorical style of the twelve commandments and the thetical method through which purely speculative facts are presented without any veil, any attenuation, and any artificial disguise as texts for studying and symphilosophizing are most appropriate for enlightened natural philosophy. If both are to be done equally well, there is doubtless more difficulty in stating something than in explaining it. There are plenty of demonstrations excellent in their form that prove to be false and trivial statements. Leibniz stated and Wolff proved. Enough said.

84. Considered subjectively, philosophy always begins in the middle, like an epic poem.

87. The most important thing in love is the sense for one another, and the highest thing, the faith in one another. Devotion is the expression of that faith, and pleasure can revive and enhance that sense, even if not create it, as is commonly thought. Therefore, sensuality can delude bad persons for a short time into thinking they could love each other.

89. Criticism is the only substitute for the equally impossible moral mathematics and science of propriety sought for in vain by many a philosopher.

90. The subject of history is the gradual realization of all that is practically necessary.

93. The doctrine of the spirit and the letter of things is interesting for the following reason among others: that it could bring in touch philosophy and philology.

96. Whoever does not philosophize for the sake of philosophy, but rather uses philosophy as a means, is a sophist.

102. Women have no sense at all for art, but certainly for poetry. They have no talent for science, but for philosophy. By no means do they lack speculation and inner vision of the infinite, but only the power of abstraction that can be learned so much more easily.

108. Beautiful is that which is simultaneously attractive and sublime.

111. The lessons of a novel ought to be of such a character that they are communicable only as a whole and cannot be proved singularly or exhausted analytically. Otherwise the rhetorical form would be far more preferable.

113. A classification is a definition comprising a system of definitions.

114. A definition of poetry can only determine what poetry should be and not what poetry actually was and is; otherwise the most concise formula would be: Poetry is that which at some time and some place was so named.

116. Romantic poetry is a progressive universal poetry. Its mission is not merely to reunite all separate genres of poetry and to put poetry in touch with philosophy and rhetorics. It will, and should, now mingle and now amalgamate poetry and prose, genius and criticism, the poetry of art and the poetry of nature, render poetry living and social, and life and society poetic, poetize wit, fill and saturate the forms of art with solid cultural material of every kind, and inspire them with vibrations of humor. It embraces everything poetic, from the greatest system of art, which, in turn, includes many systems, down to the sigh, the kiss, which the musing child breathes forth in artless song. It can lose itself in what it represents to such a degree that one might think its one and only goal were the characterization of poetic individuals of every type; and yet no form has thus far arisen appropriate to expressing the author's mind so perfectly, so that artists who just wanted to write a novel have by coincidence described themselves. Romantic poetry alone can, like the epic, become a mirror of the entire surrounding world, a picture of its age. And yet, it too can

soar, free from all real and ideal interests, on the wings of poetic reflection, midway between the work and the artist. It can even exponentiate this reflection and multiply it as in an endless series of mirrors. It is capable of the highest and the most universal education; not only by creating from within, but also from without, since it organizes in similar fashion all parts of what is destined to become a whole; thus, a view is opened to an endlessly developing classicism. Among the arts, romantic poetry is what wit is to philosophy, and what society, association, friendship, and love are in life. Other types of poetry are completed and can now be entirely analyzed. The romantic type of poetry is still becoming; indeed, its peculiar essence is that it is always becoming and that it can never be completed. It cannot be exhausted by any theory, and only a divinatory criticism might dare to characterize its ideal. It alone is infinite, as it alone is free; and as its first law it recognizes that the arbitrariness of the poet endures no law above him. The romantic genre of poetry is the only one which is more than a genre, and which is, as it were, poetry itself; for in a certain sense all poetry is or should be romantic.

117. Those works whose ideal has not as much living reality and, as it were, personality as the beloved one or a friend had better remain unwritten. They would at least never become works of art.

124. If one writes or reads novels from the point of view of psychology, it is very inconsistent and petty to want to shy away from even the slowest and most detailed analysis of the most unnatural lusts, gruesome tortures, shocking infamy, and disgusting sensual or spiritual impotence.

125. Perhaps a completely new epoch of sciences and arts would arise, if symphilosophy and sympoetry became so universal and intimate that it would no longer be unusual if several characters who complement each other would produce common works. Sometimes one can scarcely resist the idea that two minds might actually belong together like separate halves, and that only in union could they be what they might be. Were there an art of fusing individuals, or could postulating criticism do somewhat more than just postulate—and there are everywhere so many indications for

this—then I should like to see Jean Paul and Peter Leberecht [Ludwig Tieck] fused. The latter has precisely everything the former lacks. The fusion of Jean Paul's grotesque talent and Peter Leberecht's fantastic education would produce an excellent romantic poet.

139. From the Romantic point of view, the modifications of poetry, too, even the eccentric and monstrous ones, have their value as raw material and preliminary exercises of universality, provided they contain something, if only they are original.

146. As the novel permeates all modern poetry, thus satire—which through all transformations always remained among the Romans a classical universal poetry, a social poetry from and for the center of the cultured universe—tinges all Roman poetry, even the whole of Roman literature, and establishes, as it were, its tone. One has to have loved and understood Horace's satires for a long time in order to have a sense for that which is the most urbane, original, and beautiful in the prose of a Cicero, Caesar, or Suetonius. These are the eternal fountainheads of urbanity.

155. The rude cosmopolitan attempts of the Carthaginians and other peoples of classical antiquity, compared to the political universality of the Romans, appear like the natural poetry of uncivilized nations compared to the classical art of the Greeks. Only the Romans were content with the spirit of despotism and despised its letter; they alone had naive tyrants.

166. The genuine talent of the poetic Tacitus was to characterize nations and ages, to depict the great in a grand style. In historical portraits, however, the critical Suetonius is the greater master.

196. Pure autobiographies are written either by neurotics who are fascinated by their ego, as in Rousseau's case; or by authors of a robust artistic or adventuresome self-love, such as Benvenuto Cellini; or by born historians who regard themselves only as material for historic art; or by women who also coquette with posterity; or by pedantic minds who want to bring even the most minute things in order before they die and cannot let themselves leave the

world without commentaries. Autobiographies can also be regarded as mere plaidoyers before the public. Another great group among the autobiographers is formed by the autopseusts.

206. An aphorism ought to be entirely isolated from the surrounding world like a little work of art and complete in itself like a hedgehog.

216. The French Revolution, Fichte's *Theory of Knowledge,* and Goethe's *Wilhelm Meister* are the three greatest tendencies of the age. Whoever takes offense at this combination, and whoever does not consider a revolution important unless it is blatant and palpable, has not yet risen to the lofty and broad vantage point of the history of mankind. Even in our meager histories of culture, which usually resemble a collection of variants accompanied by a running commentary whose classical text has been lost, many a little book of which the noisy rabble scarcely took notice in its time plays a greater role than did all this rabble.

220. If wit is the principle and organ of universal philosophy, and if philosophy is nothing but the spirit of universality, that is, the science of all perpetually mixing and separating sciences, a logical chemistry, as it were, then that absolute, enthusiastic, and completely material wit is of infinite value and dignity, in which Bacon was one of the first, and Leibniz one of the greatest virtuosos, both leaders in the art of scholastic prose. The most important scientific discoveries are *bons mots* in their genre. They are this by virtue of the astonishing accident of their origin, the combinatory character of thought, and the baroque quality of their casual expression. In their substance, however, they are indeed much more than the mere expectation of a purely poetic wit that resolves itself into nothing. The best are *échappées de vue* into infinity. Leibniz's whole philosophy consists of some aphorisms and projects which are witty in this sense. Kant, the Copernicus of philosophy, has by his nature perhaps more of this syncretistic spirit and critical wit than Leibniz: his situation, however, as well as his education, is not so witty; his ideas have the same destiny as popular tunes: the Kantians sang them to death; thus, one is easily inclined to do him an injustice and to consider him less witty than he really is. To be

sure, philosophy is in good condition only if it must no longer wait for, and expect inspirations of, genius, but can progress steadily with a sure method by enthusiastic strength and the art of genius. But shall we disregard the few still existing products of synthesizing genius only because the combinatory art and science does not yet exist? And how could it exist as long as we are still spelling most of the sciences as if we were sixth-grade boys flattering ourselves that we have achieved our goal if we can decline and conjugate in one of the numerous dialects of philosophy—without hitherto knowing anything about syntax, or how to construct even the smallest sentences?

222. The revolutionary desire to realize God's kingdom on earth is the elastic point of progressive development and the beginning of modern history. Whatever is without relationship to God's kingdom is for it only incidental.

233. Religion is usually nothing but a supplement to or even a substitute for education, and nothing is religious in the strict sense that is not a product of freedom. Thus one can say: the freer, the more religious; and the more education, the less religion.

234. To maintain that there is only one mediator is very one-sided and presumptuous. For the perfect Christian—and in this regard, the unique Spinoza comes nearest to being one—everything should be a mediator.

238. There is a poetry whose One and All is the relationship of the ideal and the real: it should thus be called transcendental poetry according to the analogy of the technical language of philosophy. It begins in the form of satire with the absolute disparity of ideality and reality, it hovers in their midst in the form of the elegy, and it ends in the form of the idyll with the absolute identity of both. But we should not care for a transcendental philosophy unless it were critical, unless it portrayed the producer along with the product, unless it embraced in its system of transcendental thoughts a characterization of transcendental thinking; in the same way, that poetry not infrequently encountered in modern poets should combine those transcendental materials and preliminary exercises for a poetic theory of the creative power with the artistic

reflection and beautiful self-mirroring, which is present in Pindar, the lyric fragments of the Greeks, the ancient elegy, and among the moderns, in Goethe; thus this poetry should portray itself with each of its portrayals; everywhere and at the same time, it should be poetry and the poetry of poetry.

247. Dante's prophetic poem is the only system of transcendental poetry and still the highest of its kind. Shakespeare's universality is like the focus of romantic art. Goethe's purely poetic poetry is the most complete poetry of poetry. This is the great triad of modern poetry, the innermost and most sacred sphere among all the narrower and wider spheres constituting the critical selection of the classics of modern literature.

248. Singular great men are not so isolated among the Greeks and the Romans. They had fewer men of genius, but more geniality. Everything classical is of genius. The entire antiquity is a genius, the only genius that without exaggeration can be called absolutely great, unique, and unattainable.

255. The more poetry becomes knowledge, the more it also becomes art. If poetry is to become art, and if the artist is to have a thorough knowledge and scholarship of his means and goals, their hindrances and subjects, he has to philosophize about his art. If he is to become not only an inventor and worker, but also an expert in his field and also be able to understand his fellow citizens in the realm of art, he must also become a philologist.

259. A: Aphorisms, you maintain, are the true form of the universal philosophy. The form does not matter. What, however, can these aphorisms achieve and be for the greatest and most serious concern of mankind, the perfection of knowledge?
B: Nothing but Lessing's salt against decay, perhaps a cynical *lanx satura* in the classical style of Lucilius and Horace, or even *fermenta cognitionis* for the critical philosophy, marginal notes to the text of the age.

262. Every good man progressively becomes God. To become God, to be man, and to educate oneself, are expressions that are synonymous.

268. A so-called happy marriage corresponds to love as a correct poem to an improvised song.

299. With respect to ingenious subconsciousness, I think, philosophers might well rival poets.

300. When reason and unreason come into contact, an electrical shock occurs. This is called polemics.

305. Intention to the point of irony and having the arbitrary appearance of self-destruction is as naive as instinct to the point of irony. As the naive plays with the contradictions of theory and practice, so the grotesque plays with the odd displacements of form and matter; it likes the air of the casual and odd and flirts with absolute caprice. Humor deals with being and not being; its peculiar essence is reflection. Hence, its kinship with elegy and with everything transcendental; hence, also, its arrogance and its affinity to the mysticism of wit. As genius is necessary for the naive, grave and pure beauty is necessary for humor. Preferably, it hovers over lightly and clearly flowing rhapsodies of philosophy or poetry and flees from heavy bulks as well as from incoherent fragments.

344. To philosophize is to seek omniscience together.

365. Mathematics is, as it were, a sensuous logic, and relates to philosophy as do the arts, music, and plastic art to poetry.

366. Reason is mechanical, wit chemical, and genius organic spirit.

367. Authors are often thought to be insulted by comparing them to manufacturers. Yet should not the true author also be a manufacturer? Should he not devote his entire life to the business of molding literary materials into forms that in a grand manner are practical and useful? We would wish many a bungler a small part of that diligence and care that we hardly appreciate in the most common implements.

395. In true prose everything must be underlined.

424. One can regard the French Revolution as the greatest and most remarkable phenomenon in the history of nations, as an almost universal earthquake, an immeasurable deluge in the political world, or as a prototype of revolutions, as the revolution of revolutions. These are the usual points of view. One can, however, regard the French Revolution as the center and the epitome of the French national character, where all the paradoxes of this nation are concentrated; as the grotesque of the age in the most awesome dimensions, where the most profound prejudices and the strongest presentiments of the age are mingled in a horrible chaos and are interwoven to a tremendous tragicomedy of mankind to the most bizarre degree. For the elaboration of these historical views, one finds only particular traces.

Translated by Ernst Behler and Roman Struc

On the Imagination

Wilhelm von Humboldt

The field of the poet is the imagination. He is a poet only when he renders his own imagination fruitful and arouses ours to life. By means of his genius, nature, which otherwise we contemplate with our senses and analyze with reason, presents itself to the imagination; it seems to receive new radiance through him.

The fundamental problem that every artist has to solve, be he poet, painter, or sculptor, is, to put it briefly, to transform what is *real* in nature into an *image*.

Yet how does he achieve this? In doing so, does he change the objects depicted and give them other forms, colors, and characteristics? If it is the artist's goal that we recognize nature once more in his work, then he may not undertake any significant alterations. He should not so much change his object, rather he should change me, the observer or listener. I should experience the most astonishing transformation through him and feel myself in the midst of nature yet feel elevated above it; in the presence of its full beauty and sublimity, I should forget its imperfections—the narrow boundaries enclosing existence, the swift pace with which all creatures strive towards their dissolution. Thus, the artist must turn to the imagination. His craft in full consists in waking and guiding it. It does not suffice that he merely stimulate it; at the same time, he must give direction to its flight. If he does not wish to miss his goal, he must produce total empathy between himself and us, his readers, which causes us to focus constantly on the same objects and keeps us at the same level of excitement.

Whenever we wish to depict an object for contemplation by the senses or analyze a train of thought with reason, it suffices to take up the individual components one by one in turn. The imagination, however, cannot be governed in such a mechanical way. In vain does the poet describe the beauty of his beloved in most precise detail; never will her likeness impress itself upon our fantasy if he does not succeed in filling his readers with the same enthusiasm that is devouring him. So he delivers the electric shock to our imagination that brings it to life and compels it to repeat the labor previously performed by him and to follow him through the entirety of his artistic production into every detail. Thus, whoever views a painting with the eye of a true connoisseur must re-create it himself through his fantasy; and whoever reads a poet must be a poet himself to a certain degree.

If there is any capacity for immediate spontaneity in our emotions, then it is the imagination. It is completely free in its actions. If the poet nevertheless wishes to direct it, he must himself inject into it the desire, or rather the necessity, of following the path charted by him (since in every art there is a characteristic and sweeping force). If we penetrate deeper into the essence of imagination, then we discover a further characteristic, which does indeed enable its astonishing effect in the arts, but at the same time impedes the activity of the artist that much more. For its productions must be from a single cast, they can be developed only as a whole and cannot be composed of individual components. Therefore, the inner unity of their character is an essential condition of every artistic production. The individual parts of a work must not emerge as separated elements of which the whole is composed but rather as the various sides through which the whole presents itself. If this truly poetic unity is lacking—no matter how strictly the composition of a work may be carried out, no matter how consistent the logic is with which the author has joined the individual parts—then we will be confronted only by a work of mere artfulness and never one of imagination and of genius.

Therefore, only enthusiasm can awaken and command our imagination. It is the poet's task to kindle it. Perhaps that is the reason why we can never fully sense the words of a poet who writes in a foreign tongue. Enthusiasm is composed of an infinite number of relationships that exist between objects on the one hand and our sensations and our character on the other. One must have grown up in the conventions of a language, one must have thought and felt in them, in order that every expression, every word may present itself in all its nuances and awaken all the memories that the thought expressed in words is capable of strengthening. In truth, the words of a foreign language resemble dead signs, those of our own are alive to a certain extent, because they are intimately bound up with everything that stirs about us. Even when a certain expression of a foreign language is completely known to us and we have even frequently heard it spoken in its own country, it has still never penetrated to the depths of our thought, it has never aided us in discovering a new and arresting thought, it has never escaped from us spontaneously in moments of excitement and pain. All this suffices to render it to an extent foreign to us forever.

The more finely and invisibly the relationships between language and thoughts are woven, the greater does this difficulty become; perhaps it is nowhere as pronounced as among French poets. No other poetry is so strongly bound to its language. Thus, how often it becomes impossible to release a work from its linguistic bonds by means of a satisfying translation. Perhaps no other nation possesses such refined and purified sensitivity, a fineness of taste so difficult to grasp. Foreign nations, as soon as they have succeeded in forming a character of their own, frequently treat the masterworks of the French unjustly perhaps for this reason.

I return to my topic. The poet must sense enthusiasm himself, if he is to kindle ours. His secret is to ignite our imagination with the fire of his own. If he portrays nature's image to us, then, as we have seen, he must not change the essential traits of the objects depicted. Rather, he should cause us to see them in a new and different way and now effect their representation to us solely through imagination in place of the usual sensual contemplation and reasoned analysis. But since he is not permitted to affect them directly, he has no other alternative but to withdraw into his self, simply to bring forth his work and to imbue it with form, be it with brush on canvas or by means of language in the minds of men, and leave to the work itself concern for the effect intended by him. The work of a true genius will always speak to us and ignite our fantasy. Only thus do our emotions feel moved in truly poetic fashion.

Everyone agrees that without imagination there would be no poetry or art at all. But, it seems to me, it has not yet been sufficiently recognized that this capability of the mind comprises the actual essence of poetry. Too frequently it was believed that the function of the imagination was exhausted in adorning its object, instead of seeing that it is the imagination itself that must first create the object. In order to prove this, we must engage in an analysis of this capability itself. It is necessary to show what poetic imagination is in the true sense, how it differs from that of the philosopher or the historian, from the imagination evident in practical life. Only from this vantage will new light fall upon our investigation.

It is part of the essence of imagination that the limits of space and time are canceled. Its customary activity consists in making present what is absent, preserving in thought what is past, rendering real what is immaterial. In the process of constantly combining material, conditioned being with unconditional, independent being (for which I would like to use the term *ideal* being, for now), differences and gradations necessarily can be ascertained, the most important of which I would like to characterize here.

I. *Imagination alters nothing at all in the objects, but rather restricts itself to transfering them to other relationships of space and time or to generally different conditions.*

II. *It alters the objects themselves, assembles them—if possible—from varied components and develops forms for which nature supplies only the individual elements.*

During none of these operations does it traverse the boundaries set by real, limited existence itself. It does indeed form new objects, but without exempting them from the laws of natural reality. It must therefore accomplish something additional, if it is to transport our emotions into that highest condition that comprises the character of true poetry. The poet does not need to change the forms of nature at all; the more faithfully he reproduces them, the more surely will he generate pleasure and emotion. Therefore, we are glad to forgo mythological fictions. No other object demands our sympathy with greater right than the depiction of humankind and everything that relates to human existence. *Even if imagination leaves nature as it is, nevertheless it must free it from all conditions limiting and restricting its existence.* It must eliminate the constrictions that hinder the free soaring of our spirits, it must deprive things of their excluding and negative characteristics and portray them in their entire real and positive beauty with the highest degree of perfection, constancy, and uniformity. The poet does not need to lift us from earth to heaven, as it is often expressed; rather, he should diffuse the sublimity and immovable constancy of these high spheres upon the earth itself. He only needs to add the colors to things. And, as the traveler, who sees the sun appear again after gloomy and foggy weather, believes himself among other hills, other forests, in another landscape—thus, in a word, we too must find ourselves transported by the poet into another world in which, with soul-felt joy, we recognize the selfsame things once dear to us. Only in this way does he succeed in connecting our sensual-physical nature with that other that seems to intimate a more sublime origin and at the same time to afford us the highest pleasure of which we are capable.

If we now consider how the poet brings about the astonishing transformation of which we have just spoken, it is easy to conclude that he must evoke such a transformation within us too. Things, with their characteristic essence, he cannot touch; his particular gift consists in generating mere semblance, yet a semblance that is of greater permanence and depth than truth itself. Thus, he must influence our thought and our sensations, but create for us quite different organs, so to speak, than those that guide us in ordinary life. Do not expect me to reveal the secret of the poet here, which is impenetrable even to his own scrutiny. Only from a distance can we follow his tracks. If we analyze the impression that the masterworks of art leave upon our souls, however, we can reduce it without difficulty to a single factor: namely, that they release us from the limitations of present existence and transport us to that realm of deep and sublime ideas in which alone the better part of our essence finds itself.

The greatest achievement of the poet consists in uniting in his object all those features that comprise its particular character. Every art work worthy of its name equals, in the language of the mathematician, a fully given and determinate quantity. Nothing is lacking or superficial in it; it is only what it is and nothing else. But that which it is, it is completely. Therefore, the first effect that emanates from a beautiful statue, a beautiful painting, and grasps the observer consists in drawing his gaze wholly to itself and enabling him to find in this small area everything that is capable of enchanting his senses and filling his emotions. If anything is lacking here, if the painting leaves him distracted or restless, then either the artist or the observer is to be faulted. The former missed the zenith of his art, or the latter lacked the strength of receptivity. While contemplating the Apollo Belvedere, we never grow tired of allowing our gaze to wander over these truly divine forms; from every point our eye returns to the majestic whole and from it turns back again to the details; constantly our feeling of wonder grows and the work of the artist seems inexhaustible. Its sublime beauty resembles a mountain range that grows all the more gigantic, the more the eye attempts to measure it; or an abyss that grows all the deeper, the more one strains to fathom it. In contrast, how different is the impression made by a work of nature! It may be great, indeed beautiful, but the mind viewing it will soon leave it behind in order to contemplate instead its creation, its effects, the changes it has undergone, how it is related to all the other objects of creation. Ultimately, the observer has removed himself from it entirely and is occupied only with the order of the great whole of which the object is merely a part. And, instead of in it, the observer loses himself in the immeasurable All. Art, on the contrary, if I may express it this way, permits us to find the immeasurable in the individual himself.

The work of art is fully a whole; it depicts an idea to us through a particular form. Yet form and idea are so intimately united that they can no longer be separated. Therefore, the work of art compels us to produce the same union within ourselves to enliven our imagination through our thoughts and feelings, so that we are sensible of the sublime art of the poet within us. Thus, we ignite our mind by means of fantasy and are not tempted to reduce the work of the poet to a mere hieroglyph, to a sensual sign for a rational concept. For that is what constantly happens in ordinary life. In natural science or in the pursuit of truth, we must separate the visual form of phenomena from rational concepts. That is, we must separate the capabilities of our mind from one another, as in an analysis of nature.

Art as such has no excluding character. A natural object, by presenting itself as itself, indicates thereby that it cannot be anything other than what it now is. Art, on the contrary, shows us a hero in the blossom of his youth, but instead of dwelling on the inadequacies of this age, it concentrates on showing us its strength and manliness; and instead of holding us to this single, fleeting instant of existence, it permits us to run through the entire, sweeping course of life. For in the youth, we still recognize the charming and innocent features of childhood and at the same time see the firm and manly character of the grown man developing.

That interesting sculpture in Florence in which Menelaus bears Achilles' friend, killed in battle, unites the most faithful picture of death with the most impressive portrayal of life, for example, and in a manner that does not repulse us in fright but links us intimately to life and leads our thoughts to the fate of man, that great and sublime idea in which our soul always loses and then finds itself anew.

The objects of reality awaken our desire for them and our interest in them. Alternately, we calculate the use and the pleasure that they can bring us. The objects of art call forth purer sensations in us. They promote our enjoyment, they arrest us with their very being, they put our passions to rest, no base appetite is stimulated in their presence, and we do not demand to possess them exclusively. It suffices that we enjoy simply viewing them.

Art always leads us back to ourselves; it fills us with the greatest and noblest enthusiasm and thus becomes an inexhaustible source of great deeds. But first it must give man back to himself, before it can make of him a gift to his fellow man.

Thus, we have established the essential points that constitute the effect of great artworks and collected enough facts for the continuation of our investigation. As we have seen, in regard to the achievements of the imagination, there are various gradations. It bears the name "poetic" with good reason only when it has liberated nature from all those conditions restricting existence or, better, when we have released ourselves through it from the narrow circle of our daily needs, desires, and passions. If it succeeds in reaching this goal, then it puts us in a condition of elevation and of peace that is characterized by the absence of every base and impure emotional urge.

We must never forget that the poet effects that transformation only within ourselves. If he portrays nature to us in a new form, in reality he has not transformed nature at all but only the state of our emotions. We have already noted how art in its works eradicates everything that constitutes the isolated, excluding, and mutable being in the things of reality. But in no way does it stand aloof from the reproduction of the regular changes in nature, which constantly fascinate us anew, nor from those sudden catastrophes that often endow life with a sublime trait. Nor does it turn away from those situations of dread in which life seems hopeless. Otherwise, it would deprive itself of one of its most powerful tools to move our emotions. Thus, it holds us fast in its sublime sphere by extinguishing everything that reminds us of our limited and uncertain existence, raises us above our destiny and the occurrences in the world so that we completely forget our own egos and devote ourselves fully to the creations of its spirit. It thus speaks to our imagination alone. The effect of true poetry is surely proven also by the fact that we feel greater inner peace and strength when we leave the theater or after we read a poem. No matter how painful the conflict between human aspirations and the power of fate that the poet presents to us may be, we always succeed in gathering the sensations within our emotions and in restoring the necessary equilibrium again; or we acknowledge in fate itself a kindly, if stern, justice and feel determined to spite the blind force that could shatter us and not to submit to it. No matter how strong the violent emotion may be that we face in truly tragic situations, afterwards we feel within ourselves greater strength, armed to take up the afflictions of life again, to defy its pains and hazards. Only men of weak character succumb to the sublime pain, which elevates the soul instead of suppressing it and which, where it fully penetrates it, purifies it at the same time.

Without dwelling any longer on the difference between nature and art—we shall come back to it later—let us continue the analysis of imagination and show how the poet must proceed to attain his goal. If our imagination is to be captured by him and elevated to a sphere that transcends nature, then everything must be contained within the artwork itself; it must above all be independent of everything that is outside of itself. Precisely therein is the tie that binds it to us. This is so constituted that we are incapable of releasing ourselves from it and now find in the work everything that the poet placed there for our interest and our sympathy. The historian must tie together those facts that he relates and in so doing keep in mind what these in truth once were. Thus, he constantly points us back to an original that he is merely copying. The philosopher does indeed enjoy greater independence but supports his train of thought with facts that his readers and he must constantly refer to. Only the artist bases his creation upon nothing; borne solely by the pure flight of his genius, he holds himself, figuratively speaking, suspended over the void. He does indeed nourish himself from the contemplation of nature, but when he depicts it, he gives us something other than it. He does not lead us to real things but liberates us from them. A beautiful statue reminds us of nothing but itself; beside it, nature disappears; it has extinguished even its creator. It seems to exist merely through itself. People who possess no sensibility for the sublime beauty of art see in its works nothing but the objects portrayed. Those for whom the poet is in truth creating discover more.

If the artist does reproduce nature, he must assimilate it; and as he receives his object from its hands, he must generate it anew. Bacon defined art ingeniously as: "Nature enriched by humanity." But the art of the painter, the sculptor, the poet is more; it is not just nature enriched by humanity; in art, man replaces nature. In fact, the artist must destroy nature as a real object in order to create it anew as the work of his imagination.

In sensuality and in the imagination, we possess two capabilities that are closely bound to one another and yet are sharply different. Through the senses, we are dependent upon the things that surround us. Through the imagination, we can liberate ourselves from this dependency. When the senses are involved, our physical needs call attention to themselves, desires awaken, passions are excited, we exert ourselves and are dependent on the results, our physical strength begins to act, and finally we stop, exhausted. If the imagination is involved, however, then we feel free of all encumbering bonds. We do continue to be sensible of love and hate, fear and hope, but we rise above emotional excitement as real experiences and draw new strength from the pure activity of our powers. Therefore, an object of nature can never be compared with an object of art. The former always appeals to our senses or our imagination; the latter affects the imagination alone. The artist therefore must subordinate his sensual capacity to the imagination.

It can no longer be doubted that his real achievement consists in creative production. Is it not much more a creative production, a creating rather than a mere reworking of natural being, when the artist portrays this being to us in a new form and a new radiance, when he imbues it with the magical force that rejects all mere sensual desire and stimulates the highest energies of our souls? But in order to be creative, he must let the imagination dominate him, it must control him completely; senses, reason, and sensibility must obey only it.

We differentiate between two different types of imagination: the *reproductive,* which recalls to mind the objects of our sensual experience, and the *creative* imagination, which, although it does not generate any absolutely new objects (for we must always create from experience), presents those objects to us in a manner quite different from that of sensual perception, in which they could never appear thus. This type of imagination belongs intrinsically to art. The artist earns his name only when he lets himself be controlled by it.

But creative imagination is not only found in the activity of the poet. It determines the actions of every genius. And genius is always needed wherever ordinary resources have been exhausted, where traditional rules can no longer be applied mechanically or a suitable solution be chosen from among those at hand. There where every exit seems blocked, the genius must break new, hitherto unknown trails. So his singularity has been defined fittingly and cleverly as *the talent of making rules through action.* Although it is impossible to fathom his secret and to pursue his action, yet we can recognize how the imagination takes possession of all our emotions, and, even if it does enrich itself from experience, how it always generates its own means, its own raw material, instead of drawing them from experience. To express it metaphorically, albeit less precisely, in such creative moments not only are reason and reflection active, but the entire soul is seized by a fire that both warms and illuminates it.

However, there is an essential difference between the procedure of the artist and the nonartistic genius. The latter pursues a certain goal, foreign to the imagination; he does not discover for the sake of discovering, but rather to take possession of a resource that he lacks toward a practical goal, whether it is a matter of solving a scientific problem, the building of a machine necessary for a certain project, or reaching the correct decision on the battlefield, where smart and bold maneuvering is required. The artist, however, creates only for the joy of creating. His goal is contained wholly within his work. That it may be and endure, that it may speak to those who seek it out, that it be recognized—he desires nothing more.

The activity of the artistic imagination is subject to no foreign idea. It fully follows its natural penchant for invention, to shape alone, free, and independent. Neither the judgment of men nor the impression that he leaves among them is considered by the artist when he is seized by the enthusiasm of creation. Even if he were outside all human society, he would nevertheless retain the strength and youthful freshness of his genius. He would exert himself no less if he knew he were alone in the desert, or if he knew that with the last stroke of his chisel his life too would end. Thus, he creates more from a secret instinct of his emotions, from inner necessity, than from a sheer act of will.

In every successful activity, all the forces of our mind work together. Here the philosopher needs the imagination no less than the poet does, even if he must subordinate this capability to the sole dominance of speculative reason. All significant expressions of the human spirit resemble each other in that all its capabilities appear simultaneously and in closest cooperation. Yet these expressions differ in that one of the capabilities dominates the others, according to the particular purpose that has been settled upon.

There are in general three quite different states of attitude, which contain all the others.

Either we occupy ourselves with the collecting, testing, or classifying of facts; or, as in mathematics, we pursue abstract ideas or at least those that have been abstracted from objects of experience; or we conduct ourselves toward nature and its manifold richness in a purely contemplative manner, but so that we do not view things as real but rather as new creations of our imagination. This third frame of mind belongs most properly to art; and we now continue to analyze it in order to cast light upon its other characteristics, too.

We said that the imagination must dominate the poet. But nothing is more arbitrary than the imagination; left to itself, it succumbs to coincidence and aims merely at the appearance of things.

Therefore, it must unite with the other capabilities; it should dominate them but at the same time arouse and determine their activity. It is obvious that a work of art must show the greatest regularity and be constructed according to strict laws, exactly observed. But the imagination cannot simply borrow the principles of these laws from external objects, if it is to rise above them. These principles must thus come from the organization of our reason itself. But precisely in this does the chimerical imagination differ from the poetic imagination; for the one follows the impulses of the moment, giving itself over to coincidence, and the other creates according to the internal laws of our thought and feeling; the one smothers all the other capabilities of the mind or whirls them alone, the other, in contrast, fills them with a life of their own, preserves their free effectiveness, and receives from them in turn the norms and rules of their own action. For this reason, poetry joins the greatest *reality* with the most perfect *ideality*. Ideality, as we call the highest and most sublime beauty, of which nature is incapable of offering us a single example, springs from the creative activity of the imagination. Reality, in contrast, necessarily results from the combined functioning of all the other capabilities of our mind, to the extent that they are active in combination with imagination.

We have now reached the point we were striving for; let us summarize the main results of our train of thought. The poet, we said, undertakes to transform what is real in nature into an image. To do so, he must involve our imagination and compel it spontaneously to generate mental representations of that which he intends to show it. In order to set our fantasy in motion, he must first render his own creation, reshape the object borrowed from nature, and produce it anew. His fantasy should dominate in freedom, and yet assure itself of the cooperation of the other powers of the mind. Only then can a work of art elevate us above ourselves and speak directly to our spirit and heart.

If we have in fact determined the true essence of the art of poetry here, then the answer to two questions can decide the poetic worth of any given work.

Does the work possess a foundation in reality on which our senses, our thoughts, our sensations can fasten, and does this foundation present itself exclusively to our imagination?

Does one recognize the effect of the imagination by the form, either in the radiance therein that it casts upon the great and sublime ideas of mankind, or by the ease with which it treats a happy poetic sketch that delights us with its simplicity or fineness?

Whenever we search in vain for one of these two characteristics, then we are dealing with imperfect rather than true poetry.

Thus, we do not call a product poetry if, lacking that foundation in reality, the poet recites glamorous phrases, pretty verses, and even picturesque images. For even if he is able to flatter our fantasy in this clever way, we still lack that solid object on which it could attach itself, that perfect portrayal that we could contemplate and admire as a whole in all its details. Only the pure versifier is an exception here, if he has unfortunately committed himself to this genre. For perfect and continuous versification does in fact call forth a musical effect that fascinates that listener whose poetic tastes are so immature as to be content with the sweet harmony of the sheer sound of language.

In addition, we do not accord the name of poet to anyone who is merely pursuing novel effects by means of farfetched images, showy truisms, abstruse logic. He may seem clever, inventive, to us, even great and linguistically skillful—but that does not make a poet of him. He arouses our astonishment, our interest—but leaves us cold withal, because he remains unable to lead us out of and beyond ourselves.

Above all, we refuse to grant this title that is so difficult to achieve to someone who unsuccessfully claims to touch heart and feelings directly and thus fails to affect our fantasy. Even if he touches and moves us, yet he does not lift our spirit nor expand our thoughts. We avoid him all the more when at first glance he seems to be the closest to true poetry. He is a greater danger to it, however, than the others, because he degrades and destroys true good taste and poetic sensibility.

In order to form a correct idea of the art of poetry, one must not consider it as an art meant merely to please, a decoration of nature that is only reserved for the entertainment and instruction of the human race in its infancy. To be sure, such an opinion of the art of poetry is shared by most of those poets whose fantasy lacks true creativity, and who therefore scatter only a few blossoms and who must embellish their unpoetic thoughts and feelings with poetic phrases; but these poetasters are to the true poets as a scene painter is to a genuine artist.

If we are to offer a definition of art at this point, then the concept of imagination will have to play an essential role. Such a definition will either proceed from the creative capacity of the imagination or from its result, the picture of nature that it forms, according to whether one conceives of art as a particular quality or as a creation of the artist. To understand this in its full significance, one needs to remember what we have explained about the essential traits of the imagination. If we take the most important of these traits into our definition, then we can perhaps say: *Art is the capacity to portray nature solely through imagination as the free and independent activity of the imagination.*

We said the portrayal of *nature* in order to characterize therewith the most general objects, which contains all others that are at the disposal of art. For since nature extends to all objects in general, then everything that exists is necessarily a part of it, even our thoughts and sensations, in a word, everything at all to which a reality can be ascribed, be it the senses, reason, or sensibility.

Since the *beautiful ideal* is often talked about, it seems odd that I have not yet mentioned it here. But philosophers frequently use the word *beautiful* in a differing sense, and it is difficult (although not impossible) to ascertain its real meaning. Therefore, I chose a more natural procedure and based my considerations directly upon the given facts. Consequently, I investigated the impression that is left on our emotions by the great works of painting, sculpture, and poetry; from there I attempted to find out how the artist himself is affected by them, and I derived my definition of art from this source. However, it is probably still appropriate to add a few comments about the concept of the *beautiful ideal*.

It has often been asserted that the beautiful ideal arises from the selection and compilation of examples of beauty scattered throughout nature. But this designation is highly unsatisfying in my eyes. In order to unite a number of these beautiful separate parts, one must make a whole of them; or, to put it another way, in order to invest them with that harmony of which a unified figure alone is composed, one must change these parts and create them anew. It is thus a matter not merely of compilation but of new creation. The term *separate part* is itself relative; a separate part is in itself a whole and consists in turn of other, smaller parts. Which ones are meant here, then? Would one not have to despair of ever locating a complete and at the same time ideal figure? And does one really believe it would be easier to locate an arm, a hand, a finger that deserved this designation? If the painter would investigate his artistic procedure more closely, he would have to recognize that there is nothing, down to the smallest fingernail, that he can transmit directly to the canvas from nature and leave it as it is. To destroy the real object in his memory and to create it anew as the work of his imagination is the course he constantly takes—even where he is not aware of it.

The word *ideal* is the opposite of the word *real*. Everything that exists as a mental representation is ideal; the ideal in particular can have its existence only here, and in this sense we would like to use it as the sobriquet for the word beauty. Art aims to transform what is real in nature into an image. So it seeks out something that lies within itself, something ideal; but it is not actually concerned with making its object beautiful, but with making beautiful what it depicts. It remains true to its original purpose: that of *transformation into an image*. Yet the poet knows that success will be denied him if he does not surrender completely to the domination of his fantasy, if he does not let it do as it alone pleases. Thus does his work participate imperceptibly in the radiance and impetus of this capacity of the mind. Only the insignificant poets previously mentioned constantly labor to beautify their object; the great artist thinks solely of reproducing it. He releases it from his hands beautiful and sublime, without expressly having to act upon it to present it that way. The imagination impresses its character on every object it treats.

It is more difficult to explain how it can produce this unique and indisputably magic effect. We must content ourselves with the assertion that it is able to do so because it is among the highest capabilities of our mind, because it eradicates anything that restricts our existence and awakens only the highest thoughts and sensations within us. However, one observation can probably be made that, even if not capable of solving our problem entirely, at least leads us closer to a solution.

If we enter the realm of pure possibility, then we encounter there nothing but the condition of the connection and reciprocal dependence of these various elements from which objects can first take on their form for us. Divested of all real being, they are endowed merely with ideal existence, an existence that can be guaranteed to them only through their causes or their effects. In other words, the poetic imagination is completely contained within itself, but it is nevertheless destined to give us the mental representation of a being that is more vivid and more permanent than that perceived by the senses. So if we judge how the unifying bond is constituted, with which the imagination links the various parts of its compositions, then it must be remembered above all that there are no truly independent parts here, that each one is supported and preserved by all the others, just as each in turn supports and preserves the others. In this closely linked and reciprocally conditioned unity, which we encounter in every work of art, the being of each object is dependent on that of every other. Indeed, the concepts of means and end switch places, since they are equally applicable to every component; the parts make up the whole, and all details relate totally to the whole. Thus, we reproach a poet who knew no better than to make the means of his art externally visible, rather than to allow it to arise necessarily from the treatment of his object. For him, the artistic means is not part of the work. Rather, it resembles props that are constructed on the outside of a building instead of making it rest upon its own foundation. It is easy to observe, if one investigates one's own attitude carefully, that in the observation of works of art (in contrast to works of philosophy and history) one does not pursue a progressive series of ideas but often turns back, describing a constant circle and, in the analysis of the composition of the individual parts, is again and again led back from one of them to another. However, this reciprocal bond, this perfect harmony and unity of the work of art, should dominate not only the plan of its design but likewise the thoughts and sensations developed by the artist and above all the forms, colors, and tones employed by him.

Now, since this is the principal law that poetic imagination has to follow, we no longer need to wonder at that radiance it imparts to all its portrayals. For how could there be anything more beautiful and more sublime than this perfect harmony, which allows a work to rest solely upon itself and connects all its parts with one another?

Art is usually defined as the imitation of nature; and it is true that the portrayal of nature through imagination gives us a product different from nature, which, however, reminds us of nature again. In spite of that, this definition seems neither accurate nor usable to me. For what nature is supposedly being imitated? Beautiful nature, I suppose? But are there sure signs by which it can be recognized? What kind of imitation is required? The slavish imitation of the copyist? Or a different, freer kind that permits the model to be altered and embellished?

These difficulties can be avoided by the course that we have adopted. The artist must portray nature though his fantasy. That also means imitating it—but at the same time much more. Our means of expression is thus clearer and more accurate. Imitation remains inferior to its model; the artist, in contrast, raises us above our physical and real existence and thereby supplies the sure proof of being superior to it; his goal is thus established unequivocally. He must cause us to see things exclusively with our fantasy, instead of viewing them through our senses and analyzing them with reason. Furthermore, he cannot be uncertain about the manner of treating them. The extent to which he can change them is prescribed to him, that is, he can go only as far as is necessary to portray them through the imagination alone. The selection of his objects likewise affords him no difficulty. Everything that fits into the composition of the imagination, without causing disproportion or disharmony, may with perfect right and will be beautiful and sublime. As long as he lets only his fantasy have free rein and elevates and purifies it, he will remain faithful to poetry.

Therefore, the principle of the imitation of nature is to be employed cautiously; it can generate errors due to its imprecision. If it is interpreted falsely, it can shackle art and lead to an undervaluation of its great and high character.

Perhaps I may be permitted to insert one more general comment here that is significant for the entire topic of the theory of art. In thoughtful preoccupation with the beautiful, the sublime, the essence of poetry, the problem of genres, one of the two following methods can always be applied. Either one can aim at determining the characteristics that should be appropriate to the work of the artist and prescribe certain rules to him for the execution of his artistic undertaking, or one can limit oneself to elucidating to him the creative methods of the imagination and the effect necessarily generated by it—in a word: what goal the artist must set for himself, leaving to his genius alone the means of artistic execution. Both methods should always be applied together; especially the first is of inestimable value. Yet everywhere that the actual essence of art is at stake—this is important to recognize—only the second alone is applicable. For if one attempts to describe the object of artistic worth as such, then one always runs into things that stubbornly resist all attempts to express them by means of language. That is why we have so long been lacking a definition of beauty. The search was constantly for certain signs as *characteristics of objects* with the help of which the beautiful could be recognized. But that is a futile undertaking. The assessment of the beautiful is not the result of a rational analysis, rather it rests upon a decision of *taste*. One can analyze only this capacity itself as well as the sensation that the truly beautiful object generates in our emotions.

The artist would doubtlessly profit from rules that would provide him with precise directions for his creative efforts and permit their direct application. To be sure, the number of such rules is extremely small, and none of them is pertinent to the truly poetic part of his art. As far as this part is concerned, we can tell him nothing but this: That is how the effect that you must strive after is produced, that is the manner and method that you yourself must appeal to, that is the idea that you must form of your work. In the search for the means with which to transfer your ideas to canvas, to marble, you can rely only on your genius. There lies a secret that belongs entirely to you; and you would not deserve the rank you hold, if its veil could be lifted with greater ease.

Every work of art can be judged according to three different merits: according to

> *its poetic merits,*
> *its logical merits,*
> *its artistic merits.*

It can be devised with genius, thought through with precision, executed with greatness and skill. The composition of the structure is the business of reason, and therefore completely accessible to analysis and debate. Even someone who lacks taste and a knowledge of the arts will be able to judge to a certain extent here. The merits of the execution belong wholly to the artist in the truest sense of the word; only he or the true connoisseur can evaluate them; but rarely will a connoisseur in this true sense possess the competence to judge two different genres of art. The merits of a genius are comprehensible to everyone who possesses a pure and high sense of taste; but a better judge is found in someone who knows by comparison what the various arts have in common than in someone who has specialized too greatly in those differences that characterize the individual arts.

I have been treating only the truly poetic part of art here. I have attempted to explain its essence and to give a satisfactory definition of it. Here now follow a few remarks about its composition and about the differing character of the various outward forms of art that arise from the observation of examples well known to us.

That which is poetic consists in portraying nature through the imagination. Thus, two different things are present: *the object* which the author offers to us and *the form* through which he makes it appear. That which is poetic is composed of these two closely connected parts.

In art, *form* is what is essential. No matter what object, whether large or small, the artist may choose, only through his manner of treating it is he able to ennoble it and to project it into a sphere that lies above our usual field of vision. In this, all genres truly belonging to art are of equal rank and value. Surely, the historical painter is greater as a man and knows human nature better than the painter who with his brush offers us pictures of flowers and animals or of still life from nature. But he is for that reason no less a painter than the other. To electrify the imagination, to compel it to create from its foundation the picture that he offers us: This is the goal towards which every artist must strive and which solely and alone is decisive for his artistic capability. When we demand of the poet that he elevate and expand our mind, we are far from assigning him only serious and sublime objects, from forbidding him lovely and clever games, those happy and ethereal flights of a cheerful and capricious fantasy that constitute such a great charm of poetry. Not by showing us objects that amaze us by their greatness does he cause that marvelous effect in us, rather by freeing us of the burden and the tedious mementos of life. What transports us to rapture is the lightness of his flight and not at all the beauty of the regions through which he speeds us.

The objects of art are as manifold as nature itself. Everything that is receptive to the colors of the imagination falls into the realm of art.

Whatever the artist depicts, he must make tangible to the senses or adapt to our perceptive faculty. Only objects of pure thought present great difficulties for him, and for this reason good didactic poetry is found so seldom among the masterworks of any nation. In spite of all diversity, the greatest object that he can choose and to which all others ultimately relate continues to be man—man in his contact with nature as he either enjoys its gifts or struggles with the dangers with which it threatens his existence.

Among all the arts, sculpture and music are the most antithetical. The former presents only pure forms to us, and everything depends on the faultlessness and rigor of its design. Music, by contrast, offers us no specific objects at all. It imparts only a certain impulse to our sensations, more precisely, it calls to life a specific series of impulses, the rhythm and harmony of which correspond to that rhythm with which it charms our ear. Every artistic impression contains something of this double effect: By means of sensuality we imagine forms, images, and our sensibility is stimulated to a certain excitement. Thus, all arts in general share in some way with *sculpture* and with *music*.

Poetry connects these two elements with the greatest possible coequality. It links their forms closely with thoughts and sensations, because it brings forth living man in his actions and speech. This is probably the reason it generates a much deeper effect than the other arts. For the priceless merit of words is that they sketch pictures for our senses and at the same time awaken the most secret sensations of our emotions.

Since poetry possesses the possibility of this double effect, the poet can employ either of them to advantage at any time. There are poets whose efforts are directed solely at impressing our memory with a certain picture, who concentrate wholly on depicting this image from its various views and on exhausting it in all its details. In contrast, other poets are intent on transmitting a certain series of impulses to the imagination and on imparting a certain movement to it by leading it through a great variety of images. If, for example, we compare Homer and Ariosto, then the effect of the former is based upon the beauty and sublimity of his images, in the rigorous and bold manner in which he sketches them. The Italian poet, in contrast, seems to affect us only by his emotionality, through the alacrity with which he communicates it to us, through the richness of the sequence of his images. Homer never appears on the scene himself. We see only his heroes, only they speak to us, amaze us, and move us. But Ariosto constantly mingles with his figures; it does not satisfy him simply to depict his object. And so he also directs his attention to the impression that he generates in us, without concealing the fact that it is he who is attempting to determine that impression. Thus, we see here two different kinds of poetry that actually belong to two different genres, the epic and the lyric, and that can also appear in other genres, according to the specific character of a nation, a century, an individual.

For especially in this regard, the poetry of ancient peoples is different from that of modern peoples. With the ancients everything is *plastic;* there are only forms, figures, pictures. Their poetic works leave us with almost the same impression that we receive from those beautiful fragments of their sculpture rescued from the ravages of time. Modern poetry, in contrast, more resembles sonorous and moving *music,* and its objects often dissolve before our eyes into deep emotion, which is generated by its sweet and musical language. I do not propose to portray in detail this difference between our era and centuries long past. An entire work could easily be dedicated to the treatment of this topic. We will content ourselves with pointing out a few characteristics of this difference, in order to determine the path that our poetry must take if, to the extent this is possible, it is to attain the beauty and youthful freshness of that first era of our race and yet at the same time draw its nourishment from the philosophy of our century. When the poetry of the ancients is mentioned here, I have only the Greeks in mind; for the Romans had already set out in a different direction from them, even where they were imitating them, and are already closer to our own age in many ways. Among modern nations, the French seem to me to have imitated Latin poetry the most. That gives their poetry its determining character, which distinguishes it from the Greek as well as from that of their neighbors.

It would be a superfluous exertion to try to portray the singularity of the ancients in detail. Everyone knows the effect that their artworks have on us, the soaring of the spirit that they impart to us, the sublime peacefulness that they dispense upon us, the sweet melancholy to which they move us. It would be more difficult to discover the artistic process through which they were able to attain this degree of perfection. Here too, then, lies the actual task of the critic. Without flattering ourselves that we have penetrated the secret of their spirit, we are nevertheless capable of tracing a few of its decisive traits. If we analyze an artwork of the Greeks, we find a kind of artistic treatment that diverges from our own in regard to its inner structure, the selection of the elements of which it is composed, and the way in which its figures are designed.

The structure of their works is the greatest uniformity. There are rarely parts that do not connect quite naturally with the others. Yet a unity consciously to be striven for, that rigid manner of proceeding that we find so frequently in our modern poets, was unknown to the ancients. The composition of their works seems to have issued from the imagination itself; more admirable in design even if less consciously thought out, they show much less of the exertion of the poet. Their works thus bear more the character of what is natural and preserve a greater immediacy; they do not afflict our minds with fatigue and they impair the free flight of fantasy less.

They are composed of elements as great as they are simple. Sophisticated sensation is foreign to them, as is the sharpness of reason, of which our authors are full. They differentiate their characters by means of strong and prominent traits and do not resort to finer and almost imperceptible nuances that characterize the works of our century. They avoid everything that could appear affected. Only the great characteristics of the soul, the great passions springing directly from human nature are admitted into their portrayals.

Above all, it is the way in which the characters portrayed to us are sketched that is characteristic. They are always depicted through their words and deeds; they are all we see, never does the poet appear. Those cold portraits, such as, for example, the constantly repeated descriptions of feminine beauty by the Italian poets, are also foreign to the ancients. If Homer is frequently minutiose in his descriptions, he is following the custom and taste of his century in this, and furthermore this is true only in the incidental passages of his work. There where he truly wants to move us, one single adjective often suffices to place a picture before our eyes in its totality.

The poetry of antiquity thus offers us only great, brightly illuminated masses, which form before our eyes with the same ease with which they dissolve, and which, since they never become entangled, do not hinder our fantasy. With the poets of antiquity, there is nothing that does not speak to the senses or is not directed to the most natural sensations of our emotions. This naive simplicity nevertheless possesses the character of the sublime, which never fails to enrich our thinking and elevate our minds. Here everything is lightness and clarity; it is noble and sublime at once. If now we add the grace, the gentle and prepossessing harmony of their language, their richness in graphic expression, it is easy to admit that ancient poetry is the only poetry that can satisfy the imagination in its entirety, and that it will remain an unattainable model forever.

It would be unjust, however, to ignore the merits with which modern poets are able to enrich their art. If the ancients unfold before our eyes a charming picture of nature rich in forms and colors, then the poets of the modern age do offer us a more interesting picture of man and penetrate to the most hidden corners of our hearts. The distinct individuality of the ancients and of the moderns is most acutely determined by the fact that the former lived quite outside of themselves in the bosom of nature, whereas we moderns have the penchant of withdrawing into ourselves and of locking ourselves into our thoughts and sensations. Modern poetry thus grasps us with greater power, it affects our feelings more deeply, it stimulates the interest of our reason more; but it touches our fantasy less, speaks less to our senses. Its language is darker and more difficult, the situations that it depicts often enough tear our souls, and it no longer dispenses that charming and deep peacefulness by which we recognize the masterworks of antiquity. To put it briefly, it is less poetry and possesses less of the true character of art.

But what can the poet do in order to make up for these mistakes without relinquishing the merits connected with them? The answer seems simple to me. We have already distinguished the *foundation* that the poet treats from the *form* in which he clothes it. As far as the form is concerned, he should approximate the ancients as far as possible. Here they will always remain our only model. Yet everything that the philosophy and culture of our age can inspire it with should be included in the foundation of his work. It would indeed be sad to think that nothing remained for us from a succession of centuries so rich in events and great minds with which we could enrich and adorn poetic art in our own way.

That does not mean that we advise the poet to use the results of philosophy and the sciences directly and to surround himself with new and farfetched images, with thoughts that are perhaps profound but speculative and abstract. Since it is part of his vocation to generate universal interest, to involve sensuality and fantasy equally, he need only keep to the broad traits of human nature, to simple and true sensations, and to the images that the sight of nature itself offers us. The poet is able to enrich himself not through the expansion of his territory but by making it more fertile.

There is a further means to secure greater interest in his works. We said that the principal object of the poet was man, his character, and his relation to nature. Now, all our progress in the arts, in the sciences, and in political institutions should aim not only to make man more virtuous and happier (which would be a much too narrow attitude that might actually lead to missing the goal it aimed at), but at the same time greater, higher, and richer in his whole existence. He should be rendered capable of absorbing as much as he can of the things of his world and of impressing upon them in return the seal of his own greatness. In a comparison of the ancient with the modern nations, it is evident that the latter lack greatness and strength of character, but that they are deeper and richer in their thought and sensibility and possess greater variety in their lives than did the ancients. Let the poet study this variety and portray it for us in his works, let him ascend to the zenith of his century, then he will elevate our fantasy through his portrayals and strengthen our spirit and emotions with this healthy and hearty fare. If he follows this past, the poet can perform a substantial service even for philosophy and ethics. He will present to the imagination a high and ideal frame of mind that is unattainable in the real world, and thus awaken enthusiasm for virtue; he will raise man above the limits set him by the regular, if slow, progress of his own reason.

If the progress of philosophy and the sciences has expanded and enriched the character of man, then this elevated level of culture must be evident in the works of modern art as well. Here, in my opinion, lies the only possibility for philosophy to influence the art of poetry without changing its simplicity and individuality. It would be a task for the philosophical writer to describe the characters portrayed in the poetry of modern nations in their individuality and diversity and, therewith, the idea of humanity that each one of them contains when one looks at each one by itself. Such an interesting comparison would not, to be sure, decide anything about the poetic worth of the poetry of a nation; but it would show which of them has best learned to assimilate the teachings of philosophy and experience and to express that in their works of art, too. It would not be difficult to predict which nations would carry off the victory in this praiseworthy and difficult contest.

We need to realize, however, that the progress of poetry is blocked by a hurdle difficult to overcome. The greater and more momentous the theme of a poem is in itself, then the more vividly does it engage the mind and sensibility and the harder it is also to imbue it with the clarity, spontaneity, and lightness that the work of art requires. The real advantage that the modern nations have over the ancients consists in their dividing up their projects much more carefully and isolating much more the intellectual capabilities they have acquired. Since they liberated themselves from the bondage of the senses and of fantasy, they imparted greater authority to the analytic spirit and themselves drove their investigations forward, even into the profundities of philosophy. To the degree that they closed off their sensations within themselves, they fashioned characters of extreme originality. But nothing is so contrary to artistic effect as such a division and isolation of our mental forces. The poet demands man, the whole man, and we never feel all the powers of our emotions more intimately united than when he transports us on the wings of fantasy to those high regions accessible only to his genius.

Whatever is original in the passions or in the character, whatever bears the stamp of originality, seems to move away from nature and can only with difficulty be brought back to simplicity and provided with a semblance of truth. Only the genius of the poet knows how to avoid the hazards of these straits. He is capable of doing so because now he penetrates deeper into his object, portrays it in all the details that constitute its totality. If some modern poets seem more bizarre to us than sublime, if they miss the poetic effect at which they were aiming, the reason for this is less that they have chosen unusual situations or have depicted eccentric characters than that they show us only one side and do not join this side to the whole that would put it into context. No matter how extraordinary a character may appear at first glance, when the conditions and relationships of his life are investigated, it follows in a clear and natural way how this character developed and had to develop. This, at any rate, is the procedure of a great poet. He presents a character with all of its features; he surrounds it with appropriate figures in order to emphasize these features; he places it in appropriate situations. Instead of moving away from nature, it causes nature to be enhanced. Therefore, we will no longer lament that the clarity and truth of the ancients is irrevocably gone. We mourn only the lively and glowing colors with which their youthful fantasy endowed their portrayals; this is a merit that is inextricably linked to the beauty of their climate, the harmony of their language, and the promising childhood of our race.

Since the French, Italian, and English poets are already generally known, I need say nothing else about them. Anyone may judge for himself to what extent they have succeeded in combining the merits of the ancients with the progress of our modern centuries. German poetry, in contrast, is still unknown in most of Europe. Only a few authors, chosen at random, are known, and even then in very inadequate translations. Therefore, it might possibly be useful to say something about German poetry, insofar as it possesses a peculiar character common to the works of various authors. This character consists in our taking advantage of the enrichment and expansion of thought and sensibility that we owe to the progress of our age and, at the same time, in attempting to approximate as closely as possible the rigorous and true poetic method of the ancients. Rich in profound thought, in noble and delicate sensations, German poetry advances more every day toward the greatness, simplicity, and grace of the forms of antiquity. It excels above all in its depiction of character, even though it does not yet offer originals of charm equal to those known, for example, from the comic writing of the English. But German writing penetrates into the most secret crannies of the human heart, grasps its subtlest stirrings, and joins them to the entirety of the character with all its features. It succeeds in doing so with an urgency and clarity that we find otherwise only in introspection. Never does it offer us only the picture of a single action or passion, but always a specific, acting individual. The German poets place such value on this part of their art because they believe that the highest ideas can be combined in this way with the simplicity of what is natural. For there is absolutely nothing so extraordinary that it cannot be brought into association with the relationships and conditions proper to human character itself. In that case, there is no longer anything alien to us that might lie outside the boundaries of the natural and simple. So here we have found that true center to which the poet must move in order to bring his boldest schemes into the realm of our vision and sensibility.

If, for example, we examine the works of Goethe, who above all others has prepared the way here, one cannot help noticing how penetratingly this poet has dedicated himself to the study of the ancients, less to the conventions of their linguistic forms than to their true spirit. Following their tracks, he is concerned only with reproducing his object. He disdains every foreign embellishment and looks only for a faithful portrayal that will captivate us through its truth and simplicity alone. Nevertheless, it is no other than he who depicts characters exposed to the most extraordinary situations and arousing the greatest amazement; and there probably is no poet who has even given us such a profound and at the same time noble conception of love, such a new and interesting picture of the character of women. Since he chooses characters, however, who seem to originate in ordinary natural circumstances, he succeeds in leading them back to that state. Where he shatters our soul through situations full of dread, he knows how to restore peace to us at the same time by lifting the soul to a height where everything—human destiny, our desires and passions—constitute only a single and perfect harmony. His *Werther* has been applauded by all nations because people were amazed by how the poet was able to unite in the same character the violence of passions, the profound power of feeling, such excessive love, and such extraordinary intellectual aptitude, with such simple and natural taste, with such sincere, such naive love of the beauty of nature, of the innocent games of childhood.

It would probably be useful to develop more completely the singularity of this poet and others like-minded and provide an analysis of their works in detail. But that would be a special project lying beyond the goals we set ourselves here.

Translated by Ralph R. Read III

The German Chapbooks

Joseph Görres

The writings of which we are speaking here comprise nothing less than the entire, actual mass of the people in their area of influence. Literature has gained no greater extension and no broader distribution in any direction than by breaking through to the lower classes, stepping out of the closed circles of the higher classes, living with those classes, and becoming of the people, flesh of their flesh, life of their life. As blades of grass press close to one another in the field and grow up high, as root interweaves with root beneath the earth, nature, monosyllabic but untiring, always says the same thing there, but also always says something different; that is how the spirit of these works behaves. Every year in higher literature, do we not see the births of the instant devouring their own children like Saturn, but *these* books live an immortal, inexhaustible life; throughout many centuries they have busied hundreds of thousands, a vast public; never aging, they are always welcome, returning time after thousands of times; pulsing tirelessly through all classes and taken in and assimilated by countless minds, they have always remained equally entertaining, equally refreshing, equally instructive, for so many, many senses that have opened uninhibitedly to their indwelling spirit. Thus, they form the most steadfast part of literature, as it were, the kernel of its characteristic life, the most inner foundation of its entire physical composition, whereas its higher life dwells among the higher classes. Was it wise so plainly to denigrate this body of the popular spirit as the tool of sin; was it wise to disdain those writings as dull outgrowths of the rabble's wits, and therefore to mislead the people with arbitrary restrictions and violent acts? That is

162

hardly the question! For after all, we do not reproach the honey-bee for building its hexagons, nor the silkworm for weaving only silk and not braid and purple garments, and now we are beginning gradually to respect the world as nature has arranged it in its permanence without human wisdom, and having arrived at a beautiful and humane tolerance, we live and let live, because it is not proper to destroy the works of the Lord. It seems to us that it would be wise and opportune to proceed from this tolerant sentiment of the educated man toward the uneducated in this investigation; those who are not disposed to admitting that postulate, however, will find it substantiated, when what is to be proven has been proven. For that itself is the question: Whether these writings, with their external distribution, do possess a certain appropriate internal significance as well; whether the spark of formative power glows too weakly in them for higher minds; whether what is higher, all that admitted, as soon as it climbs down from the upper world into the plantlike, fettered nature of the people, loses all its inner vitality and goes native as a useless tangle of vines abounding as nothing more than a harmful weed. It is true, only tasteless water comes from the streams and wells that spring from bad earth, whereas fiery wine ripens only on a few sunny, high-arching hills; it has been rightly and incisively remarked that wild flowers have little attraction for the educated dilettante, and it is pathetic how much nature has thrown away, it is hardly worth saving for a well-to-do person, but what is really precious, she conceals deep and stingily in the many folds of her broad mantle, and only someone with a divining rod can penetrate to her treasures. Further, it also seems true that the people live a sprouting, sleepy plant life; only seldom and little does their spirit shape, and it can sun itself only in the radiance of the higher forces of the world, but their blossoming burgeons entirely beneath the earth down into the roots, to produce edible tubers there like potatoes that never see the sun. The concern thus turns out to be not so unfounded that there is nothing to be found down there but worthless scree, pebbles that streams have rubbed round and smooth in the long passage of time, dirty small change that has worn down with passing from hand to hand. But there is much to counter these arguments. First, it could appear as if the artistic divergence of the classes, by no means immediately established and delineated in sharp outlines by nature, also would not be even of such a powerful influence. In every human being, it seems to us, actually all classes are present; the times have taught us how they awoke in turn in single individuals, until finally crowns blossomed from what was unpretentious. In the higher classes, we therefore see a peasant and a burgher concealed behind external elegance, in the peasant, however, as a rule we see good taste and tone turned to flesh, as it were, turning to muscle tone itself. It would seem that the peasant imprisoned there, when he has fought his way out, probably would like to refresh himself in peasant fashion, and that in the lower classes to boot, especially on Sundays and holidays, when the week's dirt is wiped away and the body, in the state, feels inclined to dramas of the state too; the kneeling gentleman in the human being would like to rise up and look about, desirous of the golden apples that hang up above among the dark leaves. However, we do not intend to support this reasoning at all: The former would hide themselves in shame that they were surprised in a moment of weakness; the latter would be laughed at as vain parvenus and dismissed in mockery. But we do want to focus clearly on one thing: that we distinguish between vulgarity, as such simply bad and reprehensible, from popular spirit and popular sense, which merge with the former only in the case of their decadence and corruption. We will then remember the old comment that this vulgarity, spreading through all classes, by no means limits itself to the lower ones. When we see the noisy folk of the marketplace in our fine literature swarming around works of art, gawking at them fixedly and dumbly, and the beautiful forms are reflected in unpleasant distortions in the nasty puddle that collects around the noble image, then we catch scent of the rabble; baseness in the people has dispatched its representatives to the big assembly, and they now sit in council to pass judgment on life, art, and science, and periodically give an account of their actions to their constituents, and it is *one* spirit, *one* will, and *one* conviction that prevails among the allied brothers and friends. Thus, what is evil, bad, inferior, has its church, its visible governors on earth, trusted councillors, priests, knights, lay brothers, all of them riffraff, fine, coarse, bestial, polished, cheeky, dumb, all of them riffraff. We will not speak about the books of this people, it would be too extensive, we would have to attempt too much. But there is another people within this people, all geniuses in virtue, art, and science, and the blossoms of this people are present in their every action; everyone who is pure of heart and decent in his beliefs belongs to this people; they move through all classes, ennobling everything lowly, that kernel most inherent to a class, and their most specific character is inherent in them. An ideal character can be thought of as being inherent in every class, tuned more highly in the higher classes, more deeply corporeal, but still complete, in the people. Physical health is as perfect in itself and as estimable as mental harmony, and each is always conditioned by the other. We now speak about this sacred spirit that dwells in the people and has nothing to do with the unholy rabble, about whether, grown tougher, more sensual, in its descent, it is reprehensible. Thus, for instance, the spirit that remains in the French people, after one separates out everything that the depravity of centuries has burned into it, is separate from that rabble in it, it is a harmless, light, cheerful spirit of life; deft and quick in its expressions, sensitive to and touched by whatever is good. That is the splendid spirit that dwells within English sailors after one has smelted all the bestiality from them, this powerful, energetic, untiring, good-hearted nature, which, tempered like Damascus steel in the raging storm, parries the onslaught of all the elements and struggles proudly and wildly and victoriously with the sea. The proud, lofty Berber temperament of the Spaniards that bears sounding brass in its bosom and, because it is incapable of worthy achievement, prefers to rest upon its inner richness, disdaining any unseemly action. Thus, finally we recognize the genuine inner spirit of the German people, too, as the older painters show it in its better times, simple, peaceful, quiet, self-contained, honorable, bearing little in itself of sensual depth but, for all that, all the more receptive to higher subjects. Precisely the humiliation that has been imposed upon this character through the ineptitude of its leaders must complete the inner division in the essence of the nation; renouncing what the confusion of recent times has forced upon it, it must return into itself, to what is most characteristic and worthy within it, casting aside and surrendering whatever is perverse; so that it will not wholly shatter in the hostile onrush of time.

After we have considered everything in this fashion, the thought of a popular literature will no longer seem so paltry and reprehensible to us in itself as it had seemed at first glance. After we acknowledged an inherent spirit inhabiting all classes, the idea is more appealing to us too that in the general range of ideas the lowest regions may also be valid and significant, and that the great nation of literature also has its House of Commons in which the nation is represented directly. But if now there really is a circle of writings that the native spirit of those peoples we enumerated recognizes, that are always sanctioned by the many subsequent generations anew, that have always pleased the best, that the ordinary people never put aside, and that everyone has never ceased to demand, then we do well not to condemn them so lightly; those we have despised may step before us and inquire of us what we meant and upon what we base our presumption. But this is how the books upon which we have our eye are really constituted: Wherever German is spoken, they are honored and loved by the people everywhere; they are devoured by youth and still smiled upon by the old in the joy of reminiscence, no class is excluded from their influence; while they make up the only mental nourishment during the whole life of the lower classes, they reach into the upper classes, at least through the youth, in whom all class differences tend to level off, and who often find in them the external impulse for their entire future existence and absorb the enthusiasm of their life. But by no means have they restricted their effectiveness to this great national circle; as among the Germans, we find them also in general circulation among the French in the same way; as in Germany, Cologne and Nuremberg distribute them by the thousands in all directions, in France, Troyes is the storage place from where they spread out across the nation in the same numbers, though frequently more careful and correct in form than with the Germans, and they exert an incalculable influence on French spirit and character. And even this is not the limit of the field of influence of these books; while the Dutch and the English possess the most in their languages, the Italians and the Spaniards have in part translated them into their own languages, and in part produced some for themselves, so that perhaps sixty million people or more know of their existence and enjoy them more or less. If, in addition, one considers that, while generations change three times in a century, these books last for three, four, or more centuries—many, as we shall see, reach back into the grayest times of antiquity—

then they win a truly unmeasured audience, and they stand facing us no longer as objects of our tolerance but rather much more as objects of our highest reverence and our genuine respect; as venerable antiquities that have passed intact through the purifying fire of so many eras and minds. Do not believe that something base could pass this test of time and quantity by itself; it can appear intermittently, dragged in tow by what is good, but never maintain itself alone. The nation does not resemble a dead rock upon which a chisel can engrave an image at will; there must be something appealing in it that we desire to absorb; a dark instinct for the good is lacking to no creature, so whatever is good and beneficial, whatever is harmful and poisonous, is sensed easily and strongly; and without a second thought the common people cast aside anything of which that dark instinct warns them. And even though occasional errors occur and something base and feeble finds momentary entrance, soon an inner revulsion and disgust awakes, and time washes it all away in its stream and expunges any mistake. But what passes this test, what appeals to everyone, individuals and generations, what gives strong, sturdy nourishment to everyone, like bread, must necessarily possess bread's strength and strengthen life. If, therefore, coincidence seems to have been in control of the selection of these writings by how they were offered to the people, coincidence by no means prevailed over their acceptance; a great, continuous need must exist in the people, to which everyone responds, and that therefore constantly preserves them: It is precisely the base that through coincidence may remain floating on the surface for a while but must necessarily disintegrate sooner or later. And this need is precisely what strives, ineradicably implanted in human nature, to saturate the mind with thoughts and the emotions with sensations, a striving that reveals itself successfully in precisely the most surprising way on this level, where it would seem as if dark, sensual drives and the desire that it linked to their happy satisfaction would have to bind up all the forces whose field of action is located in regions that have nothing to do with bodily needs. But breaking through the firm crusts of coral in which life must defend itself against an unfriendly nature, the inner, introverted spirit pushes its feelers out into the wide, free surroundings, and it is moving to see how, groping about itself, feeling everything around and turning in all directions, it struggles towards a world view and would also like to bask in the friendly radiance that makes up the soul of all creatures. It is therefore a different hunger and a different thirst than a merely sensual one that stirs in the people here; it does not yearn for physical fare that it can transform into something bodily, it longs rather for the higher spirit that the native spirit poured from his cup into raw matter and that is now shaped as its soul. The animal in man draws its body's nourishment down to it in the depths, and ruminating and assimilating it strengthens life's juices and wins breadth and space on earth; but the god in man likes only the finest aroma of things, the delicate fragrance that breathes from them impalpably and invisibly; he nourishes himself only with life spirits that dwell concealed deep within creatures, which he then absorbs with all his nerves and assimilates as the fare of a higher heaven and transfigures in their very assimilation. This spirit must have wrested itself free from the animal; what was purely animal must have intensified in the centaur, in which the human dominates and tames the bestial victoriously, if the urge for that finer nourishment is ever to come alive within him. But that in the people, in consequence of the urge, the means to its satisfaction can be found simply proves that that transformation has long since taken place within them; that they have long since deserted that region of dull stupidity to which circumstances seemed to have bound them inextricably; that what is better now successfully reveals itself in the lower classes of society, and that a human face has sprouted atop a thoroughly sensual body, which strives upward above the horizontal animal line toward the sky, already seeking and knowing something other than what is earthly.

But that poetry awakened within the people has expressed itself in the people in a doubly different way. In the folk song, for one, in which the voice of mankind's youth first develops beyond animal noises, as the butterfly does beyond the chrysalis, testing itself by climbing joyfully up and down the scales in artless intonations, and in which the first natural accents rang out, into which the demanding, joyful, yearning emotions poured themselves, enthused in their inner courage to live. Entering the world in the way that man himself enters it, without intention, without reflection and random choice, existence as a gift of higher powers, they are by no means works of art but rather works of nature, like plants; often sung from out of the people, often sung into the people, too, they testify in every instance to a geniality inherent within the people, and express themselves productively there, and by means of the naiveté that characterizes them, as a rule proclaiming the innocence and prevalent intricacy of all the forces in the masses from which they have bloomed; but here through their inner excellence retaining the fine rhythm and the forthright sense that dwells so deep down and, touched only by what is better, acquire only what is better and preserve it. But as in these songs the lyrical spirit concealed within the people at first awakens in cheerful sound, and the inner enthusiasm reveals itself in a few artless forms and, soon turned toward the celestial, speaks and sings—as well as the heavy, awkward tongue is able to give words to its enthusiasm—of what is sacred; but then, turned toward its surroundings, again meditates on life and its manifold conditions, exults or laments and jokes; thus, the epic spirit of nature must also soon present itself in the same manner, likewise in poetry and form, and also fill with its creations the circle drawn for it in this region. Those religious and profane songs in which the emotions of the people are intimately expressed will thus soon be complemented by other poems in the character of that spirit of nature, poems in which the emotions paint and proclaim what they have seen through their viewing of the world, and likewise what is celestial now significantly characterized as sacred history, now as Romantic history moved closer to the immediately human, made a delight through beauty, liveliness, greatness, power, magic, or striking wit.

These poems are the folk sagas, which tradition has transmitted from generation to generation, since, once formed through the manner of singing natural to the voice, they have protected themselves from perishing along with those songs. Most of these sagas came into being in earliest times, when the nations, clear, fresh fountains, had just sprung from the young, bounteous earth; when man, as youthful as nature, viewed it with loving enthusiasm and experienced then the same love and enthusiasm from it; when both, not yet become ordinary to one another, undertook greatness and recognized greatness; in this period, when the spirit did not yet place demands upon its surroundings, but only sensation did, when therefore there was only natural poetry and no natural history, in this vital feeling for nature, the manifold, various traditions of the many nations necessarily had to arise, which recognized nothing lifeless and everywhere saw a hero's life, great, gigantic force in all creatures, and everywhere perceived only great, heroic action in all they saw, and made a great legend of all of history. These cantos strolled vitally through life with the songs, animated by sound; but then, when the invention of the art of writing and later that of printing placed sight before sound, life in them did indeed grow fainter, but to the same extent more stubborn, and what they lost in inner intensity they at least won back in outer extension. Thus, the songs were captured in those pamphlets that bore them into all countries as on the wings of the wind; and what more and more was gradually falling silent in the mouth of the people was at least preserved for memory by the page. But those other cantos, according to their nature, calmer, certain, bound more to sight than to sound, and therefore like magic mirrors in which the people see themselves and their past and their future, and the other world, and their own innermost secret emotions and everything that they cannot name standing precisely and clearly expressed; these creations had to find a happy organ for their free development, particularly in something that could capture them externally, because, according to their nature, they exist more in what is extensive, and now that the limitations placed upon them by the narrow capacity of memory had fallen, they could spread freely in all directions. So most of the chapbooks arose from those sagas, and, taken from oral transmission into written form, they were expanded and completed; they lost only one thing during this metamorphosis: the external, poetic form that was considered now to be useless, a mere tool for the memory, and therefore it was mistaken for ordinary prose. But few later sagas fared as well as the ancient Greek saga of the conquest of Troy, in that a Homer was found, who, taking it over from the mouth of the nation, while expanding it extensively into a great epic, transfigured it in its inner form as well, and then erected the great work inscribed on tablets of brass in the great temple of the nation. But the tradition itself, after having found a permanent organ in this manner, gradually was lost as such, while others, waiting for centuries in vain for such a deliverance, have themselves perished, reached by the progress of culture, and still others hover in the twilight, like

quiet lights, in more remote areas where time has not yet illuminated the old darkness, waiting desperately for a better future,
because mischance of circumstance would not have it that the past
give them body and substance. The history of many of these chapbooks states expressly of them that they arose in such a fashion;
others bear the character of such a descent unmistakably in their
whole being, and, if particular historical sources are consulted with
still other books, then when the nature of these sources is examined more closely, one finds again and again that they ultimately
relate to those sagas and have been assembled from them.

But as far as the didactic, instructive chapbooks are concerned,
they are thoroughly modern due simply to their inward reflective
character, and even more modern to the degree that rationality
predominates in them. And it most predominates in the oldest ones;
that marvelous view of the strange characteristics of the products
of nature, for instance in the herbal books of the time that natural
philosophy in its progress has totally destroyed, is poetic to the
same degree that it is unscientific; and precisely because they are
so old, there is so much poetry in them, so little of truth, by contrast. For to the extent that the force of nature prevails in the
individual human being and in the whole people in youthful abundance, and in swift, courageous life, to that degree he is possessed
by the intoxication of life, and he submerges with his whole being
in the fresh, warm fountain and is pure imagination, sensation,
and poetry. But when, after the whole has been rounded in powerful abundance, nature in man matures to its perfection, then he
collects himself within himself again and wrests himself loose from
himself, and now in his freedom he faces this nature and all of his
past as something objective, just as previously the object itself had
faced the totality of external nature, and only with this antithesis
does reflection and reflective thought first awaken, and with them
clear, free cognition, and the broad, untrammeled realm of thought
is then opened. All these writings, therefore, did not derive from
an earlier oral tradition, likewise did not grow from the people
themselves as did the purely poetic ones, and were by no means
so deeply interwoven with their innermost nature as those are.
They can be classified most closely with the later attempts of the
recent writers to expand this literature through other combinations foreign to the masses, with which the people had never been

familiar before, that in their effect have therefore been so ineffec-
tual and so often useless. The people have not been able to em-
brace them with the same love that they did the earlier ones with
which they grew up, and in which, astonished, they suddenly recognized their most personal property and found expressed plainly
and clearly in words what they were probably often able to articulate only with a heavy, thick tongue.

But if now we inquire about the general character that marks
all these writings in common, then above all we must be convinced that, if these creations are to take root in the people and
win their own independent existence among them, an inner sympathy between them and the nation had to exist; there must be a
factor for this elective affinity within them and an identical, corresponding one in the people, and in stroke and counterstroke
everything was then able to join in love and become one in general
desire and familiarity. We have just seen how that element that
the people gave to culture was that ancient saga poetry, which
continued to flow through all generations like a soft murmuring,
until one of the last formed it into full speech; but the parallel,
reciprocal factor in books is the thoroughly native, sensually powerful, robust, marked character in which they are thought and
written, printed with wooden blocks and strong lights and black
shadows, characterized well and fully with a few firm, coarse, bold
strokes. Only thus can poetry be something to the people, only for
the strong, robust-sounding tone does this coarsely fibered bottom
have resonance, and the strong fiber can resound onto what cuts
deep. Poetry becomes popular poetry only by adapting to its forms;
if nature has wanted to reveal its formative power in these forms,
then art must never hesitate to follow it in this metamorphosis,
and to mold again in words what nature shaped silently and
soundlessly. But the same spirit does not predominate all that
evenly in all these creations indiscriminately; through all of the
continuing development of time, art has followed the nation from
afar, and the most excellent epochs of this gradual development
are characterized by just as many superior works. When the Etruscan satires and Oscan attelans were first introduced in Rome, the
people received them joyfully and willingly; surprised, they found
their entire nature reflected in these rough, wild, barbaric creations; art wrestled with the force and the inner energy of the peo-

ple, and it wrestled again with the spirit that was able to grip so robustly, and it extracted good taste from rude comedy, between its own powers and the powers of the marvelous foreign magic, and all poetry was still popular poetry in the true sense, and there was great, sturdy, pithy Alpine nature in it all. The people have not kept themselves at this level of genuineness in recent times; a higher flight evaporating from the masses, abducting precisely what was most intellectual, must already have imparted a more phlegmatic and less elastic character, as it were, to the remainder, in contrast to what was in flight, and many of the oldest chapbooks, which appealed purely to the early, antique spirit of the people, have become foreign to the people of the present; and many more recent ones, by molding themselves to the changed native spirit, emerged at the same time in a form that does not agree with that norm. No bears roam our forests anymore, no elk and no aurochs; what was bearlike in the old sagas and creations has thus receded with them, and as sunbeams broke through the thinned-out forests, a milder spirit has also found its place in the corresponding development of art, a spirit that sometimes stands purely by itself in individual creations, sometimes merges with that earlier spirit, forming a rather median character. Thus, the untamed wildness of the bear no longer speaks from these books, but, indeed, swift, healthy, fresh spirit does, like that which drives the deer through the thicket and lives in the other animals of the forest; there is nothing tame, domestic, well tended in them, everything having become as outside in the wild forest, born in the shadow of the oak, raised on mountain clefts, roving fast and free across the heights, coming down trustingly from time to time to the dwelling places of the people, bringing its tidings of the free life outside. That is the actual spirit of those writings, far from the one that was imposed in most recent times in the first-aid manuals as a moistly warm, soothing poultice for its aches, and that, although perhaps corresponding to the needs of the moment, yet precisely thereby bears witness to the chronically ill spirit of the time.

When one weighs what we have taught about the character and the essence of these books in these few pages; when one considers, whenever vanity about our finer poetry starts to overtake us, how yet it is always the people who bring us the most fragrant and refreshing flowers from their fields and forests in spring, even if later the luxury of our flower gardens asserts itself, the most beautiful ornaments of which, though, always are found wild somewhere; when one stops to think that all poetry originally did emanate from the people, because all institutions and constitutions and the whole scaffolding of the higher classes are ultimately always based upon the people, and in the first times the same poetic, as well as political and moral, naiveté was predominant, then we probably can finally assume that all prejudice against this great organ has disappeared in the general body of art and we have cleared the path to the proper appreciation of these writings individually. Therefore, we will proceed to the observation of the particular creations in this category without further delay, in order to see to what extent what we have just said will prove itself in detail. But the order that we follow in this review of books will be this, namely, that we begin with the didactic ones, with those youngest in age, from there to the romantic, and then pass on to the religious ones, and then finally end with a broad glance at the territory we have covered from the heights we have won.

Translated by Ralph R. Read III

Lectures on Dramatic Art and Literature

August Wilhelm Schlegel

First Part, First Lecture

In the following lectures, I will attempt to connect the theory of dramatic art with its history and at the same time demonstrate the rules and models of this art.

The general philosophical theory of poetry and the other fine arts propounds the basic laws of the beautiful, which all of them have in common. Further, every art has its own theory, which is directed at instruction in the understanding of the limitations, the difficulties, and the means of that art. To do this, scientific discussions are necessary, which are useful for the artist but are hardly attractive to those lovers of art who want only to enjoy the productions of excellent minds. General theory, by contrast, analyzes a characteristic essential to human nature: the ability to be sensible of beauty, from which the need for the fine arts and our pleasure in them arise. It shows the relation between this ability and all other moral and cognitive abilities of man. It is thus very important for the thinker, but in itself it does not suffice to serve as our guide in the practice of art.

The history of the fine arts teaches us what has been accomplished, the theory of the fine arts what should be accomplished. Without some connecting link, the two would remain separated and inadequate. It is criticism that elucidates the history of art and renders its theory fruitful. The comparison and evaluation of the existing productions of the human mind must supply us with the conditions that are required for the formation of distinctive and substantial works of art.

We frequently have a false notion about criticism, as though it consisted merely in the acumen that it takes to detect the mistakes in a work of art. I have devoted a great portion of my life to this study and want first of all to explain my concepts of the true spirit of criticism.

We see hordes of people, indeed, entire nations, so caught up in the habits of their education and way of life that they cannot tear themselves away from them even when the enjoyment of the fine arts is at stake. Only what is native and traditional in their language, their customs, and in their social relationships seems natural, proper, and beautiful to them. In this exclusive manner of seeing and feeling, education can bring about a great refinement of discrimination within the narrow circle to which one has restricted oneself. But one cannot be a genuine connoisseur without universality of spirit—that is, without the flexibility that through the renunciation of personal prejudice and blind habit renders us capable of imagining ourselves placed in the peculiar situation of other peoples and other times, to be aware of them at their very core, as it were, and to recognize and esteem appropriately what ennobles human nature, everything beautiful and great beneath the external garnishings that it needs for embodiment, indeed, sometimes beneath alien disguise. There is no monopoly on poetry by certain ages and peoples; consequently, that despotism of taste, too, with which they want universally to enforce certain rules that have been perhaps arbitrarily established by them, is always an invalid presumption. Poetry, taken in the broadest sense, is the ability to devise the beautiful and to portray it visibly or audibly; it is a universal gift of heaven, and even so-called barbarians and savages have their proportional share of it. Internal excellence alone decides, and wherever this is present, one should not be concerned with superficiality. Everything must be traced back to the roots of our existence: If it came into being there, then undoubtedly it has value; but if it was only attached from the outside without a vital origin, then it can neither flourish nor experience true growth. Many phenomena in the fine arts, radiant at first glance, indeed, even some that as a whole have been honored with the name of a golden age, resemble gardens that children like to make: Impatient to see a creation made by their own hands instantly finished, they pick off sprigs and flowers here and there and plant them in the ground without further ado; at first everything looks splendid, the child gardener walks proudly back and forth among the pretty beds until soon there comes a doleful end to it as the rootless plants let their leaves and blossoms drop and only dry twigs remain, whereas the dark forest on which no artificial care has ever been applied, which grew upwards toward the sky from time immemorial, stands unshaken and fills the solitary observer with awe.

Now to the application of these concepts of versatility and universality, which have just been developed, of the true critic on the history of poetry and the fine arts. We usually limit them (although outside of this circle much more that is remarkable might still be encountered), as with the so-called universal history, to that which has had direct or indirect influence on the European culture of today: thus, to the works of the Greeks and Romans and then to those of the new European peoples who were active in this field the earliest and most significantly. It is known how, almost four and a half centuries ago, the study of ancient literature was revived by the propagation of the Greek language (Latin had never died out): The classical authors were brought to light and made generally accessible through print; the monuments of ancient art were exhumed tirelessly. All this provided much stimulation for the human mind and marked a decisive epoch in the history of our culture; it was fruitful in effects that reach down even to us and will reach into an incalculable future. But immediately a stifling misuse was made of the study of the ancients, too. The scholars, who were chiefly in possession of this study and were unable to excel through works of their own, attributed absolute authority to the ancients, convincingly, in fact, since they are exemplary in their genre. They asserted that true salvation of the human spirit could be hoped for only from the imitation of the ancient authors; in the works of the moderns, they esteemed only that which resembled the works of the ancients or seemed to. Everything else they rejected as barbaric degeneration. But it was a different story with the great poets and artists. No matter how lively the enthusiasm might be with which the ancients imbued them, no matter how much they might have intended to compete with them, the independent singularity of their minds nevertheless compelled them to walk their own path and to place the stamp of their own spirit on their creations. So it was among the Italians even with Dante, the father of modern poetry: He declared Vergil to be his teacher, but he produced a work that in form was the most different from the *Aeneid* of any that could be named, and, in my opinion, he outdid his presumed master in power, truth, scope, and depth. So it was later on with Ariosto, too, who was perversely compared with Homer: There is nothing more dissimilar. Thus it was in the plastic and graphic arts with Michelangelo and Raphael, who indisputably were great connoisseurs of antiquity. If one judges more recent painters solely by their distance from the ancients or their proximity to them, then one must be unjust to them, which Winkelmann doubtless was to Raphael. Since poets usually shared a scholarly education, a conflict arose in them, because of this, between their natural inclination and their imagined duty. When they surrendered to the latter, they were praised by the scholars; to the extent that they pursued the former, the people loved them. What keeps the heroic songs of a Tasso or Camoëns alive up to this day in the hearts and on the lips of their countrymen is certainly not their imperfect relationship to Vergil or even to Homer, rather in Tasso the delicate feeling of knightly love and honor, in Camoëns the glowing enthusiasm of patriotic heroism.

Precisely the ages, the peoples, and the classes who least felt the need for an independent poetry were the most satisfied with the imitation of the ancients. Thus, there came into being dead school exercises that could arouse cold admiration at most. But in the fine arts, mere imitation is always fruitless: Even what we borrow from others must be as if reborn within us if it is to turn out poetic. How can it help to plagiarize something foreign? Art cannot exist without nature, and man has nothing to give his fellow humans other than himself.

The genuine successors to the ancients, their rivals who continued along their path by virtue of similar aptitude and education and acted as they had, have been just as rare as the mechanical, insipid imitators have been frequent. Bribed by externalities of form, the critics have also very generously left the latter unassailed. These imitators were the proper, new classics for them, whereas they would tolerate only as raw, wild geniuses those great, vital, popular poets whom a nation simply will not do without and in whom also many a sublime trait could not be overlooked. But the absolute separation of genius and taste that they assume is a futile subterfuge. Genius is precisely the choice—unconscious to a certain degree—of what is excellent, and thus it is taste at its most effective.

Things continued something like this until a few thinkers, mostly German, attempted not long ago to settle this misunderstanding, at the same time to honor the ancients as they deserved but still to recognize the singularity of the moderns, so wholly divergent from them. They did not fear an apparent contradiction. Human nature is simple in its fundamentals, to be sure; but all research shows us that no basic force in all of nature is simple in such a fashion that it cannot divide and scatter in opposite directions. The whole play of living movement is based upon agreement and antithesis. Why should this phenomenon not repeat itself in the history of humanity as a whole? Perhaps with this thought, the true key to the ancient and modern history of poetry and the fine arts might be found. Those who assumed this have invented the term *romantic* for the characteristic spirit of modern art, in contrast to the ancient or classical. Not inappropriately, to be sure. The word derives from *romance,* the term for those vernacular languages that had developed through the mixture of Latin with the dialects of Old German, just as modern culture is a fusion of the heterogeneous components of Nordic tribes and the fragments of antiquity, whereas the culture of the ancients was much more monolithic.

This tentatively proffered view would be quite convincing if it could be shown that the same antithesis between the aspirations of the ancients and the moderns runs symmetrically—indeed, I would like to say systematically—through all the expressions of artistic capability (to the extent that we know them) and reveals itself in music and in the plastic and graphic arts as well as in poetry, a problem that remains to be worked out in its entirety, although excellent individual insights have already been observed and recorded.

To mention writers who have written in foreign countries and at an earlier time than this so-called school prevailed in Germany: In music Rousseau recognized this antithesis and showed that rhythm and melody were the dominant principle of ancient music and harmony that of modern music. But in a biased way he rejects the latter, in which we cannot agree with him at all. Hemsterhuis makes this ingenious pronouncement about the plastic and graphic arts: The ancient painters were probably too much sculptors, the modern sculptors are too much painters. That strikes the real point: for, as I will more clearly explain subsequently, the spirit of all the art and poetry of antiquity is plastic, just as that of modernity is picturesque.

By means of an example from another art, architecture, I will try to clarify what I mean by giving recognition to these apparent opposites. In the Middle Ages, there prevailed and developed to fullest maturity, especially in the final centuries, a type of architecture that has been called Gothic and should have been called Old German. When with the revival of classical antiquity in general the imitation of Greek architecture also came into fashion and often was applied all too perversely without consideration of the difference in climate, customs, and the purpose of the buildings, the zealots of this new fashion condemned the Gothic style completely, calling it tasteless, gloomy, barbaric. It was easiest to pardon the Italians for this; the preference for ancient architecture was almost in their blood on account of the inherited ruins of ancient buildings and the climatic relationship with the Greeks and Romans. But we Northerners do not intend to be so easily talked out of the mighty, solemn impressions upon entering a Gothic cathedral. Rather, we intend to endeavor to explain and justify those impressions. Scant attention will teach us that Gothic architecture does not merely testify to extraordinary mechanical skill but also to an admirable display of inventiveness; upon closer observation, we will recognize its deep significance and that it comprises a complete, self-contained system just as the Greek does.

Now for the application! The Pantheon is no more different from Westminster Abbey or Saint Stephen's in Vienna than the structure of a tragedy by Sophocles from a drama by Shakespeare. The comparison of these marvels of poetry and architecture could probably be extended even further. But does our admiration of the one really compel us to the disparagement of the other? Can we not admit that each in its own way is great and marvelous, even though the one is quite different from the other and should be? Let the example stand. We do not want to dispute anyone's preference for the one or the other. The world is vast and many things can exist in it side by side. But a one-sided, instinctive preference does not make a connoisseur by any means. What does, on the contrary, is the free consideration of divergent views while renouncing personal inclinations.

For our purpose, namely, to justify the main divisions that we make in art history and according to which we consequently intend also to treat the history of dramatic literature, it might suffice merely to have pointed out the very striking antithesis between the ancient or classical and the romantic. Since, however, biased admirers of the ancients always continue to assert that all deviation from them is nothing but a quirk of the latest critics who might talk about it mysteriously but are unable to support it with any valid concept, I will try to give an explanation of the source and spirit of the romantic, and then let you judge whether the use of the word and the recognition of the issue are thus justifiable.

The culture of the Greeks was a perfect, natural education. Born of a beautiful and noble race, endowed with receptive senses and a blithe spirit, under a gentle sky, they lived and flourished in a perfect, healthy existence and, through the rarest advantage of circumstances, achieved everything that men caught within the strictures of finiteness can. Their entire art and poetry is the expression of the consciousness of this harmony of all forces. They invented the poetics of joy.

Their religion was the worship of natural forces and of earthly life, but this situation, which among other peoples darkened the imagination with horrid images and hardened the heart to cruelty, here had great, dignified, and generous form. Superstition, elsewhere the tyrant of human designs, seemed to want to lend a hand in their freest development: It nurtured the art that adorned it, and out of idols came ideals.

No matter how the Greeks flourished in the beautiful and even in the moral, however, we can concede no higher character to their culture than that of a purified, ennobled sensuality. It is obvious that this must be taken as a generalization. Individual insights of philosophers, flashes of poetic inspiration, are exceptions.

Man can never turn away entirely from the infinite; a few forlorn memories will testify to his forfeited homeland, but much depends on the prevailing direction of his efforts.

Religion is the root of human existence. If it were possible for man to deny all religion, even unconscious and instinctive religion, then he would become wholly superficial and no longer possess an inner self. If this center is displaced, then in consequence the entire effectiveness of the powers of the disposition and the intellect must redefine themselves.

And, indeed, this happened in modern Europe with the introduction of Christianity. This religion, as sublime as it is beneficent, regenerated the exhausted and sunken Old World; it became the guiding principle in the history of modern peoples; and even now, when many fancy they have outgrown their upbringing, they are influenced much more by it in regard to all human matters than they themselves realize.

Next to Christianity, the most decisive influence on the shape of Europe since the Middle Ages has been the Germanic line of the Nordic conquerors, who instilled new life-forces into a degenerate race of men. The stern nature of the North presses man back upon himself, and what is withdrawn from the free development of the senses must, in noble temperaments, enhance earnestness of disposition. Thus, the ingenuous heartiness with which the Old German tribes took up Christianity so that nowhere else did it penetrate so deeply to the core, prove itself so vigorously effective, and so interwoven with all human feelings.

From the raw but faithful courage of the Nordic conquerors there came into being, through the admixture of Christian sentiment, chivalry, whose aim consisted of preserving the use of weapons from any brutal and lowly misuse of force, into which it so easily sinks, by vows regarded as sacred.

To the knightly virtues was added a new and more decorous spirit of love as an enthusiastic dedication to genuine womanliness, which now for the first time was revered as the zenith of humanity and, erected by religion itself under the banner of virginal motherliness, caused all hearts to intuit the mystery of pure love.

Since Christianity was not satisfied with certain external acts, as was the polytheism of the ancient world, but involved the whole inner man with his slightest impulses, the feeling of moral independence sought refuge in the sphere of honor: equivalent to a worldly moral philosophy next to the religious one, which often asserted itself in contradiction to the latter but nevertheless was still related to it to the extent that it never calculated the consequences, rather unconditionally sanctioned principles of action as dogmas exalted above all examination by carping criticism.

Chivalry, love, and honor are, next to religion itself, the objects of the natural poetry that poured out in the Middle Ages in incredible abundance and preceded a more artistic formation of the romantic spirit. This era also had its mythology, consisting of knightly tales and legends, but its marvels and heroism were quite the opposite of the old mythology.

A few thinkers who, furthermore, comprehend and trace back the characteristics of the moderns just as we do have placed the essence of Nordic poetry in melancholy, and, understood properly, we have no objection to that.

Among the Greeks human nature was self-sufficient; it had no feeling of defect and strove for no other perfection than what it really could attain through its own powers. A higher wisdom teaches us that, through serious error, mankind has forfeited the position originally alloted to it, and the entire lot of our earthly existence is to strive to regain it—but, left to ourselves, we are unable to do so. That sensual religion wanted only to acquire external, transitory blessings; immortality, to the extent that it was believed in, stood in the dark distance like a shadow, a pale dream of this alert, bright day of life. In the Christian view, everything is reversed: The contemplation of the infinite has destroyed the finite; life has become a shadow world and a nighttime, and only in the hereafter does the eternal day of essential existence dawn. Such a religion must awaken to clear consciousness the presentiment that slumbers in all feeling hearts that we yearn for a bliss unattainable here, that no external object will ever be able entirely to fill our souls, that all pleasure is a fleeting illusion. And if the soul, now resting, as it were, under the weeping willows of banishment, breathes out its desire for the new foreign homeland, what else can be the keynote of its songs than melancholy? And so it is: The poetry of the ancients was the poetry of possession, our poetry is that of yearning; the former stands firmly on the ground of the present, the latter sways between memory and presentiment. Do not misunderstand this by thinking that everything dissolves in monotonous lament and that melancholy always has to express itself obtrusively. Just as bitter tragedy was nevertheless possible in the serene world view of the Greeks, so all moods up to the most merry can pass through romantic poetry, whose origin is explained above; but it will always bear traces of its origin in a nameless something. With the moderns, feeling has in general become more fervent, fantasy less corporeal, thought more contemplative. To be sure, in nature the boundaries become diffuse, and things are not so strictly divided as must be done to hold fast to a concept.

The Greek ideal of humanity was perfect concord and symmetry of all powers, natural harmony. The moderns, by contrast, have come to the awareness of inner dissension, which makes such an ideal impossible; therefore, the aim of their poetry is to reconcile these two worlds between which we feel divided, the intellectual and the sensual, and to fuse them inseparably. Sensual impressions must be hallowed, as it were, through their mysterious alliance with more noble feelings; the mind, in contrast, wishes to record its presentiments and ineffable contemplation of the infinite metaphorically.

In Greek art and poetry, there is primal, unconscious unity of form and content; in the modern, to the extent it has remained true to its own peculiar spirit, a more intimate penetration of both as of two opposing things is sought after. The former has resolved its problem to perfection; the latter can be content with its aspirations toward the infinite only by approximation and, due to a certain appearance of imperfection, is all the more in danger of being misjudged.

It would lead us too far to point out the characteristics indicated in the individual arts—architecture, music, and painting (the moderns have had no sculpture of their own)—to show their antithesis in the formation of the same arts of the ancients, and to attempt to discover their similar aims.

We cannot inspect more closely here the genres and forms of romantic poetry in general either but must return to our objective of dramatic art and literature. The division of these, as of the other branches of art, into ancient and romantic points out the way we are to take.

Let us first speak about the ancients; then about their imitators, the genuine and the supposed successors among the moderns; finally about those poets among the latter who, unconcerned about classical models or even diverging from them knowingly, have trod their own path.

Among the ancient dramatists, the Greeks are the really important ones. In their earlier epoch, the Romans were mere translators of the Greeks in this branch, later imitators and not always fortunate imitators. Moreover, less by them has survived. Among the modern peoples, the effort to restore the old theater and, where possible, to perfect it has been effective especially in Italy and France. Individual attempts of this kind in the tragedy have also been made more less among the other peoples, particularly later on; on the other hand, in comedy the form of the genre, as we find it with Plautus and Terence, has certainly been more universally prevalent. The tragic theater of the French is the most brilliant of all the intended imitations of ancient tragedy; it has acquired the greatest reputation and thus also deserves the closest scrutiny. Modern Italians, such as Metastasio and Alfieri, follow the French. The romantic drama, which, to be precise, can be called neither tragedy nor comedy in the sense of the ancients, has been native only in England and Spain, and in both instances it began to blossom at the same time, somewhat more than two hundred years ago, there with Shakespeare and here with Lope de Vega.

The German stage is the youngest of all; it has experienced the most varied influences from all its predecessors: It is, therefore, only most appropriate that we come to it last and thus best be able to evaluate its direction up to now and disclose its future prospects.

If I promise to survey the history of the Greek and Roman theater, then that of the Italian and French, finally that of the English and Spanish in the few hours that are allotted to these lectures, then it is obvious that I can give only surveys of them that summarize the essentials from a general viewpoint. Even though I am limiting myself to *one* genre of the poetic art, the mass of what exists therein is still incomprehensible and would remain so, even if I emphasized only one variety. One could lecture oneself to death on epilogues. In ordinary literary histories, the poets of *one* language and *one* genre are listed one after the other without any distinction, about like the Assyrian and Egyptian kings in the old world histories. There are people who have an irrepressible passion for book titles, and it is easy to grant them an increase in numbers through books about book titles. But actually it still seems as if in the history of a war one tried to name all the soldiers in the rank and file who had fought in it. One speaks only of the generals and of those who performed outstanding deeds. In the same way, the battles of the human intellect also, if I may put it that way, have been won by only a few heroes of genius. The history of the development of art and of its various shapes can therefore be presented by characterizing a modest number of creative minds.

Second Lecture

Concept of the dramatic. Overview of the theater in all nations. Theatrical effect. Importance of the stage.

Before we discuss the historical as outlined above, it will be necessary to preface this with a short explication of the concepts of the dramatic, theatrical, tragic, and comic.

What is dramatic? The answer might seem easy to many of you: where many characters are introduced, speaking, but the poet does not speak at all in his own person. Yet this is only the first, external basis of the form; it is the dialogue. If the characters express convictions and opinions to one another, but without effecting a change in their conversational partners, if both find themselves in the same emotional state at the end as at the beginning, then the conversation can be noteworthy due to its contents, but it arouses no dramatic interest. I would like to make this clear by means of a more imperturbable genre not intended for the stage, the philosophical dialogue. When in Plato, Socrates quizzes the windbag sophist Hippias about what the beautiful is, and he is quick to give a superficial answer, but afterwards is forced by the disguised objections of Socrates to give up his first explanation and to grope for other concepts, finally, humiliated and resentful, taking to his heels before the superior sage who has proven his ignorance, then this conversation is not just philosophically instructive but is also entertaining as a little drama. And this lively movement in the chain of thought, this suspense about the conclusion, in a word the dramatic in Plato's dialogues has rightly been praised.

The great attraction of dramatic poetry can be comprehended even in this alone. Activity is the true enjoyment of life, indeed is life itself. Merely passive enjoyments can lull us into sluggish comfort in which, if any inner alertness is present, boredom will soon set in. Most people, through their position, or also if they are not capable of unusual exertion, are narrowly encircled by insignificant activities. Their days are repeated according to the soporific law of habit, their life proceeds only imperceptibly, and from the raging torrent that was formed by the first passions of youth, it becomes a stagnant swamp. They seek to rescue themselves from the discomfort that this engenders in them by all kinds of games that always consist in a mild, arbitrarily set busyness that struggles with difficulties. But among all games, the drama is indisputably the most entertaining. We see action when we ourselves cannot act meaningfully. The highest object of human activity is man, and in dramas we see humans measure their strengths against one another in friendly or hostile concourse, or influence one another through their opinions, convictions, and passions as rational and moral beings, and determine their mutual relationships decisively. By separating off everything that is not of the essence, everything through which in reality our daily needs and the petty activity that they require interrupt the progress of essential actions, the art of the poet is able to compress our attention and expectations more suspensefully in a narrow space. In this manner, he gives us a small-scale picture of life, an excerpt of what is mobile and progressive in human existence.

This is not yet all. Even in a lively oral tale, one is accustomed frequently to introduce characters speaking and accordingly to change one's tone and voice. Only, the narrator in his own name fills the gaps that these speeches would leave in the vividness of the story related by depictions of the accompanying actions or other incidents. The dramatic poet does without this aid, but he finds a rich substitute for it in the following invention. He demands that each of his figures be presented by a real human being; that the human equal his fictional being as much as possible in age, sex, and form, indeed, take on all his characteristics; that he accompany every speech with suitable expression in voice, face, and gestures, and add the external actions that otherwise, to make it clear to the listeners, the narrative would require. Even more: These representatives of the creatures of his imagination should also appear in the attire appropriate to class, era, and country; partly to resemble them even more, partly also because something characteristic lies in the clothing. Finally, he wants to see them set in a location that is fairly similar to that in which the action is supposed to have taken place, because this likewise contributes to vividness: He sets them in a scene. All this leads us to the concept of theater. It is obvious that in the form of dramatic poetry, that is, in the presentation of an action through conversations without any narration, the requirements of the theater as its necessary complement are already contained. We admit that there are dramatic works that were not meant for the stage by their authors, and that would not make any particular impression there, either, whereas they are highly readable. But I doubt very much whether they would make as equally lively an impression on someone who had never seen a play or heard a description of one as they do upon us. We are already trained to add the performance in our mind when we read dramatic works.

The invention of dramatic art and of the theater seems quite natural. Man has a great disposition for mimicry; by transposing himself spiritedly into the situations, convictions, and passions of others, he comes to resemble them, even if involuntarily, in his outer appearance. Children constantly set their identities aside: It is one of their favorite games to play at being the adults whom they have the opportunity to observe, or whatever else occurs to them; and in the happy flexibility of their imagination, anything will work to equip them with the trappings of assumed dignity, be it that of a father, a schoolmaster, or a king. The only step required for the invention of drama, namely, to separate the mimic elements and fragments out of social life and to assemble them collected into *one* mass vis-à-vis social life, nevertheless did not happen in the case of many peoples. In the very extensive descriptions of ancient Egypt in Herodotus and others, I do not remember a trace of drama. The Etruscans, in contrast, otherwise so similar to the Egyptians in many things, did have theatrical games, and strangely enough, the Etruscan name for actor, *histrio,* has survived in living languages to this day. The entire Near East, the Arabs and Persians, have no dramas, in spite of an otherwise rich poetic literature. Europe in the Middle Ages also did not. After the introduction of Christianity, the plays traditional among the

Greeks and Romans were abolished, partly because they had reference to heathen attitudes, partly because they degenerated into brash immorality; and after that they did not appear again for a thousand years. Even in the fourteenth century, we do not find a trace of dramas in Boccaccio, who otherwise depicts the entire composition of social life very precisely. In place of them, they merely had the *conteurs, ménétriers* and the *jongleurs.* On the other hand, it can by no means be assumed that the invention of drama took place only once on earth and was always transmitted from one people to another. The English circumnavigators report that among the island peoples of the South Seas, who were still on such a low level of intellectual capability and development, they nevertheless saw crude drama, in which an ordinary event of life was imitated for amusement. To go to the other extreme: In a people whose social constitution and intellectual development undeniably derive from a distant antiquity, among the inhabitants of India, there were dramas long before they experienced any foreign influences. As has only recently become known in Europe, they possess a rich dramatic literature, extending back about two thousand years. Of their plays, we know as a sample only the lovely *Sakuntalā,* up until now, which, in its foreign climatic coloring, bears such a striking resemblance to our romantic drama in its structure that one might suspect that the English translator, [Sir William] Jones, worked toward this similarity from a love of Shakespeare, did not other scholars confirm his fidelity. Dramatic art seems to have been a favorite pastime in India at the courts of native princes; and it was suited to this by the fineness of social tone that prevails in it. Ujjayini is especially named as a seat of this art. Under Muhammadan domination, it was forced to disappear: The native language was foreign to them, since Persian had become the language of the courts; the mythology interwoven so densely with the literature conflicted with their religious concepts. There is no nation at all, devoted to Islam, that has achieved anything in dramatic poetry or has even had a notion of it. The Chinese, in contrast, have their permanent national theater; presumably permanent in every regard; I do not doubt that they leave the most proper Europeans far behind in the establishment of arbitrary rules and in the fine observation of insignificant properties.

When the new European theater began after the Middle Ages,

in the fifteenth century, with allegorical and clerical plays, called morality plays and mysteries, this probably occurred without any stimulus being received from classical dramatists, who did not come into circulation until later. In those crude beginnings lay the seed of romantic drama as a specific contribution.

With theatrical entertainments being so widespread, it is striking how much nations otherwise equally ingenious vary in their dramatic talent, so that this talent appears to be something specific of its own and essentially different from the gift of poetry. The contrast between the Greeks and Romans here should not surprise us, for the Greeks were a thoroughly artistic people and the Romans a practical one. Among the latter the fine arts were introduced only as an unhealthy luxury, leading to and promoting decadence. They so exaggerated this luxury, as far as the theater was concerned, that the perfection of the essential elements soon had to be neglected in favor of the decorative ornaments. Among the Greeks, too, dramatic talent was nothing less than general: Theater was invented in Athens, it was perfected in Athens exclusively. The Dorian dramas of Epicharmus probably constitute only a minor exception. All great creators of drama in Greece were born in Attica, were educated in Athens. As far as the Greek nation extended, with however much fortune it practiced the fine arts almost everywhere, outside of Athens it nevertheless had to imitate the creations of the Attic stage, without being able to compete with them.

The great difference in this matter between the Spanish and their neighbors, their relatives in race and language, the Portuguese, is most perplexing. The Spanish have an immeasurably rich dramatic literature, in productivity their dramatists equal the Greeks, who are often said to have written more than one hundred plays. No matter how they may otherwise be judged, no one has ever denied their imagination. This was recognized by the fact that the Italians, French, and English used the ingenious inventions of the Spanish, often without crediting their source. The Portuguese, in contrast, who compete with the Spanish in other genres, have done practically nothing in this one, indeed have not even had a national theater. Rather, itinerant Spanish players came to visit them, and they preferred to put up with a foreign dialect on the stage, not quite comprehensible without study, and did not devise plays for themselves or even translate and imitate.

Drama is by no means the most prominent of the many artistic and literary talents of the Italians, either, and this insufficiency seems almost to have been inherited by them from the Romans, just as their great mimic talent for clowning likewise stems from oldest times. The extemporized *fabulae Atellanae,* the only originally native dramatic form of the Romans, may be no more perfect in regard to plan than the so-called *commedia dell' arte,* extemporized comedy with stock roles; presumably, the seed of carnivals of today lay in the old Saturnalias, a wholly Italian invention. Therefore, the opera and the ballet arose among the Italians, too: theatrical entertainments in which dramatic meaning is entirely subordinated to music and dance.

If the German spirit did not develop in the field of drama with the same productivity and facility as in other parts of literature, then perhaps this insufficiency stems from a true characteristic. Germans are a speculative people, that is, through reflection they want to get to the bottom of everything with which they occupy themselves. For this very reason, they are not practical enough, for in order to act determinedly and with skill, one must believe that one has finished one's lessons and not always return to a testing of the theory of one's business; one must even have become entrenched in a certain conceptual one-sidedness. But in the organization and execution of a drama the practical mind should dominate: It is not granted to the dramatic poet to dream enthusiastically, he must take the straightest path to his goal; and the German so easily loses sight of his goal in face of the paths to it. Further, nationality in drama may and must emerge most decisively, and German nationality is modest; it does not raise its voice; disparagement of one's worth is not seldom connected with the noble effort to understand all foreign merits and to assimilate them. Therefore, our stage has often experienced more foreign influences than was proper. But our task is not simply to repeat tolerantly Greek or French, Spanish or English theater, rather, it seems to me, we are seeking a form that contains the truly poetic of all those forms, while excluding that which is founded on conventional tradition; but in content, German nationality should prevail.

After this fleeting glance, cast as it were on the map of dramatic literature, we now return to the discussion of basic concepts. Since, as we have shown above, the prerequisite for visual portrayal and the claim to it is already present in dramatic form, a dramatic work can thus always be observed from a double viewpoint, to what extent it is poetic and to what extent it is theatrical. The one can very well be separated from the other. Do not misunderstand the term *poetic* here: I do not mean meter and rhetorical devices; without higher invigoration these achieve the least on the stage; rather, I mean the poetry in the spirit and composition of a play; and this can take place to a high degree, even if it is written in prose, just as conversely. But what makes a drama poetic? Indisputably, whatever it is that makes works of other genres poetic. First, it should be a coherent, closed, satisfying whole. However, this is only the negative condition of the form of a work of art, through which it is distinguished from phenomena of nature that flow together and never quite exist on their own. For poetic content, it is necessary that it reflect within itself and graphically present ideas, that is, necessary and eternally true thoughts and feelings that transcend earthly existence. What ideas these can and should be in the various dramatic genres will be the object of our investigation in what follows here; in contrast, we will also show that in their absence a drama becomes something prosaic and empirical, that is, something composed merely by reason from the observation of what is real.

What makes a dramatic work theatrical, that is, fit to appear advantageously on a stage? Whether it possesses this characteristic is often difficult to determine in the individual case. There is usually much argument about this, particularly when the egotism of the authors and actors is involved; each blames the other for a failure, and whoever represents the case of the poet then appeals to a perfection of portrayal on the stage that he had in his mind, for which the means simply were not present. But in general, answering this question is not so difficult. The task is to produce an effect on an assembled crowd, cause it suspense, arouse its sympathy. Thus, the poet shares a part of his business with the popular orator. How does the latter principally reach his goal? Through clarity, quickness, and emphasis. He must carefully avoid anything that exceeds the usual measure of patience and mental capacity. Further, many people gathered together are a distraction to one another as long as their eyes and ears are not yet directed at a common goal outside of their circle. Thus, the dramatic poet, as well as the popular orator, must draw his listeners out of themselves right at the outset through strong impressions; he must command their attention virtually physically. There is a kind of poetry that softly stimulates a mind attuned to lonely contemplativeness, somewhat like gentle breezes coax chords from an Aeolian harp. This poetry, no matter how excellent it may be otherwise, would fade away unheard without other accompaniment on the stage. A lilting concertina is not designed to lead and excite the march of an army. That takes penetrating instruments but particularly a decisive rhythm that quickens the pulse and increases the tempo of our senses. To make this rhythm in the progress of a drama visible is the principal requirement. If this succeeds, then the poet may perhaps be permitted to tarry in his swift course and indulge his own inclinations. There are points where sometimes the most garish or embellished storytelling, the most enraptured lyric poetry, the most profound thoughts and most remote allusions, the cleverest plays of wit, the most glittering sleights of hand of high-flown fantasy are in place and where the prepared listener, including those who cannot quite comprehend all this, will follow it with eager ears as music fitting their mood. Here we find the great art of the poet in exploiting the effect of these contrasts, which makes it possible to emphasize peaceful quiet, introspection, indeed the indolence of exhaustion just as strikingly as in other cases the most violent motion, the stormiest passions. But in consideration of what is theatrical, we must not forget that something must always be determined in reference to the capabilities and inclinations of the listeners, something that varies according to the nations in question and the degree of artistic education in each case. Dramatic poetry is, to a certain extent, the most mundane of all genres, for it does not hesitate to step out into the tumultuous swirl of social life from the quiet of its own enthusiasm. More than any other, the dramatic poet must vie for external favor, for loud applause. But he should only seem to condescend to his listeners, in fact, he should be lifting them up to himself.

The following circumstance deserves to be weighed in its effect upon the assembled crowd, to gain insight into its full importance. In everyday life people show each other only their exterior selves. Mistrust or indifference hold them back from letting others see their inner selves, and to speak about what lies closest to our hearts with emotion and pain would not be appropriate to the tone of fine society. The popular orator and the dramatic poet find the means to tear down these barriers to conventional, custom-bound reserve. By transporting their listeners into such a lively emotional state that the external signs of it break out involuntarily, each perceives the same emotion in the others and thus people who were strangers until then suddenly become intimates in an instant. The tears that an orator or playwright compels them to shed for a defamed innocent, for a hero going to his death, makes them all friends and brothers. It is incredible what an intensifying force the visible community of many has for an ardent feeling that otherwise usually withdraws into solitude or only reveals itself in the familiarity of friendship. The belief in the validity of this becomes unshakable through its transmission; we feel strong among so many comrades; all our emotions flow together in one great, irresistible stream. For this very reason, the privilege of being permitted to influence the assembled crowd is vulnerable to a very dangerous abuse. Just as one can inspire crowds unselfishly to what is noblest and best, they can on the other hand also be entangled in webs of sophistic deceit, they can be blinded by the gleam of false magnanimity, the ambitious crimes of which are portrayed as virtue, indeed as sacrifice. In the agreeable disguise of rhetoric and poetry, a seduction creeps imperceptibly into our ears and hearts. The comic poet above all must be on guard, since in light of his task he always veers toward this precipice, that he not give vent to what is vulgar and repulsive in human nature but express himself positively. If through the view of the community the shame even in such base inclinations, which usually pushes them back within the limits of decency, is overcome, then the enjoyment of what is bad soon breaks out with untrammeled brashness.

This demagogic force in good and evil has always from the very beginning properly attracted the attention of lawmakers to drama. Through sundry measures, states have attempted to mold it to their purposes and guard against abuse. The task here is to unite the unhindered movement necessary for the flourishing of the fine arts with the considerations demanded by the codes of laws and ethics in each case. In Athens the theater blossomed in almost unlimited freedom under the protection of polytheism, and the morality of the public preserved it from decadence for a time. The comedies of Aristophanes, incredibly permissive according to our customs and opinions, in which the state and the people are ruthlessly ridiculed, were the watermark of popular freedom in Athens. Plato, by contrast, who lived in this very Athens, who saw or predicted the decay of art, intended to have dramatic poets banned entirely from his ideal Republic. Few states have judged it necessary to endorse such a stern sentence of condemnation; but then few have judged it wise to leave theater to itself without any supervision. In many Christian countries, dramatic art has been considered worthy of extending its hand to religion by treating sacred subjects; especially in Spain, competition in this area has produced many a work that certainly does not disavow devotion or poetry. In other states, under other circumstances, this has been considered offensive and problematical. But where an ongoing supervision is judged necessary, and not just of the poet and the actor in retrospect for what is presented on the stage, then it is perhaps hardest to apply precisely where it would be the most important: namely, to the spirit and overall impression of the play. Owing to the nature of dramatic art, the poet must put many words in his characters' mouths of which he is in no way a proponent; he desires his convictions to be judged according to the context of the whole. In contrast, it could also be that a play could be quite inoffensive in regard to the individual speeches and would pass any test directed merely at them, whereas it intended a pernicious effect as a whole. In our own times, we have experienced plays often enough—and they have been successful in Europe—that overflow with surgings of good-heartedness and high-minded exploits, and in which the hidden intent of the author nevertheless, unmistakable to the sharper eye, is to undermine the stern moral principles and the reverence for what should be sacred to man, and thereby to bribe his lazy and slack contemporaries. Yet if anyone wanted to concern himself with the moral defense of the so maligned Aristophanes, whose excesses seem quite impermissible by our standards, then he would have to point to the intention of the whole of his plays, in which he at least proves himself a patriotic citizen.

All of the above is designed to make the importance of the object of our observations clear. The theater, where the magic of several arts can be united, where the most sublime and profound poetry sometimes has the most skilled acting as its interpreter, acting that at the same time is eloquence and fluent portraiture; while architecture supplies a gleaming setting and painting its illusionary perspectives; and music too is called upon for aid in stirring our emotions or to intensify even more through its tones those already aroused; the theater, finally, where the entire social and cultural education that a nation possesses, the fruit of centuries of continued efforts, can be presented in a few hours. The theater, I say, has an extraordinary appeal for all ages, races, and classes and has always been the favorite entertainment of gifted peoples. Here the prince, the statesman, and general see the great world events of bygone days, similar to those in which they themselves had a hand, laid out according to their inner motives and relationships; the thinker finds inducement for the deepest reflections on the nature and lot of man; with attentive eyes, the artist follows the groups rushing by, which he impresses upon his fantasy as spores of future paintings; receptive youth opens its heart to every uplifting feeling; age rejuvenates itself through memory: childhood itself sits in intuitive expectation before the colorful curtain, which is about to rustle open and disclose marvels still unknown; they all find refreshment and cheer and for a time are relieved of the cares and pressures of daily life. But since dramatic art, along with the arts that accompany it and stand in its service, can so decline through neglect and mutual deterioration of the artists and the audience, that the theater sinks to the most vulgar and insipid time killer, truly harmful, thus it certainly is not a question of mere chatter when we occupy ourselves here with observations of the works that the most excellent peoples have produced for theater in their best times, and with the means for perfecting such a significant art.

Seventh Lecture

Life and poetic character of Sophocles. Evaluation of his tragedies individually.

With the year of his birth, Sophocles falls almost midway between that of his predecessor [Aeschylus] and of Euripides, so that he stands about half a generation distant from each; the dates are imprecise. But for the greatest part of his life, he was a contemporary of both. He often competed with Aeschylus for the tragic laurel, and he outlived Euripides, who also attained great age. It seems that a kindly Providence, to speak in terms of the old religion, intended to reveal to the race of man the dignity and happiness of its lot in this one man, by endowing him with everything divine that can embellish and elevate the emotions and the intellect, as well as all conceivable blessings of life. To be born of wealthy and respected parents as a free citizen of the most civilized city-state in Greece was only the first prerequisite thereto. Beauty of body and soul, and uninterrupted use of both forces in perfect health to extreme old age, an education in the choicest abundance of gymnastics and music, of which the former were powerful enough to impart energy, and the latter harmony, to beautiful temperaments; the sweet bloom of youth and the mature fruit of age; the possession and uninterrupted enjoyment of poetry and art, and the practice of serene wisdom; love and esteem among his fellow citizens, fame in other states, the favor and grace of the gods: these are the most general characteristics of the history of this pious, sacred poet. It is as though the gods, among whom he early dedicated himself especially to Bacchus as to the giver of all joy and the shaper of previously primitive mankind by depicting his tragic rites, had wished to make him immortal, they postponed his death for so long; and since that was not possible, they closed his life as gently as possible, to permit him to exchange one immortality for the other imperceptibly, the long duration of his earthly existence for the immortality of his name. As a youth of sixteen, he was chosen for his beauty to dance, playing on the lyre according to Greek fashion, before the chorus of youths who performed the paean around the erected trophy after the battle of Salamis (in which Aeschylus had joined and had described so splendidly); so that the most beautiful unfolding of the blossom of his youth coincided with the most glorious epoch of the Athenian people. He filled the post of general, along with Pericles and Thucydides, already approaching old age; in addition, the priesthood of a native hero. At the age of twenty-five, he began to perform tragedies, he achieved victory twenty times, more often second place, never third; he continued his efforts with increasing success past his ninetieth year, indeed, perhaps some of his greatest works stem from that period. There was a story that he was sued by an elder son or sons, because he loved one grandchild from another spouse more tenderly, as though he had become childish with age, and was no longer capable of administering his property. Instead of any defense, he is supposed to have declaimed his newly composed *Oedipus at Colonus,* or, according to others, the magnificent choral song from it that extols Colonus, his birthplace, to the judges; and the judges were said then to have adjourned in admiration without further ado, and he was accompanied to his home in triumph. If it is true that he did write the aforementioned second *Oedipus* so late in life in all its distance from the harsh turbulence of youth, it still bears the traces of it in its mature gentleness, and it thus affords us the picture of a most affectionate and dignified old age. As fabulous as the divergent legends about the manner of his death are, they nevertheless agree and have as their true significance that he died while busy with his art or with something related to it, without illness; so that, like a gray swan of Apollo, he breathed out his life in song. And thus I adjudge the story to be genuine, according to which the Lacedaemonian general who had fortified his ancestral burial grounds was warned by a double vision of Bacchus to conduct the burial of Sophocles at that very place, and therefore he sent a herald to the Athenians; just as everything else, that serves to illuminate the transcendent venerableness of this man. I called him pious and sacred in his own meaning of the words. But although his works breathe the greatness, charm, and simplicity of antiquity, yet among all Greek poets he is the one whose sentiments are the most related to the spirit of our religion.

Only one natural gift was denied him: a resonant voice for song. He could call forth and guide only the harmonious flow of other voices and therefore, for his part, is said to have suspended the previously existing custom that the poet act in his plays himself, and he is said to have played the zither, appearing as the bard Thamyris, only a single time (again a very significant trait).

To the extent that Aeschylus, who developed tragic poetry from its initial primitive state to the dignity of his cothurnus, preceded him, Sophocles stands in a historical artistic relationship to him, in which, to be sure, the undertakings of that original master were at his disposal, so that Aeschylus appears as the planning precursor and Sophocles as the perfecting successor. It is easy to observe the more elaborate composition of the dramas of the latter: the restriction of the chorus in relation to dialogue, the development of rhythms and the pure Attic diction, the introduction of several persons, the richer plot structures, the multiplicity of incident and more complete development, the calmer retention of all plot elements, and the more theatrical emphasis of the decisive ones, the more perfect rounding off of the whole, even considered externally. But there is something else through which he outshines Aeschylus and earned the good fortune to have had such a precursor, and to vie with him toward the same objects: I mean the inner harmonic perfection of his emotions, by means of which he fulfilled every duty towards beauty from his own inclination, and whose free impulse was accompanied by self-awareness grown clear to the point of transparency. It is hardly possible to exceed Aeschylus in boldness: but I think that Sophocles seems less bold only due to his wise moderation, since he sets to work everywhere with greatest emphasis, indeed perhaps applying more rigor; just as a man who knows his limitations exactly, all the more confidently insists upon his rights with them. Just as Aeschylus likes to project everything into the primal world of the raging Titans, Sophocles, in contrast, seems to have the gods appear only when necessary: He formed humans better, appropriate to antiquity in general— which does not mean more moral and less flawed, but more beautiful and nobler than real people, and by taking everything most humanly, its higher significance also devolved upon him. By all appearances, he was also more moderate in scenic decoration than Aeschylus, perhaps had more selective beauty, but did not seek such colossal pomp.

The ancients praised his native sweetness and charm as characteristic of this poet, on account of which they called him the Attic honeybee. Whoever has penetrated to a feeling for this characteristic may flatter himself that he has understood the sense of ancient art, for the sentimentality of today, far from agreeing with that judgment, thinks much in Sophocles' tragedies to be unbearably harsh, in the portrayal of physical suffering as well as in the attitudes and arrangements.

In relationship to the great productivity of Sophocles, who is supposed to have written one hundred thirty plays according to some (of which Aristophanes, the grammarian, declared seventeen to be apocryphal, however), and eighty according to the most moderate estimates, little of his work has remained for us, to be sure, since we have only seven of them. Yet chance has been kind to us, since several of these were recognized by the ancients as his most excellent masterpieces, such as the *Antigone,* the *Electra,* and both of the *Oedipus* plays; they have also come down to us almost unmutilated, with an uncorrupted text. The first *Oedipus* and the *Philoctetes* have usually been admired over the others without reason by recent critics; the former because of the artistic intricacy, in which a series of interdependent causes inevitably brings about the terrible catastrophe, which intensifies even curiosity (so seldom the case in Greek tragedies); the latter because of the masterly character portraiture and the beautiful contrasts between the three main figures, next to the simple structure of the play, where with so few characters everything is derived from truest motivation. But with Sophocles, almost every one of his tragedies shines with its individual merits. In the *Antigone,* heroism is depicted in purest womanhood; in the *Ajax,* masculine sense of honor in all its strength; the *Electra* distinguishes itself with energy and pathos; in the *Oedipus at Colonus* gentle emotion prevails, and all of it displays the greatest charm. I do not undertake to weigh the value of these plays against one another; yet I do admit to a certain preference for the latter-named piece because it seems to me to express the personality of Sophocles the most. Since this play is dedicated to the glorification of Athens and especially of his native deme, he seems to have fashioned it with particular love.

The *Ajax* and the *Antigone* are usualy understood the poorest. Readers cannot comprehend why the dramas stretch out so long after what we customarily call the catastrophe. I will comment on this again below.

Among all the tales of fate that the old mythology contains, the story of Oedipus is perhaps the most thought-provoking; yet others seem to me to intend greater significance, as, for example, that of Niobe, which quite simply presents on a huge scale both human hubris and the punishment ordained for it by the gods, without such intricacy. What gives the plot of *Oedipus* a less elevated character is the very intrigue that it contains. In the dramatic sense, intrigue is the intricacy that arises from the collision of intentions and coincidences, and this obviously takes place in the destiny of Oedipus, since everything that he and his parents do to evade the horrors prophesied leads him toward them. But what gives this plot a great and fearful significance is the circumstance, usually overlooked, that it is precisely Oedipus himself who solved the riddle of the Sphinx concerning human existence, for his life remained an indecipherable riddle, until it was elucidated for him all too late in the most frightful way, since everything was irretrievably lost. It is a striking picture of overweening human wisdom, which always aims at generalizations without its possessors being able to apply it to themselves correctly.

The harsh conclusion of the first *Oedipus* reconciles one to the violent, suspicious, and overbearing nature of Oedipus to the extent that one's feelings do not amount to a resolute indignation against such a horrible fate. From this side, the character of Oedipus thus had to be sacrificed, though it is elevated by his paternal concern and his heroic zeal in the rescue of the people: zeal that hastens his downfall through his honest investigation of the causes of the crime. It was also necessary, for the contrast to his subsequent misery, to have him appear still arrayed in the full pride of his sovereignty as he meets Tiresias and Creon. What is suspicious and violent can already be seen in his earlier actions; the former to allay his fears when Polybus assures him that the accusation of his being raised as a foundling was untrue; the latter in the so bloodily concluded strife with Laius. His character seems to have been inherited from both his parents. The wanton frivolity of Jocasta with which she mocks the oracle as not having been confirmed by events, but soon thereafter performs atonement upon herself, has not been transmitted to him, to be sure; rather, he is honored by the purity of his emotions, with which he so scrupulously flees the prophesied crimes, and through which his desperation, at having committed them nevertheless, naturally must be intensified to the extreme. His blinding is frightful, as enlightenment lies so near at hand; for example, when he asks Jocasta what Laius looked like, and she replies that his hair had turned white, otherwise his figure had not been dissimilar to that of Oedipus. On the other hand, it is a frivolous trait that she does not properly notice the similarity to her husband, by which she should have recognized him as her son. On closer analysis, the most extreme propriety and significance can thus be proven in every trait. Only because it is customary to praise Sophocles as correct, too, and to extol the excellently observed probability in this *Oedipus* above all, must I remark that this very play is a proof of how in this matter the old artists followed quite different principles than those critics have. For otherwise it would indeed be a great improbability that Oedipus had not inquired about the circumstances of Laius's death in so long a time, that the scars on his feet, and even the name that he bore because of them, had not aroused Jocasta's suspicion, and so forth. But the ancients did not plan their artworks for prosaic, calculating reason, and an improbability that is discovered only through analysis, that does not lie within the circumference of the presentation, counted as none at all. Even Aristotle, otherwise little inclined to grant the imagination room for free play, expressly posits this principle.

The difference in character between Aeschylus and Sophocles is displayed nowhere more strikingly than in the *Eumenides* and the *Oedipus at Colonus,* since both plays have a similar purpose. That is, Athens is to be glorified as the sacred residence of equity and generous humanity, and crimes of the heroes of foreign families that have been paid for are to be solemnly expiated in this city through a higher mediation; from this the Attic people are prophesied continuous well-being. With the patriotic and freedom-breathing Aeschylus, this takes place through a forensic act; with the pious Sophocles, through a religious one: namely, Oedipus' consecrating himself to death, since he is bowed by the consciousness of involuntary crimes and long misery, to whom the gods virtually make a declaration of honor, as if the frightful example they had made of him were impersonal, intending only a serious lesson for mankind in general. Sophocles, for whom all of life is a continuing religious service, loves as a rule to embellish to the utmost the last instant of life, like an instant of higher celebration, and he imparts a quite different emotion thereby than that which the thought of mortality in general arouses. That the tormented and exhausted Oedipus finally finds rest and peace in the grove of the Furies, at the very place from which every other man flees in uncanny horror, he whose misfortune resulted directly from having done, unconsciously and without warning from any inner feelings, that from which all men recoil, this contains a deep and mysterious meaning.

Attic culture, circumspection, moderation, justice, generosity, and magnanimity were presented more majestically in the person of Pallas by Aeschylus; Sophocles, who so liked to draw everything divine into the realm of humanity, developed it in Theseus. Whoever wishes to become better acquainted with Hellenic heroism, in contrast to barbaric heroism, I would refer to this character.

In Aeschylus, so that the persecuted man be rescued and partake of the land of blessings, the nocturnal terror of the Furies must first make the blood of the spectators congeal and their hair stand on end, the entire rage of these goddesses of vengeance must first exhaust itself: The transition to their peaceful departure is all the more marvelous; it is as though all of mankind were being redeemed by them. In Sophocles they do not appear themselves but rather are kept completely in the background; they are not even called by their own names but only by discreet terms. But this very darkness appropriate to these daughters of the night, and the distance, favors a quiet horror in which the physical senses do not participate at all. That the grove of the Furies is finally draped in the loveliness of a Southern spring completes the sweet charm of the poetry, and if I were to choose a symbol for Sophocles' poetry from his own tragedies, then I would describe it as a sacred grove of the dark goddesses of fate, in which laurels, olive trees, and grapes flourish, and the songs of nightingales sound unceasingly.

Two of Sophocles' plays, according to Greek temperament, relate to the sacred rights of the dead and the importance of burial: In the *Antigone* the entire plot is posited on them, and in the *Ajax* a satisfying conclusion is arrived at only through them.

The feminine ideal in the *Antigone* is of great rigor, so that it alone would be sufficient to put an end to all the sweetish notions of Greekness that have recently become stock in trade. Her resentment, when Ismene refuses to participate in her bold resolve; the manner in which she rejects the offer of Ismene, remorseful for her weakness, at least to accompany her heroic sister in death, borders on harshness; her silence and her speeches against Creon, with which she goads him to carry out his tyrannic decision, testify to unshakable masculine courage. Yet the poet has found the secret of revealing lovely feminine emotion in a single line, where she answers to Creon's assertion that Polynices had been an enemy of the fatherland:

I am here not to join in hate, but to join in love.

And she holds back the outburst of her feelings only as long as they could have rendered the firmness of her resolve ambivalent. As she is being led irrevocably to her death, she pours forth the most delicate and moving laments for her harsh premature death, she, the chaste virgin, does not disdain to bemourn her lost bridal rites and the unenjoyed marital blessings. However, she does not betray with a syllable any inclination for Haemon, indeed nowhere does she mention this amiable youth. Barthelemy does assert the contrary; but the line to which he refers belongs to Ismene, according to the better manuscripts and the context. It would have been weakness to be chained to life still, after such a heroic resolve, by this individual inclination; to have left universal gifts, with which the gods embellish life, without melancholy would not have been appropriate to the piety of her dispositions.

At first glance, the chorus in the *Antigone* can appear weak by acceding to the tyrannical commands of Creon without objection and by not even attempting to present the young heroine in a good light. But she must stand wholly alone with her resolve and with her deed to be truly glorified, she must never find a support, a hold. The submissiveness of the chorus also increases the impression of the irresistibility of the royal commands. Thus, painful references must be intermixed even in the last speeches to Antigone, so that she completely drain the cup of earthly suffering. The case is quite different in the *Electra*, where the chorus had to be so involved and encouraging to the two main characters, since powerful moral feelings resist their acts, just as other feelings spur them on; such an inner conflict does not occur at all in Antigone's deed, merely external threats are supposed to prevent her from acting.

After the completion of her deed and her suffering for it as well, the punishment for Creon's hubris remains, which will avenge Antigone's demise: Only the destruction of his entire family and his own despair is a worthy death rite for the sacrifice of such a precious life. For this reason, the spouse of the king, hitherto unmentioned, must appear towards the very end, solely to hear of the disaster and to kill herself. It would have been impossible to Greek feelings to consider the work concluded with the demise of Antigone without any expiatory requital.

The matter is similar in the *Ajax*. The hubris, for which he is punished with dishonoring madness, he pays for with the deep shame that drives him to the point of suicide. The persecution of the unhappy warrior may go no further, and since the intention is to defile his corpse by refusing it burial, Ulysses steps in to help, the very warrior whom Ajax considered his mortal enemy, and to whom Pallas had shown the vanity of human existence by the example of the confounded Ajax in the terrifying opening scene: He appears virtually as moderation personified, which would have protected Ajax from his downfall, if he had possessed it.

Suicide is frequent in the old mythology, at least in that unskilled in tragedy; but it occurs mostly, if not in madness, then after a suddenly experienced disaster, in a state of passion that affords no place for reflection. Such suicides—see those of Jocasta, Eurydice, Haemon, Deianira—occur only secondarily in the tragedies of Sophocles; the suicide of Ajax is a contemplated decision, a free deed, and for that reason worthy of being the main object of the drama. It is not the final, ruinous crisis of a creeping mental illness, as so often in enfeebled recent times; even less the more theoretical satiety with life upon which the conviction of life's worthlessness is based, which brought so many later Romans to shorten their days, as much from Epicurean as from Stoic principles. Through no unmanly despondence is Ajax untrue to his rough heroism. His madness is past, also his first disconsolation after awakening from it; only after total return to himself, when he plumbs the depths of the abyss into which his hubris has plunged him by divine ordainment, when he views his situation as irredeemably in disarray: his horror besmirched by the weapons of Achilles being denied him, the outbreak of his vengeful rage at this injustice miscarried, and in his blindness deflected onto defenseless multitudes, he himself after a flawless hero's life an amusement to his enemies, a mockery and abomination to the Greeks, a disgrace to his praiseworthy father, if he were to return to him like that; he decides, according to his motto, "Live honorably or die honorably," that only this last way out remains. Even the dissimulation, perhaps the first of his life, by which he calms his comrades, in order to carry out his resolve unhindered, must be credited to him as a strength of soul. He assigns Teucer to his young son, the future consolation of his deserted parents, as a

206 · *August Wilhelm Schlegel*

guardian and, like Cato, does not die until he has settled his family's affairs. Like Antigone in her feminine delicacy, in his last speech he seems in his wild way still to feel the splendor of the sunlight from which he is parting. His raw courage disdains compassion, and arouses it all the more penetratingly. What a picture of awakening from the delirium of passion, when the tent opens where he sits lamenting amidst the slaughtered multitude.

Just as Ajax in his ineradicable humiliation casts his life away in quick resolve, so Philoctetes bears his weary burden with patient perseverance for years of misery. His persistence ennobles him, just as despair does Ajax. Where the instinct for self-preservation comes into no conflict with its moral underpinnings, then it is possible for it to express itself in its full strength. Nature has equipped all sentient beings with it, and the emphasis with which it resists the intervention of hostile forces in its existence is a proof of its excellence. It is true, Philoctetes would no more want to live in the presence of the human society that had cast him out, and in dependence on its superior power, than would Ajax. But he finds himself facing Nature alone, he does not despair in view of her intimidating countenance, and nevertheless penetrates to the very bosom of his guardian. Banned to a desolate island, tormented by a stubborn wound, lonely and helpless as he is, his bow provides him with nourishment from the birds of the forest, the cliff bears soothing herbs, a spring offers him fresh water, his cave affords him shelter and coolness in the summer, in frosty wintertime he is warmed by the noon rays or by burning brushwood, even the raging attacks of pain must finally exhaust themselves and dissolve in restorative sleep. It is those arty decorations, that irksome, stifling overabundance, that causes indifference to the value of life; strip it of all alien garnishings, overload it with suffering so that naked existence itself barely remains, and still the sweetness of it will course through the veins with every heartbeat. The poor wretch! He bore it for ten years, still he lives, he still clings to life and to hope. What intimate truth speaks from all of this! What is most deeply moving about Philoctetes, though, is that he, whom abuse of power has cast from society, encounters a second, more pernicious evil, deceit, as soon as society approaches him again. The anxiety that he might be robbed of his last resource, his bow, would be too painful for the spectator, if

we did not know from the very outset that the open, straightfor-
ward Neoptolemus would not be able to carry to the end the role
of betrayal that he learned against his will. Not without justification does the deceived Philoctetes turn away from men, and back
to those lifeless comrades with whom his inborn need for compan-
ionship has made him familiar. He calls upon the island and its
volcanoes as witnesses of this new injustice befalling him, he believes that his beloved bow senses pain at being torn from him;
finally he takes melancholy leave of his hospitable cave, from the
springs, from the wave-dashed cliff, too, from where he had so
often looked out to the sea in vain: so loving are the pristine emotions of man.

In his *Laokoon,* Lessing declared himself against Winckelmann
in regard to the physical sufferings of Philoctetes and the way of
depicting it, and, in his *Critical Forests,* Herder contradicted Lessing in turn. The two last-named writers also made excellent comments on the drama on that occasion, although we must agree
with Herder that Winckelmann was right to maintain that Sophocles' Philoctetes suffers like Laokoon in the famous group, namely,
with the suppressed pain of a hero's soul that never wholly succumbs.

The Women of Trachis seems to me to be in value so far below
the other extant dramas of Sophocles that I would like to find
some encouragement for the supposition that this tragedy, though
in the same era, in his school, was composed perhaps by his son
Iophon, and was attributed through error to Sophocles. Some
things in the composition as well as in the style of the play can
seem suspicious; various critics have already remarked that the
monologue of Deianira, which begins without cause, does not have
the character of Sophocles' prologues. Even if on the whole the
artistic maxims of the poet are observed, this happens superficially; one misses the deep emotions of Sophocles. However, since
no one of the ancients seems to have doubted its authenticity, and
even Cicero confidently cites the lament of Hercules as from a
work of Sophocles, it must suffice to say that the tragedian remained below his standard here for once.

Moreover, this raises the question that can busy the critic far
more in regard to the works of Euripides: To what extent the
invention and execution of a drama must originate exclusively from

one person in order for him to be considered its author. Dramatic literature frequently offers us examples of dramas that were composed by several writers in common. It is known of Euripides that a learned servant, Cephisophon, helped him in the execution of his plays; perhaps he pondered their outlines with him, as well. It does seem that schools of dramatic art had been formed in Athens at the time, of the kind that always happens to arise when poetic capability is pursued with public enthusiasm, abundantly, and with great vigor: schools of art that contain pupils of such excellence and of such kindred spirits that the master can entrust them with a part of the execution, indeed of the composition of a work, and yet put his name on the whole without harm to his reputation. The painting schools of the sixteenth century were so constituted, and everyone knows what sharply discerning criticism is required to distinguish in many of Raphael's pictures, for example, how much actually comes from the master himself. Sophocles had educated his son Iophon in the art of tragedy, he could easily afford to have him help in executing the plays, especially since the tragedies, in order to compete for the prize, had to be finished and rehearsed by a certain time; conversely, he might also work on passages in works originally outlined by his son, and the plays created in this way, in which touches of the master are unmistakable, were then naturally circulated under the more famous name.

Thirty-seventh Lecture

Schiller. Overview of his works. Description of the influence of Goethe and Schiller. Chivalric drama, sentimental drama, drama of family. Prospects for the future.

In these circumstances, Schiller appeared, equipped with all the traits to impress both more noble spirits and the general public. He was still very young when he composed his first works, ignorant of the world whose portrayal he was undertaking and, although an independent genius, bold to the point of recklessness, nevertheless in many ways dominated by the models mentioned above of Lessing, Goethe in his earlier works, and Shakespeare, as he was able to understand him without knowledge of the original.

Thus the works of his youth were created, *The Robbers, Love and Intrigue,* and *Fiesco.* The first, wild and horrible as it was, was powerful in its effect, totally twisting some youthfully enthusiastic minds. The unsuccessful imitation of Shakespeare is unmistakable: Franz Moor is a prosaic Richard III, ennobled by none of the characteristics that in the latter temper our abhorrence with admiration. *Love and Intrigue* can scarcely move us through its exaggerated tone of sentimentality but can well torture us through its embarrassing impressions. In its outline, *Fiesco* is the most perverse, in its effect, the weakest.

Such a noble spirit could not long persist in such aberrations, although they afforded him applause that would have made the continuation of the delusion pardonable. He had examined the dangers of coarseness and of headstrong spite of all moderating discipline in himself and threw himself into his own education with incredible exertion and a kind of passion. The work that characterizes this new epoch is *Don Carlos.* In part very deep in its character portrayal, it still cannot entirely deny the old swaggering abnormity, which is simply garbed in finer form. The situations are forceful in their pathos, the story plot is complicated to the point of epigrammatic hairsplitting, but the poet's dearly won thoughts about human nature and the social contract were so valuable to him that he presented them extensively instead of expressing them through the course of the action, and he has his characters philosophize about themselves and others, so that the length of the play grows far beyond the limits prescribed for the theater.

Historical and philosophical studies thereafter seemed to divert the poet for a time from his theatrical career, to the advantage of his art, to which he returned a mature and much enriched mind, finally truly enlightened about his ends and means. Now he turned entirely to the historical tragedy and attempted to attain truly objective portrayals by divesting himself of his own personality. In *Wallenstein,* he had striven so conscientiously for historical thoroughness that in the face of it he could not entirely master his subject matter, and an occurrence of modest proportions disintegrated into two dramas and a rather didactic prologue. In the forms of his plays, he followed Shakespeare closely, only he tried to limit the change of time and place, so as not to overwork the imagination of the spectators. Also, he cared about better-conveyed tragic dignity, did not have any insignificant characters appear, or at least did not let them speak in their natural tones, and relegated the people, here the army, to public events, to the prologue. To be sure, the love between Thekla and Max Piccolomini is actually an episode and otherwise bears the stamp of a time quite different from that presented, but it gives occasion for the most moving scenes and is presented tenderly as well as nobly.

Mary Stuart is planned and executed with greater skill and equal thoroughness. Everything is carefully balanced; one can criticize individual parts as offensive, for instance, the quarrel of the two queens, the wild outbursts of Mortimer's passion, and the like; but one will hardly be able to shift anything without disordering the whole. The effect is unfailing. Mary's final scenes are truly regal, religious impressions are presented with dignified seriousness, only the perhaps superfluous concern for exercising poetic justice on Elizabeth after Mary's death sends the spectator home somewhat cooled.

With a marvelous subject matter such as the history of the *Maid of Orleans,* Schiller believed he could permit himself more freedom. The design is looser; the scene with Montgomery, an epic admixture from the *Iliad,* misses in tone; the purpose of the poet in the strange and incomprehensible appearance of the Black Knight is ambiguous; Schiller has not competed successfully with Shakespeare in the character of Talbot and in many other parts; and I do not know whether the indulgence in magic coloring, which is then not all that brilliant, compensates for the stricter pathos whose loss is entailed. The history of the Maid of Orleans is most precisely documented, her higher mission was believed in by the Maid herself and in the main by her contemporaries, and evoked the most extraordinary results. The poet could disregard the miracle, if the skeptical spirit of his contemporaries dissuaded him from presenting it as true; the true and humiliating martyrdom of the betrayed and deserted heroine would have shaken us more deeply than the rosily cheerful one that Schiller attributes to her, in contradiction to history. Shakespeare's portrayal, although more partisan due to his national viewpoint, is nevertheless far more historical and thorough. Yet the German play remains a beautiful rescuing of the honor of a name debased by brash mockery, and its dazzling effects, supported by the rich ornamentation of its language, earned it ample success on the stage.

I can agree the least with the principles that guided Schiller in *The Bride of Messina,* and which he himself explains in the foreword. But a discussion of them would lead me too far astray into the area of theory. It is supposed to be a tragedy in the form of antiquity but with romantic contents. Its entirely fictionalized story is clothed in a costume so vague and so devoid of all inner probability that the portrayal is neither truly ideal nor truly natural, neither mythological nor historical. Romantic poetry does try to fuse that which is most distant, to be sure, but it cannot assimilate veritably incompatible things: The mentality of the people portrayed cannot be simultaneously heathen and Christian. I do not intend to censure the obvious borrowings: The entire play is put together from two main components, from the pictures of Eteocles and Polynices, who, disregarding the intercession of their mother Jocasta, are fighting for sole possession of the throne, and from the brothers driven to fratricide due to jealousy in love, in Klinger's *Twins* and in *Julius of Tarent.* In the introduction of the choruses, too, although they have much lyric verve and beautiful passages, the intention of the ancients has been missed: By each of the enemy brothers having his own partisan chorus, which struggles with the opposing one, both of them cease to be a true chorus, that is, a voice of sympathy and observation elevated above everything personal.

The last of Schiller's works, *William Tell,* is, in my opinion, also the most excellent. Here he has completely returned to the poetry of history; the treatment is true, heartfelt, and, considering Schiller's lack of acquaintance with Swiss character and customs, of admirably true local color. It is true that he had a splendid study model in the eloquent paintings of the immortal Johannes Müller. This spirit-lifting Old German moral tale, breathing piousness and sturdy heroism in its portrayal, deserves to be performed in the celebration of the five-hundredth anniversary of the founding of Swiss freedom, in full view of Tell's chapel, on the shore of the Lake of Lucerne, under the open sky, with the Alps as the background.

Schiller was in the most mature abundance of his intellect when an untimely death bore him away; up to then, his long-since-undermined health had continued to obey his powerful will and exhaust itself completely in praiseworthy exertion. How much more he would have been able to achieve, since he was devoted exclusively to the theater and with every work was increasing in certain, skilled mastery! He was a virtuous artist in the real sense, who celebrated the true and the beautiful with pure emotions and offered his personality as sacrifice in the unceasing striving for them, far from the petty egotism and the jealousy all too frequent even among outstanding artists.

In Germany it has always been the case that the appearance of major original minds always produces an army of imitators, thus Goethe and Schiller, in the main without blame, brought about on our stage much that was faulty and degenerate.

Götz von Berlichingen generated a deluge of chivalric plays in which nothing is historical except the names and other external details, nothing chivalric except the helmets, shields, and swords, nothing Old German except, presumably, the brutality, for the convictions are as modern as they are vulgar. Out of chivalric plays came horseman plays that ultimately deserve more to be performed by horses than by people. What I said about one of the most popular of them can also be applied to those that through superficial memory of olden times do engage our imagination to some degree:

> With vanguard horns and castles and breastplate
>   Joan is resplendent:
>   Faith! and the play would delight me, weren't words
>   in it, too.

Besides this one, the most popular genres are the dramas of family and the sentimental drama, two spurious genres from the promotion of which, by means of precept and example, Lessing, Goethe, and Schiller cannot be absolved (the latter two in their early compositions *Stella, Clavigo, The Siblings, Love and Intrigue*). I do not want to name names, but let me assume that two writers of equal talent and theatrical insight had dedicated themselves to these genres; they both misjudge the essence of dramatic poetry and propose an allegedly moral goal; but morality would appear to the one only in the limited range of domesticity, to the other as softheartedness: What fruits would this bear, and how would the applause of the crowd finally decide between the two competitors?

The drama of family is supposed to depict the daily life of the middle classes. Extraordinary incidents that produce intrigue will be banned; to compensate for this lack of action, resort will be taken to quite individualized character sketching, which a practiced actor may reinforce to a certain veracity, which, however, sticks to external details, like a poor portrait painter trying to attain verisimilitude through pockmarks, warts, manner of dress, and the way of tying one's neckerchief; the motifs and situations at times become capricious and droll, but never become truly merry because the prosaically serious purpose, always kept present, prevents this. The quick turns of the plot of comedy usually stop this side of family life, which reduces everything to routine. It is impossible to render housekeeping poetic: The dramatic family portrayer will have as little to say about a happy and peaceful household as a historian about a nation in internal and external peace. He will thus have to interest us in the nuisances and narrowness of domestic life, portrayed with painful precision: vexations in doing one's official duties, in the education of one's children, discord between husband and wife that goes on and on, bad conduct of the servants, but above all, worry about food. The spectators understand such portrayals only too well, for everyone knows about feeling the pinch; it could be therapeutic for them to review the relationship of their expenditures to their income once a week in the theater; but their emotions will hardly be uplifted and refreshed, because the spectators see on stage what they have at home all day long.

The sentimental poet, in contrast, relieves their emotions all the more easily. His general doctrine is actually that a so-called good heart makes up for all missteps and intemperance, and that virtue does not need to be measured strictly according to principles. Just give your natural instincts free rein, he seems to say to his audience, look how charming it makes my naive girl when she owns up to everything. If he is able to captivate us by means of loose pathos, more sensual than moral, but at the end to reconcile everything nicely by having some magnanimous philanthropist walk in handing out money by the fistful, then this pleases overindulged

hearts very well; they feel as though they themselves had performed noble deeds, yet without having to reach into their own
pockets; all costs are covered by the generous purse of the poet.
Indisputably, the pathetic genre will thus win out over the play
of domestic economy in the long run, and that is what really has
taken place in Germany. But what is depicted to us in these dramas not only as natural and permitted but also as moral and noble
surpasses all reason, and this seduction is far more dangerous than
that of the frivolous comedy because it creeps into unguarded
minds, without repulsing them through external indecency, and
uses the most sacred names as a cloak.

This poetic and moral decay of contemporary taste resulted in
the circumstance that the writers who are the most popular on the
stage vie only for instantaneous applause, unconcerned about the
judgment of connoisseurs and about true respect; but those who
have both in mind, as well as higher goals, cannot decide to give
in to the demands of the crowd, and if they compose dramatically,
they want to disregard the stage. Therefore, they remain inadequate in the theatrical part of their art, which can attain mastery
only through practice and experience.

The repertoire of our stages therefore offers in its paltry wealth
a hodgepodge of chivalric plays, drama of family, and sentimental
dramas, which only infrequently alternate with works of greater
and more cultivated style by Shakespeare or Schiller. In between,
we cannot do without the translations and adaptations of foreign
novelties, particularly of the French epilogues and operettas. Since
the individual work is of little worth, we are stimulated merely by
the fleeting appeal of novelty, to the great detriment of the art of
acting, since many insignificant roles must be memorized hastily,
only to be forgotten again immediately. On top of that, to make
the vulgarity of our theater almost incurable, comes the hopelessly
bad organization of everything that has to do with producing plays.
The acting societies should be under the supervision of insightful
connoisseurs and practitioners of dramatic art who themselves are
not actors. Engel was in charge of the Berlin Theater for a time,
and witnesses in general assure us that he raised it to unusual
heights. What Goethe achieves in the direction of his Weimar
Theater in a small town and with small means is known by all
connoisseurs. He can neither create nor reward unusual talents,

but he accustoms the actors to order and training, with which they otherwise want to have nothing to do, and through this often gives his performances a unity and harmony that is lacking in larger theaters, where everyone acts as the mood strikes him. Faulty memorization and imperfect diction I have censured elsewhere. I have heard famous actors mangle their lines so badly that a beginner in Paris would not be forgiven. I know that in a certain theater, placed in the sad necessity of performing a work in verse, the roles were rewritten in prose so that the actors would not be disturbed in their beloved flat naturalness by observing the meter. How many "bushy haired fellows" (as Shakespeare called such people) do we have to put up with, who think they are affording the public pleasure when they merely pose awkwardly on the boards, and all the while consider the words that the poet has assigned to them only as a necessary evil. Our actors do exhibit a less lively striving to please than the French. Through the establishment of the permanent so-called national theater, with which something good for the prosperity of art is thought to have been achieved in some capitals, all competition has been completely stifled. The actors are granted exclusive privileges, they are guaranteed lifetime salaries: Now they no longer need to fear more skillful rivals, they do not depend on the fickle favor of the public, and are only concerned with using their position most comfortably as a sinecure. In this way, the national theaters are a true welfare agency for talents gone stale or neglected because of laziness. Hamlet's question to the players: "Are you getting rusty?" is always timely and unfortunately must almost always be answered affirmatively. The actor, with his loose way of life (which will not change because it just lies in the nature of things), needs a certain frivolous enthusiasm for his art in order to achieve something extraordinary. He cannot strive passionately enough for applause, for fame, for every glittering reward that is accorded to him immediately for his accomplishment. The instant is the field he harvests, time is his most dangerous enemy, because he is incapable of producing anything permanent. As soon as he is seized by the bourgeois anxiety of how to secure a modest income for himself and his family, progress is no longer possible. We do not mean to say that we should not provide for the later years of proven artists. But the actors who have lost their attraction due to age, illness, or other circumstances should be given salaries so that they stop acting, not so they continue. In general, we should not let actors imagine that they are such important and indispensable people. Nothing is rarer than a truly great actor; but nothing is more frequent than the ability to play parts as middling as we usually see them: There is convincing evidence in every society theater in a somewhat clever circle. Finally, the relationship between theater management and writers is as disadvantageous as possible in Germany. In France and England the author of a play has a certain share of the proceeds of each performance; this procures him a continuous income as soon as a few of his plays have maintained themselves favorably in the theater. If the play fails, however, he receives nothing at all. In Germany, the theater management pays a certain sum in advance and at its own risk for the manuscripts. This can cost them a great deal; if the play is exceptionally successful, on the other hand, the author does not receive an appropriate reward.

The exertions of poets not working immediately for the theater diverge in very different directions; here, too, as in other subjects, a ferment of concepts is going on, which incurs the accusation of chaotic anarchy from foreigners, in which however the way is pointed to a still unreached higher goal.

The deeper foundation of aesthetics among the Germans, a people by nature more speculative than practical, has led to the fashioning of artworks, and especially tragedies, according to more or less misunderstood abstract theories, which then naturally can have no effect in the theater, which are indeed not performable at all and have no inner life.

Others have acquired the spirit of the ancient tragedians with genuine feeling and sought out the most suitable information to modify the simple, native forms of antiquity to the constitution of our stage.

Truly excellent talents have thrown themselves into romantic drama but mostly with a breadth that is permitted only to the novel, disregarding the compression that dramatic form requires. Or from Spanish drama they have seized only the musically fantasizing and picturesquely tricky sides, without the firm stance, the drastic power, and the theatrical effectiveness.

What path should we take now? Should we seek to accustom

ourselves once more to the long-banned form of the French tragedy? Repeated experience has proven that it can have no particular success even in the hands of a Goethe or a Schiller, due to the way it is modified through translation and through the tone of the performance, as it inevitably must be modified.

The tragedy in imitation of the Greeks in a more genuine manner is more related to our mentality; the crowd, however, does not comprehend it; it will always remain a learned artistic enjoyment for a few cultured people, approximately like the contemplation of the statues of antiquity.

Lessing already noted the difficulty of introducing in the comedy national customs that still are not provincial, since with us the tone of social life is not set by a common middle ground. If we demand pure comedies, I would strongly advise the use of rhymed verse; perhaps with the artistic form, characteristic contents too would gradually result.

Yet this does not seem to me to be the most urgent need: Let us first of all develop the serious, high genres in a manner worthy of the German character. In these, it seems to me, our taste is thoroughly inclined to the Romantic. What attracts the crowd the most in our half-sentimental, half-droll dramas, which transport us now to Peru, now to Kamchatka, now to the age of knighthood, while the convictions remain modern and sentimental, is always a question of the Romantic, as can be seen even in the most insipid magic operas.

The significance of this genre was lost for us before we really found it; fantasy has run away with itself in the inventing of such whimsies, and the intentions of the plays are sometimes smarter than those of their originators. The term *Romantic* is wasted and desecrated on crude and unsuccessful products on a hundred theater programs; may we be permitted to ennoble it to its true significance again through criticism and history. Recently, the effort has been made to revivify the remnants of our old national poetry and traditions in many ways. These can supply the poet with a basis for a marvelous festival play; but the worthiest genre of romantic drama is the historical.

The most splendid laurels for the poet are to be plucked on this field by the poets who care to emulate Goethe and Schiller. But our historical drama should be generally national, it should not attach itself to anecdotes from the lives of individual knights and petty princes who had no influence on the whole; at the same time, it should be truly historic, molded from profound knowledge, and it should transpose us to our great past. The poet should let us view this mirror even if we blush with shame at what the Germans once were and what we should become again. He should warn us that, if we do not weigh the lessons of history better than before, we Germans, formerly the leading and most glorious people of Europe, whose freely chosen monarch was recognized without opposition as the sovereign over all of Christianity, are in danger of disappearing entirely from the ranks of independent peoples. The higher classes have long alienated the totality of the people through their preferences for foreign customs, through their zeal for foreign culture, which can never be more than a scrawny fruit in a greenhouse; for even longer, for three centuries, internal discord has been consuming our most noble strengths in civil wars, whose ruinous consequences are revealing themselves only now. May all who have the opportunity to affect public awareness exert themselves finally to resolve the old misunderstanding, and to assemble all right-minded men around unfortunately deserted objects of veneration, by the true devotion to which our ancestors experienced so much well-being and fame, as around a sacred banner, and let them feel their indestructible unity as Germans completely! What panoramas our history offers, from the most primeval times, from the wars with the Romans, to the solid formation of the German Empire! Then the chivalric shimmering era of the house of Hohenstaufen, then the politically more important house of Hapsburg, closer to us, which has fathered so many great princes and heroes. What a field for a poet who, like Shakespeare, knows how to seize the poetic side of great world events! But we Germans are always so unconcerned about our most important national issues that even the merely historical portrayal of them is still greatly in arrears.

Translated by Ralph R. Read III

On the Process
of the Poetic Mind

Friedrich Hölderlin

If the poet has once mastered the mind; if he has felt and assimilated the common soul that is shared by all and is individual to everyone, has held it fast, has assured himself of it; if, further, he is certain of the free movement, of the harmonic interchange and advance in which the mind is inclined to reproduce itself in itself and in others; if he is certain of the fine progress prescribed in the ideal of the mind and of its poetic way of inference; if he has realized that a necessary conflict arises between the most primary demand of the mind, which aims at communality and some simultaneity of all parts, and between the other demand, which commands it to move outside of itself and to render itself in itself and in others in fine progress and interchange, if this conflict always holds him fast and draws him onward along the way towards fulfillment; if, further, he has realized that just that communality and relatedness of all parts, those mental contents, would not be tangible, if they were not different from the sensual contents, according to degree, even discounting the harmonic interchange, even with the similarity of the mental form (of simultaneity and association); further, that that harmonic interchange, that advance would, in turn, not be tangible but an empty, easy shadow play, if the interchanging parts, even with the difference in the sensual contents, do not remain the same in sensual form during the interchange and advance of the mind; if he has realized that that conflict between intellectual content (between the relatedness of all parts) and intellectual form (the interchange of all parts),

219

between the pausing and the advance of the mind is solved by the form of the subject matter in all parts remaining identical in the very advance of the mind, in the interchange of intellectual form, and that it replaces just as much as must be lost of the original relatedness and unity of the parts in the harmonic interchange; that it constitutes objective contents in contrast to intellectual form and gives the latter its full significance; that, on the other hand, the material interchange of the subject matter, which accompanies what is eternal in the intellectual contents, the multiplicity of the same might satisfy the demands of the mind that it makes in its progress and that are retarded through the demands for unity and eternity in every moment; that precisely this material interchange constitutes the objective form, the shape, in contrast to the intellectual contents; if he has realized that, on the other hand, the conflict between the material interchange and the material identity is resolved by the loss of material identity, of passionate progress, wary of interruption, replaced by constantly resounding, all-equalizing intellectual content, and the loss of material multiplicity that comes about due to more rapid advance toward its goal and impression due to this material identity is replaced by constantly interchanging, ideal, intellectual mental form; if he has realized how, inversely, precisely the conflict between intellectual, peaceful content and intellectual interchanging form, as incompatible as they are, so too the conflict between material interchange and material, identical advance towards the principal moment, as incompatible as they are, makes the one as well as the other tangible; if he, finally, has realized that the conflict of the intellectual content and the ideal form, on the one hand, and of the material interchange and the identical advance, on the other hand, unite in the rest points and principal moments and, to the extent that they are not reconcilable in them, just here and just for this reason become tangible and are felt—if he has realized this, then for him everything depends on the receptivity of the subject matter to ideal content and to ideal form. If he is certain of and the master of the one as of the other, of the receptivity of the subject matter as of the mind, there can be no mistake in the principal moment.

And how must the subject matter be constituted that is chiefly receptive to the ideal, to its contents, for metaphor, and to its form, the transition?

The subject matter is either a series of occurrences or views describing or painting realities subjectively or objectively, or it is a series of efforts, ideas, thoughts, or passions denoting necessities subjectively or objectively, or a series of fantasies forming possibilities subjectively or objectively. In all three cases, it must be capable of ideal treatment, namely, if a genuine basis is present for the occurrences, for the views that are to be related, described, or for the fantasies that are to be formed, if the occurrences or views issue from real efforts, the thoughts and passions from a real circumstance, the fantasies from fine sensation. This basis of the poem, its significance, should form the transition between the expression, that which is depicted, the sensual subject matter, that which is actually expressed in the poem, and between the mind, the ideal treatment. The meaning of the poem can be twofold, just as the mind can, the ideal, just as the subject matter, too, the portrayal, can be twofold—namely, to the extent that it is understood as applied or unapplied. Unapplied, these words express nothing but the poetic process, as it is noticeable, genial, and governed by judgment, in every genuinely poetic enterprise; applied, these words indicate the adequacy of the circle of poetic effect in question to that process, the possibility lying in the element to realize that process, so that one can say that in every element in question, both objectively and actually real, something ideal faces that which is ideal, something living that which is living, something individual that which is individual, and the question is only what is to be understood by this circle of effect. It is that in which and on which the poetic enterprise and process in question is realized, the vehicle of the mind through which it reproduces itself in itself and in others. *In* itself the circle of effect is greater than the poetic mind, but not *for* itself. To the extent that it is observed in the context of the world, it is greater; to the extent that it is held fast by the poet and assimilated, it is subordinated. According to its tendency, according to the contents of its aspiration, it is opposed to the poetic enterprise, and the poet is led astray all too easily by his subject matter since, in that if it is taken out of the context of the living world it resists poetic restructuring, in that if it does not choose to serve the mind merely as a vehicle, in that even if it is chosen correctly, its initial and first development in regard to this is antithesis and a spur in regard to poetic fulfillment, so that its second development must be unfulfilled in part and fulfilled in part, as aforesaid.

But it must be shown how, regardless of this conflict, in that the poetic mind remains at its enterprise with the element and circle of effect in question, the latter would nevertheless favor the former; and how that conflict would be dissolved, how a receptivity for poetic enterprise would still inhere in the element that the poet chooses as vehicle; and how he would realize within it all the demands—the entire poetic process, in its metaphorical, its hyperbolic, its character in a mutual effect with the element that, to be sure, resists in its initial tendency and is even opposed, but unites with the former at the middle point.

Between the expression (the depiction) and the free, ideal treatment lies the foundation and the meaning of the poem. This is what gives the poem its seriousness, its stability, its truth; it protects the poem so that the free, ideal treatment will not become empty mannerism and the depiction became vanity. It is the intellectually sensual, the formally materialistic part of the poem; and if the ideal treatment is more unifying in its metaphors, its tradition, its episodes, whereas the expression, the depiction, is more divisive in its characters, its passion, its individualities, then the meaning should stand between the two; it distinguishes itself by being opposed to itself everywhere: instead of the mind comparing everything that is opposite in form, dividing everything united, holding fast everything free, generalizing everything specific, because according to the meaning, what is treated is not merely an individual whole, nor a whole bound together with its harmonic opposite into a whole, but rather a whole in general, and the connection with the harmonic opposite is also possible through an opposite in individual tendency, but not in form; that the meaning unites through opposition, through the contact of extremes, since these are comparable not according to contents but in the direction and the degree of their opposition, so that it also compares what is the most contradictory and is thoroughly hyperbolic, that it does not progress through opposition in form where the first is related to the second according to contents, but rather through opposition in content where the first is equal to the second according to form, so that naive and heroic and ideal tendencies contradict themselves in the object of their tendency but are comparable in the form of the conflict and aspiration and united according to the law of activity, thus united in what is most universal, in life.

So in this way, through this hyperbolic process, according to which the ideal, the harmonically opposed and connected, is considered not only as beautiful life but as life in general, thus also as capable of another condition, and specifically not of another harmonically opposite one but of a directly opposite one, of a most extreme one, so that this new condition is comparable to the previous one only through the idea of life in general—for that very reason, the poet gives the ideal a beginning, a direction, a meaning. The ideal in this shape is the subjective basis of the poem, the basis of departure and return, and since the inner, ideal life can be conceived of in various moods, can be observed as life in general, as something generalizable, as something transposable, as something separable, then there are also various kinds of subjective substantiations; either the ideal mood is conceived of as sensation—then it is the subjective basis of the poem, the principal mood of the poet in the whole enterprise, and precisely because it is grasped as a sensation, it is considered by means of substantiation as something generalizable—or it is grasped as an aspiration, then it becomes the principal mood of the poet in the entire enterprise; and since it is grasped as aspiration, this means that it is considered through substantiation as something fulfillable, or if it is grasped as intellectual contemplation, then this is the principal mood of the entire enterprise, and precisely because it was grasped as such means that it is considered as something realizable. And thus the subjective motivation demands and determines an objective one and prepares it. Thus, in the first case the subject matter is conceived of first as something general, in the second as fulfillable, in the third as what is happening.

If free, ideal, poetic life has been fixed, and if significance has been given to it, according to how it was fixed as something generalizable, as fulfillable, as realizable, if it is connected to its direct opposite, in this way, through the idea of life in general and if taken hyperbolically, then an important point is still lacking in the process of the poetic mind, through which it gives its enterprise not mood, tone, not even meaning and direction, but reality.

Considered as pure, poetic life, according to its contents, of course, this poetic life remains completely united with itself, as if by virtue of the harmonic in general and of temporal deficiency, a thing connected with the harmonic opposite; and only in the interchange of forms is it opposed; only in the manner, not in the base of its advance, is it wielded or aimed or, better, tossed; only coincidentally is it more or less interrupted; considered as life determined and founded through poetic reflection by virtue of the idea of life in general and of the lack of unity, it begins with an idealistically characteristic mood; it is no longer a thing connected with the harmonic opposite at all; it is present as such in a certain form and progresses in the interchange of moods, where each time the succeeding one is determined by the preceding, and is opposed according to contents, that is, according to the organs by which it is comprehended, and to that extent is more individual, more general, fuller, so that the various moods are connected only where that which is pure finds its opposition, namely, in the manner of its advance, as life in general, so that purely poetic life can no longer be found; for in each of the changing moods, it is connected in a particular form with its direct opposite, thus is no longer pure; on the whole, it is present only as advance and, according to the laws of advance, only as life in general, and there prevails absolutely from this viewpoint a conflict of the individual (the material), the general (the formal), and the pure.

The pure, which is comprehended in every particular mood, conflicts with the organ by which it is comprehended; it conflicts with what is pure in the other organ; it conflicts with the interchange.

As a particular organ (form) has a characteristic mood, that which is general conflicts with the pure, which it comprehends in this mood; as advancement in totality, it conflicts with the pure that is comprehended within it; as characteristic mood, it conflicts with the next adjacent mood.

That which is individual conflicts with the pure that comprehends it, it conflicts with the next adjacent form; as something individual, it conflicts with that which is general in the interchange.

The process of the poetic mind in its enterprise thus cannot possibly end with this. If it is the true process, then something else must be detectable in it, and it must be shown that the manner of the process that gives the poem its meaning is only the transition from that which is pure to this detectable something, just as it is in reverse, from the latter to that which is pure. (Means of connecting mind and signs.)

Now, if that which is directly opposed to the mind, the organ in which it is contained and through which all opposition is possible, could be observed and comprehended not only as that through which the harmonically connected is formally opposed but also through which it is formally connected; if it could be observed and comprehended not only as that through which the various unharmonic moods are materially opposed and formally connected but through which they are also materially connected and formally opposed; if it could be observed and comprehended not only as that which as connective is merely formal life in general and as particular and material is not connective, only opposing and dividing; if it could be observed as something material that connects; if the organ of the mind could be observed as that one which, in order to make the harmonic opposite possible, must be receptive to the one as to the other harmonic opposite, so that to the extent that it is a formal opposition for the purely poetic life, it must also be a formal connection, so that, to the extent that it presents material opposition to certain poetic life and its moods, it must also be materially connecting, so that that which limits and determines is not just negative, that it is also positive, that, while it is considered isolated concerning harmonic connections, it is opposed to the one as well as the other, but both considered together are the union of both, then that act of the mind that in regard to the meaning had only one prevalent conflict as a result will be just as unifying as it was opposing.

But how is it understood in this quality? As possible and as necessary? Not merely through life in general, for it is rightly this to the extent it is considered merely as materially opposing and formally connecting, determining life directly. Also not merely through unity in general, for it is rightly this to the extent it is considered merely as formally opposing, but in the concept of the unity of the united, so that, of the harmonically connected, the *one* as well as the *other* is *present as regards opposition and unification,* and that, *in this regard, the mind in its infinity is tangible,* which appeared as something finite through opposition; that that which is pure, conflicting with the organ in itself, is present to itself in precisely this organ and thus here becomes alive; that, where it is present in different moods, the one following immediately after the basic mood is only the lengthened point, which leads thither, namely, to the middle point, where the harmonically opposed moods meet one another, so that precisely in the strongest contrast, in the contrast of the first ideal mood and the second artificially reflected mood, in the most material opposition (which lies between harmonically connected mind and life, meeting at the middle point, present in the middle point), that exists precisely in this most material opposition, which is opposed to itself (in regard to the point of unification towards which it is striving), in the conflicting, advancing acts of the mind, if they arise only from the reciprocal character of the harmonically opposed moods, that precisely there is the most infinite portrayed most tangibly, most negatively-positively and hyperbolically; that through this contrast in the depiction of that which is infinite in the conflicting advance to the point and its meeting at the point replaces the simultaneous inwardness and the differentiation of the harmonically opposed and living sensations lying at its base and, at the same time, is depicted more clearly by the free consciousness and more cultivated, more universally as a world of its own according to its form, as a world in the world, and thus as the voice of the eternal to the eternal.

Thus, the poetic mind, in the process it observes in its enterprise, cannot be satisfied with a harmonically opposite life, not even by comprehending or grasping it through hyperbolic opposition; if it has gone this far, if the enterprise is lacking neither in harmonic unity nor in meaning and energy, neither in harmonic spirit in general nor in harmonic interchange, then it is necessary, if the one (to the extent that it can be considered by itself) is not either to cancel itself out as something indistinguishable and become empty infinity, or if it is not to lose its identity in an interchange of antitheses, be these ever so harmonic, thus it no longer can be anything whole and unified but, on the contrary, will deteriorate into an infinity of isolated moments (like a series of atoms)—I say: It is necessary that the poetic mind with its unity and harmonic progress give itself also an infinite viewpoint in its

enterprise, a unity where in the harmonic progress and interchange everything would go forward and backward and through
its prevalent characteristic relationship to this unity gain not just
objective context for the observer but also felt and tangible context and identity in the interchange of antitheses, and it is its last
task to have a thread, a memory, in the harmonic interchange, so
that the mind might never remain present to itself in the individual
moment and then again in an individual moment but continue in
one moment as in another and in the various moods, just as it is
wholly present to itself *in the infinite unity,* which is now the separation point of the unified as unified but is then also the uniting
point of the unified as opposites, finally, even both at the same
time, so that that which is harmonically opposite in it is neither
opposed as something unified nor unified as something opposed
but rather as both in *one* is felt inseparably as something unifiedly
opposed and indivisible and is discovered as felt. This sense is actually poetic character, neither genius nor art, poetic individuality,
and to this alone is granted the identity of enthusism, to it the
perfection of genius and of art, the realization of the infinite, the
divine impetus.

So this is never merely the opposing of that which is unified,
also never merely the relationship, unification of the opposing and
the changing; what is opposed and unified is inseparable in it. If
this is so, then it can be passive in its purity and subjective entirety, as primal sense, to be sure, in the acts of opposing and
unifying, with which it is effective in harmonically opposed life,
but in its last act, where the harmonically opposed is understood
as that which is the opposed harmonic, that which is unified, as
mutual effect, as one within it; in this act, it can and may by no
means, understood through itself, become itself the object, if instead of an infinitely united and living unity it should be a dead
and deadly unity, something that has become infinitely positive;
for if unity and opposition are bound inseparably in it and are
one, then it can appear to reflection neither as something opposa-
ble-unifiable nor as something unifiable-opposed, thus it cannot
appear at all, or only in the character of a positive void, of an
infinite stagnation; and the hyperbole of all hyperboles is the boldest and last attempt of the poetic mind, if in its process it ever
makes the attempt to grasp original poetic individuality, the poetic

ego, an attempt through which it might preserve this individuality and its pure object, that which is unified and living, harmonic, reciprocally effective life; yet it must; for since it is supposed to be freely everything that it is in its enterprise and must, by creating a world of its own—and instinct by nature belongs to that world of its own, in which it exists—since it thus should be everything freely, thus it must also assure itself of this, its individuality. But since it cannot perceive it through itself and by itself, an external object is necessary and, indeed, one through which pure individuality should be bound to take some one among various particular ones, neither solely an opposing one nor solely a relating one, but a poetic character that it can assume so that thus in pure individuality as well as in other characters the now chosen individuality and its character, now determined by the subject matter, is perceptible and can freely be held fast.

Within subjective nature, the ego can be perceived only as something opposing or as something relating; within subjective nature it cannot, however, be perceived as the poetic ego in a threefold characterization, for as it does appear within subjective nature and is differentiated from itself and differentiated by and through itself, then that which is perceived, always taken together only with that which perceives and the perception of both, must comprise that threefold nature of the poetic ego and neither grasped as the perceived by the perceiving, nor as the perceiving grasped by the perceiving, nor as the perceived and perceiving grasped by perception, nor as perception grasped by the perceiving; in none of these three abstractly assumed qualities is it conceived of as pure, poetic ego in its threefold nature, as opposing that which is harmonically opposite, as (formally) unifying that which is harmonically opposite, as perceiving as one that which is harmonically opposite, the opposition and the unification; on the contrary, it remains with and for itself in real contradiction. Thus, only to the extent that it is differentiated not from itself and in and through itself when it is made specifically differentiable by a third, and if this third, to the extent that it was freely chosen, to the extent also that it does not cancel pure individuality in its influences and determinants, but can be observed by it, where it then considers itself at the same time as something determined by choice, something empirically individualized and characterized, only then is it possible that the ego should appear in harmonically opposed life as unity, and conversely the harmonic opposite should appear as unity in the ego and become an object in beautiful individuality.

a. But how is it possible? Universally?

b. If it becomes possible in such a way that the ego may perceive itself and conduct itself in poetic individuality, what result arises from that for poetic portrayal? (It perceives in the threefold subjective and objective attempts the striving towards pure unity.)

a. If man, in this isolation, in this life with himself, in this contradictory middle condition between the natural context of a naturally present world and the higher context of a world also naturally present but chosen in advance with free choice in this sphere, known in advance, and in all its influences not determining him without his will—if he has lived in that middle condition between childhood and mature humanity, a beautiful life freely between the mechanically beautiful and the humanly beautiful, and has perceived and experienced this middle condition, how he must simply continue in contradiction with himself, in necessary conflict with (1) the aspiration for pure selfhood and identity, (2) the aspiration for significance and differentiation, (3) the aspiration for harmony; and how in this conflict each one of these aspirations must cancel itself out and show itself to be unrealizable; how he thus must be resigned, relapse into childhood, or exhaust himself in fruitless contradictions with himself; if he persists in this condition, then there is one thing that will draw him out of this sad alternative; and the problem of being free like a youth and of living in the world like a child, of the independence of a cultured man and the accommodation of an ordinary man, is solved by following this rule:

Place yourself by free choice in harmonic opposition to an external sphere, just as you are in harmonic opposition in yourself, by nature, but imperceptibly, as long as you remain within yourself.

For here, in following this rule, is an important difference from the behavior in the previous condition.

In the previous condition, namely, in that of isolation, harmonically opposed nature could not become perceptible unity for the reason that the ego, without canceling itself, could neither posit and perceive itself as an active unity without the reality of differentiation, thus canceling the reality of perception, nor as passive unity, without the reality of unity, its criterion of identity, namely, of canceling activity, and that the ego, by striving to perceive its unity in the harmonic opposite and the harmonic opposite in its unity, must posit itself absolutely and dogmatically as active unity, or as passive unity; it therefore comes into being because, in order to perceive itself through itself, it can replace the natural, intimate connection in which it stands to itself and through which differentiation is made difficult for it only through an unnatural (self-canceling) differentiation, because it is by nature one in its difference with itself, so that the difference necessary for perception, that it gives itself freely, is possible only in the extreme, thus only in striving, in attempts at thought that, realized in this manner, would only cancel themselves, because, in order to perceive its unity in the (subjective) harmonic opposite and the (subjective) harmonic opposite in its unity, it must necessarily abstract from itself to the extent that it is posited in the (subjective) harmonic opposite, and must reflect upon itself to the extent that it is not posited in the (subjective) harmonic opposite, and conversely; but since it cannot make this abstraction from its being in the (subjective) harmonic opposite or make this reflection upon nonbeing in it without canceling itself and the harmonic opposite and the subjective harmonic opposite and unity, then the attempts that it nevertheless makes in this fashion must be attempts such that, if they were realized in this manner, would cancel themselves.

This is thus the difference between the condition of isolation (the intuition of his being) and the new condition, where man places himself in harmonic opposition to the external sphere, through free choice, so that, precisely because he is not so intimately connected to it, he can abstract from it and from himself to the extent that he is posited in it, and can reflect on himself to the extent that he is not posited in it; this is the reason why he goes out from himself; this is the rule for his procedure in the external world. In this way, he reaches his destiny, which is: perception of the harmonic opposite in himself, in his unity and individuality, and again, perception of his identity, his unity and individuality in the harmonic opposite. This is the true freedom of his being, and if he is not too attached to this external, harmonically opposed sphere, does not become identical with it as with himself, so that he can never abstract from it, nor attaches himself too closely to himself, and can abstract too little from himself as an independent, if he neither reflects too much upon himself nor reflects too much on his sphere and his time, then he is on the right path to his destiny. The childhood of ordinary life, where he was identical with the world and could not abstract from it at all, was without freedom, therefore without perception of himself in the harmonic opposite, and of the harmonic opposite in himself, actually without stability, independence, actual identity in pure life; this time will be considered by him as the time of wishes, where man strives to perceive himself in the harmonic opposite and that in himself as unity by giving himself up entirely to the objective life, but where the impossibility of a perceptible identity in the harmonic opposite shows itself objectively, as it has already been shown subjectively. For, since in this condition he does not know himself at all in his subjective nature but is merely objective life in that which is objective, he can strive to perceive the unity in the harmonic opposite only by proceeding in his sphere, from which he can abstract just as little as the subjective man from his subjective sphere, just as the latter does in his. He is placed within it as within the harmonically opposed. He must strive to perceive himself, attempt to differentiate himself from himself within it, by making himself something opposing, to the extent that it is harmonic, and something unifying, to the extent that it is opposed. But if he strives to perceive himself in this diversity, then he must either deny to himself the reality of this conflict, by finding himself with himself, and consider this conflicting procedure an illusion and caprice, which expresses itself so that he perceives his identity in the harmonic opposite—but then also this, his identity, is, as something perceived, an illusion—or he may consider that distinction real, that, namely, he conduct himself as something unifying and differentiating according to whether he should find present in his objective sphere something to differentiate or to unite, thus posit himself as dependent as something unifying and as something differentiating; and because this is supposed to take place in his objective sphere, from which he, absolutely dependent, cannot abstract without canceling himself, so that he can recognize his act neither as something unifying nor as something opposing himself. In this case, he can again not perceive himself as identical, because the different acts in which he finds himself are not his acts. He cannot perceive himself at all, he is not something distinct; it is his sphere in which he conducts himself thus mechanically. But even if he now wanted to posit himself as identical with it, the conflict of life and personality, which he always strives and must strive to unify and to perceive as one, to dissolve in greatest intimacy, then it avails nothing, to the extent that he conducts himself in his sphere in such a way that he cannot abstract from it, for he can perceive himself precisely for this reason only in the extremes of antitheses of opposition and unification, because he lives too intimately within his sphere.

In a too subjective condition as in a too objective one man seeks in vain to attain his destiny, which consists of perceiving himself as a unity contained in the divine, harmonically opposed, as well as conversely, perceiving the divine, the unified, harmonically opposed contained as a unity within himself. For this is possible only in beautiful, sacred, divine sensation; in sensation that is beautiful because it is neither merely pleasant and happy nor merely noble and strong, nor merely unified and peaceful, but is all that at once and can be alone; in sensation that is sacred because it is neither merely devoted selflessly to its object, nor merely resting selflessly on its inner foundation, nor merely hovering selflessly between its inner foundation and its object, but is all that at once and can be alone; in sensation that is divine because it is neither mere consciousness, mere reflection (subjective or objective) with the loss of inner and outer life, nor mere striving (subjectively or objectively determined) with the loss of inner and outer harmony, nor mere harmony, like intellectual contemplation and its mythic, metaphorical subject, object, with the loss of consciousness and unity, but because it is all this at once and can be alone; in sensation that is therefore transcendental and can be this alone, because in the unification and mutual effect of the above-named characteristics it is neither too pleasant and sensual, nor too energetic and wild, nor too intimate and enthusiastic, neither too selfless—that is, devoted too unselfishly to its object, nor too selfless—that is, too arbitrarily resting on its inner foundation, nor too selfish, that is, too undecided and empty and hovering uncertainly between its inner foundation and its object, neither too reflected, too conscious of it, too sharp and for this reason unconscious of its inner and outer foundation, nor too agitated, too contained within its inner and outer foundation, for this reason unconscious of its inner and outer harmony, nor too harmonic, for this reason too little conscious of its self and its inner and outer foundation, for this reason too undetermined, and less receptive of the real infinite, which is determined through it as a certain, real infinity, as lying external to it, and capable of less duration. In short, because it is present in its threefold characteristic and can be this alone, it is less exposed to partiality in any one of the three characteristics. On the contrary, all the forces originally grow out of it, which those characteristics possess certainly more determinedly and more perceptibly, but also more isolatedly, just as those forces and their characteristics and expressions concentrate within it again and through mutual context and living determination, enduring for itself, as organs of it, and gain freedom, as belonging to it and not limited to themselves in its limitation, and completeness, as comprised in its totality—those three characteristics may express themselves as efforts to perceive the harmonic opposite in the living unity, or the latter in the former, in the more subjective or more objective condition. For precisely these different conditions emanate from it as the unification of the same.

Suggestion for Representation and Language

Is not language like perception, of which we were speaking and of which it was said that in it the unified was contained as unity and vice versa, and that it was of a threefold variety (see above)?

And must not the most beautiful moment for the one as for the other come where the actual expression, the most intellectual language, the most vital consciousness, where the transition from a specific infinity to a more general one is found?

Does not the strong point lie right here, through which the character and the degree of the sequence of sketches, their manner of relating, and the local color as well as its illumination are determined?

Will not all judgment of language be reduced to examining it for *the most certain and feasibly least treacherous criterion* of whether language is a genuine, beautifully described sensation?

Just as perception intuits language, thus does language remember perception.

Perception intuits language after (1) it was still unreflected, pure sensation of life, of the specific infinity in which it is contained, (2) after it had repeated itself in the dissonances of inward reflection and aspiration and composing of poetry, and now, after these vain attempts to find and to reproduce itself inwardly again, after these tacit intuitions, which must also have their time, goes out beyond itself and finds itself again in total infinity, that is, through insubstantial, pure mood, as if through the echo of the original, living sensation, which it gained and was able to gain through the total effect of all inner attempts, becomes master and possessor of its entire inner and outer life through this higher, divine receptivity. In precisely this instant, where the original, living sensation, now refined into the pure mood receptive of an infinity, finds itself as the intellectual whole in the living whole, in this instant one can say that language is intuited; and if now a reflection results, as in the original sensation, then it is no longer dissolving and generalizing, distributing and cultivating, even to pure mood, it returns to the heart everything that it took from it; it is invigorating art, just as previously it was intellectualizing art, and with one wave of the magic wand after another, it calls forth our lost life more beautifully, until it feels itself to be wholly itself, as it originally felt. And if it is the course and the destiny of life itself to develop to the highest form from original simplicity, where eternal life is present for man for just this reason, and where he takes in everything all the more intimately as something most abstract, then from this highest opposition and unification of what is living and intellectual, of the formal and material subject-object, to restore life to the intellectual, form to the living, love and heart to man, and gratitude to the world, and finally, after fulfilled intuition and hope, whenever, namely, in the expression of that highest point of cultivation the highest form was present in the highest life and not merely in itself, as at the beginning of the actual expression, nor in striving as in the continuation of the same; where expression evokes life from the mind and the mind from life, but rather where it has found original life in the highest form; where mind and life are equal on both sides and perceive their finding, the infinite in the infinite, after this third and last perfection of the heart and life, not simply original simplicity; where man feels uninhibited as in a limited infinity, also not merely achieved simplicity of the mind; where precisely that sensation, purified to a pure, formal mood, takes on the entire infinity of life (and is the ideal), but rather the mind, revived from infinite life, is not happiness, not the ideal but a successful work of a creation and can be found only in the expression and outside of the expression can only be hoped for in the ideal issuing from its specific, original sensation; how, finally, after this third perfection, where the specific infinity has been called so far into life, the infinite infinity has been so far intellectualized that one is equal to the other in mind and life, how after this third perfection the specific becomes more and more vital, the infinite becomes more and more intellectualized, until the original sensation ends up as life, just as it began in the expression as mind, and the higher infinity, from which it took its life, likewise is intellectualized, just as it was present in the expression as something alive—thus, if this seems to be the course and the destiny of man in general, then it is also the course and the destiny of all and any poetry, and as on that level of cultivation where man has issued forth from his original childhood and in opposed attempts struggled up to highest form, to pure echo of that first life and thus feels himself to be infinite mind within infinite life, as man on this level of cultivation really just begins to enter life and intuits his effect and his destiny, so the poet at that level has also struggled up from an original sensation through opposed attempts to the tone, to the highest, pure form of the same sensation and sees himself comprehended entirely in his entire inner and outer life by that tone, at that level he intuits his language, and with it actual perfection for existing and at the same time for all poetry.

It has already been said that a new reflection enters at that level, which restores to the heart everything that it has taken from it, which is invigorating art for the mind of the poet and the spirit of his future poetry, as it was intellectualizing art for the original sensation of the poet and his poem. The product of this creative reflection is language. While the poet, namely, feels himself comprehended by the pure tone of his original sensation in his entire inner and outer life and looks around in his world, it is for him just as new and unknown—the sum of all his experiences, of his knowledge, of his contemplation, of his thought, art, and nature as it is portrayed within him and outside of him; everything is as if for the first time, just for that reason uncomprehended, undetermined, dissolved into pure subject matter and life, present for him, and it is preeminently important that in this instant he assumes nothing as given, proceeds from nothing positive, that nature and art, as he has become acquainted with them and sees them, do not speak until a language is there for him, that is, until that which is now unknown and unnamed becomes known and named for him in his world in such a way that it has been compared and found in agreement with his mood; for if a specifically structured language of nature and art were there for him before reflection on the infinite subject matter and the infinite form, then he would not be within his circle of effect to that extent; and the language of nature or art, that *modus experimendi* of the one or of the other, would be, first, to the extent that it is not his language, not a product issuing from his mind and his life but the language of art, as soon as it is present to me in a specific form, already in advance a determining act of the creative reflection of the artist, which consisted in his taking from his world, from the sum of his outer and inner life that is more or less my own too, that he took the subject matter from this world to designate the tones of his mind, to call forth from his mood the life underlying it through this related sign; that he thus, to the extent that he names this sign to me, borrows the subject matter from my world, causes me to transpose this subject matter into the sign, where then the important difference is between me as something determined and him as something determining; that he, by making himself understandable and intelligible, progresses from lifeless, immaterial mood that for this reason is less opposable and more unconscious simply by explaining it (1) in its infinity of agreement a comparative totality of related subject matter, according to form as well as to substance, and through ideally interchanging world, (2) in its determination and actual finiteness through the depiction and enumeration of its own subject matter, (3) in its tendency, its generality in the particular, through the antithesis of its own subject matter to the infinite subject matter, (4) in its proportion, in the beautiful determination and unity and stability of its infinite agreement, in its infinite identity and individuality and bearing, in its poetic prose of an all-containing moment, in which and towards which all named pieces relate and are united negatively and for that reason expressly and sensually, namely, the infinite form with the infinite subject matter, so that through that moment the infinite form assumes a configuration, the interchange of the weaker and the stronger, the infinite subject matter assumes a resonance, an interchange of the shriller and the softer, and both finally unite negatively in the slowness and swiftness, in a standstill of motion, always through it and the activity underlying it, the infinite, beautiful reflection, which is universal limitation, is universally relating and unifying at the same time.

Translated by Ralph R. Read III

On the Marionette Theater

Heinrich von Kleist

One evening in M., where I was spending the winter of 1801, I met Mr. C. in a public park. He had recently been hired as the principal dancer at the opera and was enjoying immense popularity with the audiences.

I told him that I had been surprised to see him several times in a marionette theater that had been erected in the marketplace to entertain the populace with short dramatic burlesques interspersed with songs and dance.

He assured me that the pantomime of the puppets brought him much satisfaction and let it be known quite clearly that a dancer who wanted to perfect his art could learn a thing or two from them.

From the way in which he expressed himself, I could tell that it wasn't something he had just now thought up, so I sat down next to him to find out the reasons for such a remarkable claim.

He asked me if I hadn't, in fact, found some of the dance movements of the puppets, particularly of the smaller ones, very graceful.

I could not deny this. A group of four peasants dancing the rondo to a quick beat could not have been painted more delicately by Teniers.

I inquired about the mechanism of these figures. How was it possible to manipulate the individual limbs and extremities in the rhythm of movement or dance without having a myriad of strings on one's fingers?

He answered that I shouldn't imagine each limb as individually positioned and moved by the operator during various moments of the dance.

Each movement, he said, had its center of gravity: it would suffice to control this within the puppet; the limbs, which are only pendulums, follow mechanically of their own accord—without further help.

He added that this movement is very easy; whenever the center of gravity is moved in a *straight line,* the limbs describe *curves.* Often, when shaken in a rather haphazard manner, the entire puppet moves with a kind of rhythm which resembles dance.

This observation seemed to me to shed some light on the enjoyment he claimed to get from the marionette theater. But I was far from guessing the inferences which he would later draw from it.

I asked him if he thought that the operator who controlled these puppets would himself have to be a dancer or at least have some idea of the beauty in the dance.

He replied that if a job is mechanically simple, it doesn't follow that it can be done entirely without sensitivity.

The line which the center of gravity has to follow is indeed quite simple and in most cases, he believed, straight. In the cases in which it is curved, the law of its curvature seems to be at least of the first or at most of the second order; even in the latter case the line is only elliptical, a form of movement of the body's extremities (because of the joints) which is most natural, so this hardly demands great talent on the part of the operator.

But, seen from another point of view, this line could be something very mysterious, for it is nothing other than the *path taken by the dancer's soul;* and he doubted if this could be achieved unless the operator transposed himself into the marionette's center of gravity; that is to say, the operator *dances.*

I replied that the job of the operator had been presented to me as something done without sensitivity, somewhat like turning the handle of a barrel organ.

"Not at all," he answered. "In fact, there is a rather ingenious relationship between the movement of his fingers and the movements of the attached puppets, somewhat like that of numbers to their logarithms or the asymptotes to the hyperbola."

And yet he believed that even the last trace of human volition to which he had referred could be removed from the marionettes, that their dance could be transferred completely to the realm of mechanical forces and that it could be produced, as I had thought, by turning a handle.

I expressed my astonishment at the attention he was paying this species of an art form intended for the masses. It wasn't only that he thought a greater development possible; he himself seemed to be occupying his time with it.

He smiled and said he was confident that if a craftsman were to make a marionette according to his specifications, that he could perform a dance with it which neither he nor any other skilled dancer of his time, not even Vestris herself, could equal.

I said nothing and looked down at the ground. Then he said, "Have you ever heard of those artificial legs made by English craftsmen for those unfortunate individuals who have lost their limbs?"

I said that I hadn't seen anything of this kind.

"That's too bad," he replied, "because if I tell you that these unfortunate people can dance with them, I fear you won't believe me. What am I saying—dance? The range of their movements is rather limited, but those they can perform are executed with a calmness, ease, and grace which amazes any thinking observer."

I said, somewhat lightly, that he had, of course, found his man. A craftsman who could make such a remarkable limb could surely construct an entire marionette according to his specifications.

As he lowered his eyes, somewhat perplexed, I asked, "What are the specifications you are thinking of presenting to his artistic skill?"

"Nothing," he answered, "that isn't to be found here as well: symmetry, flexibility, lightness—but of a higher degree; and particularly a natural arrangement of the centers of gravity."

"And what advantage would this puppet have over living dancers?"

"Advantage? First of all a negative one, my dear friend; and that is that it would never behave *affectedly*. For affectation appears, as you know, when the soul (*vis motrix*) can be found at some point other than the center of gravity of movement. Because the operator controls only this point with the wire or thread, all the other limbs are what they should be: dead, mere pendulums, governed only by the law of gravity—an excellent quality hard to find in most of our dancers.

"Take, for example, P., the one who dances Daphne," he continued. "Pursued by Apollo, she turns to look at him. Her soul seems to be in the small of her back; she bends as if she's going to break, like a naiad after the school of Bernini. Or look at young F., who dances Paris. When he stands among the three goddesses and offers the apple to Venus, his soul is located (and it is a fright to perceive) in his elbow.

"Such mistakes are unavoidable," he said, "now that we have eaten from the Tree of Knowledge. But Paradise is locked and the cherubim behind us; we have to travel around the world to see if it is perhaps open again somewhere at the back."

I laughed. Certainly, I thought, the human spirit can't be in error when it doesn't exist. But I could see that he had more to tell me and asked him to continue.

"In addition," he said, "these puppets have the advantage of being practically weightless. The inertia of matter, that property most resistant to the dance, does not affect them, for the force which raises them into the air is greater than the one which draws them to the ground. What would our dear G. give to be sixty pounds lighter, or if a weight of this size came to her aid while she performed her entrechats and pirouettes? Puppets, like elves, need the ground only so that they can touch it lightly and renew the momentum of their limbs through this momentary delay. We need it to rest on, to recover from the exertions of the dance, a moment which is clearly not part of the dance. We can only do our best to make it as inconspicuous as possible."

I said that, regardless of how cleverly he might present his paradoxes, he would never make me believe that a mechanical puppet could be more graceful than the human body.

He said that it would be impossible for man to come anywhere near the puppet. Only a god could equal inanimate matter in this respect; and here is the point where the two ends of the circular world meet.

My wonderment increased, and I didn't know what to say to such extraordinary claims.

It seemed, he said as he took a pinch of snuff, that I had not read the third chapter of the Book of Genesis carefully enough; if a man wasn't familiar with that first period of all human development, it would be difficult to discuss the later ones, not to mention the final one.

I told him that I was well aware of how consciousness could disturb the natural grace of man. Before my very eyes, one of my young acquaintances had lost his innocence, all because of a chance remark, and had never again, in spite of all conceivable efforts, been able to find his way back to its paradise. But what conclusions, I added, can you draw from that?

He asked me to which incident I was referring.

About three years ago, I related, I was at the baths with a young man who at the time was remarkably graceful in all respects of his education. He was about fifteen years old, and only faintly could one see in him the first traces of vanity—as a result of the favor shown him by women. It just so happened that in Paris we had seen a statue of a young boy pulling a thorn from his foot; the cast of the statue is well known and can be found in most German collections. Now, just as my young friend was lifting his foot on to a stool to dry it, he was reminded of the statue while he looked into a tall mirror; he smiled and told me what he had discovered. I had, in fact, noticed the same thing at the same moment. But—I don't know if it was to test the security of his grace or to provide a salutary counter to his vanity—I laughed and said that he must be seeing things! He blushed and raised his foot a second time in order to show me, but the attempt failed as anyone might have suspected it would. Somewhat confused, he raised his foot a third time and then a fourth; he raised it probably ten times: in vain! He was unable to reproduce the movement—what am I saying? The movements he made were of such a comical nature that I could barely contain my laughter.

From that day, beginning at that very moment, an inconceivable change came over the young man. He stood in front of the mirror for days. One attraction after the other left him. Like an iron net, an invisible and incomprehensible power enveloped the free play of his gestures. After a year had passed, nothing remained of the grace which had previously given pleasure to those who saw him. There's a man still alive who was a witness to that strange and unfortunate event. He can confirm it, just as I have described it, word for word.

"At this juncture," said Mr. C. amiably, "I have to tell you another story, and you'll easily see how it fits in here.

"While on my way to Russia, I spent some time on the estate

of a Livonian nobleman, Mr. von G., whose sons were just then passionately interested in fencing. The elder in particular, who had just come back from the university, was somewhat of a virtuoso. One morning when I was in his room, he offered me a rapier. We parried, but it just so happened that I was better than he. His passion caused him to be confused. Almost every thrust I made found its mark, and finally his rapier flew into the corner of the room. As he picked it up, he half-jokingly, half-irritatedly, said that he had met his master. But then he added that there was a master for everyone and everything and that now he intended to lead me to mine. His brother laughed loudly and called out, 'Go ahead, go down to the stall!' Together they took me by the hand and led me out to a bear that their father, Mr. von G., was raising on the farm.

"Somewhat astounded, I walked up to the bear. He was standing on his hind legs, his back against the post to which he was chained, his right paw raised ready for a battle. He looked me straight in the eye. That was his fighting posture. I wasn't sure if I was dreaming, since I was standing face to face with such an opponent. 'Go ahead, attack,' said Mr. von G. 'See if you can hit him!' When I had recovered somewhat from my surprise, I lunged at him with my rapier. The bear moved slightly and warded off my thrust. I tried to mislead him by feinting thrusts, but the bear did not move. I attacked him again with all the skill at my command. I most certainly would have left my mark on a human breast, but the bear moved only slightly and warded off my thrust. I now felt the same as had the young Mr. von G. The bear's seriousness robbed me of my composure. I alternately thrust and feinted; sweat poured off me: all in vain! He not only averted my thrusts like the finest fencer in the world, but made no move when I feinted to deceive him. This was something that no fencer in the world could equal. He stood, his paw still raised for battle, his eye fixed on mine as if could read my soul in it, and when my thrusts were not meant seriously, he didn't move.

"Do you believe this story?"

"Of course," I said, applauding joyfully. "I'd believe it from any stranger, it's so probable! And all the more so from you!"

"Now, my dear friend," said Mr. C., "you have everything you need to understand my argument. We see that in the organic world,

as reflection grows darker and weaker, grace emerges more brilliantly and commandingly. But just as the section drawn through
two lines suddenly appears on the other side of a point after passing through infinity, or just as the image in a concave mirror turns
up before us again after having moved off into the endless distance, so too grace itself returns when knowledge has gone through
an infinity. Grace appears purest in that human form which has
either no consciousness or an infinite one, that is, in a puppet or
in a god."

"Therefore," I said, somewhat bewildered, "we would have to
eat again from the Tree of Knowledge in order to return to the
state of innocence?"

"Quite right," he answered. "And that's the last chapter in the
history of the world."

Translated by Christian-Albrecht Gollub

From Twelve Lectures on Rhetoric

Adam Müller

Lecture VII—On German Language and Writing

As nature intends, I have given honor and precedence to the living word. I have laid an especially great stress upon this sublime matter with regard to Germany—because our nation has deserted the living word and because among all European states the Germans, especially, have granted the most to the pen's supremacy. But mainly I have stressed this matter because Germany is especially ordained for the living word. And because Germany above all others could show the word's power and infinite mobility!

In an earlier lecture, where it was appropriate, I complained about the innumerable dialects, idioms, scholarly and socially cliquish forms of our language. No European language has been so variedly individualized according to the conditions and locations, the mountains and the valleys, as well as according to the border contacts with its neighbors. No language has been expressed in such heterogeneous material. How would it be, and would I still complain about those dialects, if this language had a core in which all those peculiarities could meet, in which all the breadth and shortness, all the hardness and softness, all the roughness and gentleness, all the cultivation and all the innocence of the various German dialects could harmonize among themselves? Thus, how would it be if, by means of contact and interconnection, the unequal would be ennobled, if the immense scale of expressions

246 · *Adam Müller*

and tones in this language really could present itself in a single voice, and if all sharp contrasts were subdued and tempered among themselves in such a way that they would be subordinated to the same harmonious and philosophical law?

The universal does not originate by a casting off of the particular. Virtue does not originate through an annihilation of those powers which, through their misuse, procreate vice. Language's perfection does not originate through a mere differentiation of the dialects, as was believed thirty years ago. Then, one presumed to brand a single Meissen or Thuringian dialect as the main dialect— *Hochdeutsch,* as one called it—and one wanted to find in this dialect's constant purification and polishing the whole cultural-linguistic business! It is not true that, with the Tuscan dialect's cultivation, everything has been done in Italy now which could be done for the language of that magnificent country, even though Florence could demonstrate a much better calling as a legislator of Italy's language than Meissen or Thuringia for Germany. In Florence and the neighboring towns, everything great and important which Italy's soil has produced really has converged repeatedly. Florence lay in the midst of the power, the wealth, I might even add in the midst of that country's destinies. But there, too, the higher spirit and the vital principle of language gets lost if one would choose to check the vital forces' course which must flow into the center incessantly from all borders and shores of the country.

What would purity and smoothness be without power? What would beauty of form be without character? And how do we obtain the language's power and character other than by allowing the most lonely mountain valleys, the remotest shores, and all the places in which man expresses himself with his voice, according to nature, to have an incessant effect on the center, and other than by allowing culture to be refreshed constantly by innocence?

One imagines the business of the refining and cultivating of a language to be so easy because one forgets language's sacred nature! Is it, then, merely the Austrian's incivility that he does not speak Standard German [*Hochdeutsch*], or the Neapolitan's that he does not speak Tuscan? Does not every province of a country have its very weighty reasons when it forms the tones so differently? Can the Swiss, in an arbitrary manner, change the fact that the broad, rough tones of his fellow countrymen in the mountains and the style of his national chronicles appeal more to him than that Saxon book language which, worst of all, has in reality only been written, but never spoken?

For many years, I have concerned myself with German pronunciation; yet, today I am not able to name a place in Germany where the language is spoken well, or at least better than elsewhere. I have, indeed, come across persons of whom it would be said in Swabia, in Franconia, in Saxony, at the Elbe's mouth, as well as in Austria: they speak well. But no locality has this privilege to itself. The localities are, so far as language is concerned, equally good. In a truly republican manner, each region must carry weight. All the localities must lend their voice if a good German speaker is to come into existence. And so I have always found that those who spoke well had lived and spoken in quite different places in Germany. They had perceived and felt what is really German hidden under the roughness of the mountain tones and hidden under the soft, Low German sounds which the German lowland speaks. In the towns and in the country, at the southwestern borders where the Romance languages touch Germany, and at the northeastern borders where the Slavic languages touch Germany— in short, out of the most various dialects, they had perceived and felt what is really German.

Now if what they had heard were to be written down, then this would be the best German indeed for today and for tomorrow— the richest, noblest, and, in the higher sense of the word, the most cultivated German. But for the more distant future as well? Certainly not. A dictionary extracted from such good and living languages cannot acquire legislative power over a people that is innerly free. It is better if such a cultivated language flows back again into its dialects and incessantly refreshes itself anew in nature's bath. It is better if whatever effort, diligence, and skillfulness have attained always rejoin nature's ancient voice, the voice of the mountains and valleys. It is better if this genuine and living Standard German [*Hochdeutsch*] does not, in an ignoble way, constantly intermingle with its dialects but unites with them. Thus, no dictionary can help and no capital city can help, which can only nourish the delusion that in linguistic matters there are privileged places. No academy can help. An academy's entire art would, indeed, consist merely in the cleaning, polishing, and refining of the language, and in prescribing a strict diet for it, and in producing an artificial meagerness. For the language, one must speak, must travel, must learn how to listen to its dialects. One must learn how to perceive (from the Austrian, Swiss, Frankish, and Lower Saxon dialects, etc.) what is German. The greatest authors and speakers of the German language—Goethe, Schiller, Herder, Johann Müller, Gentz, etc.—owe a great part of their linguistic ability to the fact that they had lived here and there in Germany, or that they had been transplanted from the North to the South, from the West to the East of the country. How would our language, above all, be able to charm everyone with its variety, with all of life's thousandfold customs and modes which it now expresses individually, if only the dialects really had been mingled well with each other for twenty years, or if only the naive roughness of its natural tones and dialects were no longer separated from the cultivated flatness of the Standard German [*hochdeutschen*] book language. And then, through each series of tones in this thus ennobled third, middle language, *Germany* would resound. Whereas, for all that, one always hears only Paris (i.e., France, incessantly converging towards one capital) resounding through the French language.

So Germany would be if she spoke. But as matters are now, she does not speak, does not listen, but *writes* and reads. I have saved my soul by saying what we lack and how matters ought to be. Now, to be sure, I must deal with what exists—with our nation's art of writing, since at present there is not much to praise about its art of speaking. I have indicated sufficiently what I think about our correct writers of Standard German [*Hochdeutsch*]. Thirty years ago, they already appointed themselves reciprocally as classical authors. They undertook to govern literature in *Allgemeinen Deutschen Bibliotheken* and *Gelehrten Zeitungen;* they declared their meeting to be the golden age of literature, without hesitation and without further asking the nation itself. But if we look at the nation's real writers, then we are forced, not only in our country but also in our neighboring countries and in literature in general, to differentiate between two very different forms of eloquence. For the sake of distinctness, I must refer to an author who unites both forms in himself—Goethe. Compare the eloquence in *Werther* and in *Wilhelm Meister*. You will notice a great difference. There is a certain cothurnus, a noble solemnness in the style of *Werther*, whereas *Meister*, like the antique comedy, seems to go only in socks. As to grace, loveliness, and mobility, *Wilhelm Meister* will carry off the prize; as to dignity, decorum, and a certain omnipresent fullness of the breast, that novel cannot be compared to *Werther*. It certainly cannot be overlooked that *Werther's* author is a little too deeply entangled in life's seriousness and that, on the other hand, *Meister's* author has elevated himself a little too mischievously, playing above life. Nor can it be overlooked that the former stands a little drunk below, the latter a little too sober above the level of the quiet life and that *Werther's* author is too deeply enmeshed in life's mystery, whereas the author of *Meister* undertakes a little too boldly to imitate the meshing of destiny's nets. It cannot be overlooked that, in *Werther*, Goethe is much more an orator than a poet, although he places the opponent of his hero and his hero's love a little unrhetorically in the shadow. And although he treats Albert, the society of Ratisbon, the laws of civil order, and everything which strives to enter into the hero's fanciful dreams a little harshly, it cannot be overlooked that, in *Meister*, Goethe is much more a poet than an orator. But we will disregard the poet's mind. It seems to me that there is the same difference between the style of *Werther* and *Wilhelm Meister* as between J. J. Rousseau and Diderot. Nobody will fail to recognize the same cothurnus, the same solemnness and self-controlled dignity in Rousseau as in *Werther*. On the other hand, he will recognize something closely related to *Wilhelm Meister*, something pleasing, light, mobile, amusing in Diderot's style. One must be a German in order to feel and to appreciate the style of *Meister;* one must be a Frenchman in order to feel and appreciate Diderot's style. But every cultivated citizen of our continent is susceptible to *Werther* and Rousseau and is capable of a true judgment on that point. This important difference we express in the following manner. There are two kinds of pens. *One* pen wingedly accommodates itself to all change of times and forms without exactly being transmuted in the manner of Proteus. Nevertheless, according to the subject, this pen becomes serious, light, extraordinary, ordinary, deep, and shallow—in short, becomes, in a certain sense, all that it depicts. This pen rules in *Wilhelm Meister* and in Diderot.

The *other* pen which, on the contrary, is wielded like an iron pencil, like the stylus of the ancients, is the one which should engrave, as in wax or in wood and stone for eternity, eternal feelings and thoughts. Above all, however, it should engrave the author's serious opinions. If the winged pen receives its law rather from things, circumstances, from nature—in short, from the *eye* of man, then it is rather the mind, it is the *heart,* which leads the hand which writes with that second, iron pen.

Let us leave Rousseau, Diderot, and Goethe and choose for our understanding still higher examples. Who does not remember that pen which, at the end of the most unsurpassable of all novels, *Don Quixote,* is hung up as a souvenir by the author himself in the consciousness of success, like a gloriously wielded weapon, like the sword which the author carried in the Battle of Lepanto? Can I have meant by my winged pen another, less important pen? Is there a mood in nature, is there any sort of shading in life's infinite chiaroscuro, can a human face in all its transformations express an emotion, is there a temperature from the feverish chill to the highest ardor of passion which the human heart can actually endure which this pen were not able to reproduce? And, yet, this pen never repeats nature. And, yet, we do not get back merely for a second time what is found outside in things. We really receive nature secondhand with that quite different, deeper intelligibility which the world assumes when we see it being reflected from the artist's soul. The child seeks the sun, but the sun dazzles. The child gets accustomed to looking at illuminated nature, but to avoid the sun's direct light. But nature also dazzles, dazzles and disperses if one looks at it too long. We need a second, milder reflex; and, finally, we return to that person whom the ray of nature illuminates in the same way as the ray of the sun illuminates nature, i.e., we turn to the artist. From the artist now, we receive an intelligible and clear reflection which is of the proper mildness and calmness, without dazzling and without dispersion. That is—I must repeat it once again—what Milton has Eve ask so tenderly and beautifully when Jehovah wants to teach her how to speak: she asks that she should be allowed to learn from Adam because she understands him better. The world, humanized by the artist's hand, expresses itself most perceptibly in thoughts, in images, and especially in living words; but even the mute pen, by means of apparently very monotonous movements, can express what I have described. The mute pen can be expressive because Cervantes's style has been expressive. But Cervantes would not be able to do this solely by means of the pen. That a god can speak also through the hand we know as a matter of fact from Cervantes. Also, the winged pen must be led by sacred opinions if it is to accomplish its greatest, although the opinions themselves need not be prominent.

Regarding the other pen, which I called the *iron* one, I could quote Bossuet, I could quote Machiavelli. Let me return, however, to the one who stands next to my heart, next to my inclination, and next to all our worry—to Burke. His reflections on the French Revolution—which one may read in German or in English because the masterly translation often leaves it doubtful to whom this great work belongs more, to the German mind or to British eloquence—show very clearly what I call the iron pen. For this kind of style, the old metaphor of the river is particularly valid. Whereas the winged style presses in from all sides and around all forms like the air, and like the air deeply penetrates into the matter and arbitrarily changes its own state, its climate, so the other style eternally flows identical with itself and equally clear and equally deep, in one direction, from an elevated side, like a river's water. There is in all the language's fluidity a certain iron direction, which runs like an arrow towards a definite target. I wish to be understood correctly: I mean not only in the thoughts and the opinions about which I do not speak here, but also the word, expression, and everything the pen gives are directed toward a definite side. The iron style stands and runs as in battle array toward its definite enemy, whereas in the winged style the words stretch, bend, and sway in all directions and group themselves freely and playingly. All moments of nature occur in Cervantes's style, whereas Burke's froths and roars, here in a certain sublime uniformity, and there it moves on with quiet power and reflects the stars of the sky more mildly, but always makes itself heard clearly by a certain gentle-harmonious billowing of the waves.

Let us return from the most sublime examples to the most immediate ones. Is not that winged pen exactly the charm of all writings which proceed from feminine hands? What is it that enchants us in Madame de Sévigné's letters other than this soft, tender, and yet so sensitive, coaxing, and yet so serious touching on all situations of life? This lady moves in a seemingly limited world. It is the heart's secrets and labyrinths and then, again, the heart's manifold collisions with the world and with society. But how flexibly does this pen "wind around" all of life's forms—its writing *breathes;* like lightly stirred airs, the words play in confusion. Lady Montagu's letters are just the same. All things, past which her marvelous journey leads, appear in the most distinct outlines, as though looked at through a very clear Southern air. Therefore, it is also so natural for women that they love the basically purposeless letter writing, the carrying to and fro of quiet *Weltanschauungen* and of each experience of the heart, whereas most men do not put pen to paper for a letter without a strong reason. There must exist something which can be moved, be shifted, be gotten, be gained by means of legal proceedings, if a letter written by a man is to be mailed.

In the course of our examination of this important distinction between the two main kinds of style, are we not also forced back to that which I stated to you as the scheme of all human distinctions in general? Can I find for the cumbersome expression "winged pen" a more significant name than "feminine pen"? And for the iron pen, a better one than "male pen"? Is it not true that the male destination, as a whole, includes being directed in each moment towards a definite purpose, with all the soul's thoughts, skills, and inclinations? Whereas the female existence, limited to a narrow sphere, plantlike, I might even say, grows outwards in all directions and gently bows itself under the storms of the elements in which it lives, bows in all directions and does not directly intervene in the activities of the rest of the beings, but brings and gives flowers, fruits, and fragrance in the soft course of the seasons.

This is exactly the feeling which (amidst all the turmoil of the richest, most colorful life) Cervantes leaves behind—at the end, where he hangs his pen beside his weapons. It is the feminine qualities—let us say it frankly now—the *characteristic poetic* of Cervantes's style which attracts the educated man in such a way; whereas the women—although they themselves write with the winged pen—if they follow their natural inclination, nevertheless prefer to read the products of the more austere, prosaic pen. There are a hundred women who prefer to read *Clarissa, Héloïse,* and *Werther* to one who prefers to read *Meister* or *Don Quixote.* Thus we have touched again the area of poetry. Furthermore, the style of *Don Quixote* or *Wilhelm Meister* belongs as little as the content, as the thought of these works, to the area of rhetoric. Finally, we would find ourselves restricted to an utterly male, serious, and uniform condition; we would find ourselves forced out of free fantasy's area into civil and public life, into the tumult of the marketplace and the *ecclesia*. For the sake of justice, which is our highest law, we had to separate the two kinds of style; for how much injustice has been committed since people, on the one hand, starting from the ideal of a certain uniform classical style, did not want to admit that the romantic play of the poetic pen was a true art of speech and was a style. On the other hand, they did not want to acknowledge as a pen at all—compared to the poetic pen— the one which has to do with the seriousness of practical life, as it expresses itself in the written transactions of the citizens, peoples, and in scholarship.

A great fellow countryman, Johannes von Müller, who died recently, stood on a strange threshold between both kinds of style. Nevertheless, he never took off the cothurnus of which I spoke, even though he often seemed to change his mind's form and direction. He belongs to rhetoric. During each moment of his life, he strove in a manly manner toward definite purposes. But a certain poetic susceptibility induced him to change his aim so often that he sometimes emits the false semblance of a poet, however much his sound nature innerly opposed such semblance (like all lies in general). Not often has such a mass, not perhaps of knowledge— since this concept would be too dry and too cold for the vital warmth, for the enthusiasm with which this man knew what he knew—but of life's pictures crowded into a human soul as they did into his. Despite a certain insusceptibility for the poets themselves, which was peculiar to him, seldom has an orator been able to animate, to complement the words of the ancient ages as he did. Seldom has any human ear been able to discriminate the voices of antiquity in such a way as did his ear. I might even call him a conjurer in the same way as I called Burke a seer of antiquity. In his early youth, the study of history appealed to him, attracted him, and, unfortunately, enchanted him for his whole life with certain magic formulas of glory, of friendship, and of freedom, and with a constant battle cry and call to arms. With those formulas, which he did not utter without a certain solemnity, he himself coaxed back and conjured up the spirits of antiquity. What was toilsome work for Müller was a natural state of the soul for Burke. Therefore, Burke knew how to call and dismiss the spirits, whereas Müller conjured them up, gathered them in ever-denser masses around him, until he finally lost himself in the crowd. To Burke they appeared as spirits and glorified, so to speak; to Johannes Müller they appeared in a certain undue clearness, with a semblance of ordinary life and in its colors and manner, so that they themselves occupied a place and confused the world and the era in which Müller stood and to which they did not belong.

This excellent man called his study of history a stride through the centuries, and he was of the opinion that the way stood free to return to his native country at will. He did not feel how he was confused by the overly great clarity of his soul's eye. He drew the outlines of the individual figures so exactly, he made himself at home instantly, I might say, in every lodging of his wandering around the world in such a way that it was painful for him to tear himself away from it. Thus, his whole life became an uninterrupted chain of vehemently taken-up friendships and bitter separations, of undue hopes and untimely despairs. Besides a heart which instantly took roots where he stood and began an edifice as if for remote centuries after him, nature had given him the unfortunate gift of a winged imagination which carried him too easily from one country into the other, from one century into the other. Consequently, he possessed a quality in excess which I demand from the orator—empathy for his opponent. This spokesman of his century, with his divine talent for the language, could lead no great cause, plead no great suit, because he embraced his opponent too vehemently, because he entered too deeply into the need and into the situation of his adversary. Therefore, he displayed an unembarrassed attitude and astonishment when anyone reproached him that he had left his party. In his soul, both friend and foe were excellent people; basically, there was no struggle between them because they both had inflamed and bribed his imagination in the same way. So he appears at his life's end arrayed against the side toward which the entire activity of his life's more beautiful half was directed. And nothing accompanied him into death but the touching belief in that idea for which he had found in his rich life no other name but the incomplete name of friendship.

He had felt life in friend and foe, at least the beat of the heart, although not higher life. Why should he not die with the belief that they would have reciprocal feelings in the future, even if his beautiful soul bled because he left them behind in disunion and because of the belief that it was not given to him to walk hand in hand with the masters of the earth, or to elevate himself together with them above the earth on fame's sunny cloud?

Johannes von Müller's life is a great, instructive example for us at this point in our reflections! We have strictly separated rhetoric from poetry. We have taken away from rhetoric the wings which carry us away over countries, oceans, and times. We have fixed rhetoric in the present and restricted its scope to the seriousness of life, to civil acts. Rhetoric could not recognize its essence without poetry in the same way as a man does not recognize what he is until his social intercourse with women. We had to repudiate the traditional theories of rhetoric because they look at rhetoric alone, because they isolate rhetoric from its opposite and separate it from its relation to poetry.

The fate of Johannes von Müller's great oratorical talent showed the difference between rhetoric and poetry in a more lively way than this cold and dead theory. He did not know, he did not understand poetry's characteristics. Listen to him talk about Homer, whom he admires. He does not treat him like a poet, but like an orator, who has definite purposes of instruction, of political enthusiasm. He does not understand poetry's female nature, mysterious in itself. He does not understand the independence of poetic products. Otherwise, I would not know how to explain the entire problem, the enigma of his character, his rich poverty, his fainthearted determination, the quick vanishing of his enthusiasms, the effeminate hardness of his style, his faithless faith, and, above all, the lack of taste, even in his most excellent works. The people's laws interested him much more than their customs. But only the poetic art opens the view into the people's secret households, of which, strictly speaking, nothing is related in Johannes von Müller's stories.

So much for a great man's defects. For our understanding, a clear picture of what he had been and also an analysis of his nature was necessary. This business (accomplished not without emotion) by which we sought to summarize all the genuine orator's features that we had sketched in earlier lectures, reminds us to say now that through his life, among all errors, he had aimed at what is highest of all, and that he also had felt the nearness of the divine in many great moments of his eventful life. There was something Promethean in him; he carried the fire of heaven in his breast; but to behold the features of the divine itself was denied to him. He knew and understood the bellicosity of earthly powers, but the breeze of their peace never really cooled his restless soul. Because he looked nature herself in the face, she, therefore, dazzled him everywhere and always. I repeat, nature can calm only if she is reflected from the soul of the artist, the poet. Burke's social life was divided between the artists and the orators of his fatherland. No recent Englishman has understood Shakespeare and the poets of antiquity as he did.

*Translated by Dennis R. Bormann
and Elisabeth Leinfellner*

On the Origin of Language

Jacob Grimm

(Read at the Prussian Academy of Sciences
9 January 1851)

The question, the object of which I have just indicated and which was already placed in competition eighty years ago, recently was proposed twice to the Philosophic-Historical Class [of the Academy] by a great philosopher in our midst. That is, Herr von Schelling suggested that such an assignment be repeated now, but immediately thereafter withdrew the suggestion. Soon thereafter, he gave us information in a lecture of his own about the dissatisfaction that Hamann had displayed toward Herder's prize essay, crowned by the Academy, as well as samples from a Latin poem by a still unknown author about the origin of language. It is greatly to be regretted that in so doing, he nowhere wants to give his own view or hint at it; from that new prize competition, if it were firmly grasped and closely unfolded, one would probably be able to deduce a good bit, as it hardly seems possible to render such a suggestion concretely without the opinion of the formulator of the question, and of such a formulator, breaking through in its design. There is only one thing that we can presume without a doubt, that Herder's solution, at least for our time, does not satisfy him at all, for otherwise it would have been superfluous to bring it up anew.

No matter how inclined or indisposed one may be towards the results achieved and achievable in 1770, it cannot be disputed that since then the position of linguistic research has been changed essentially or totally, and therefore even the attempt may seem desirable to apply what research offers us today to that question in

258 · Jacob Grimm

a renewed answer, since the greater cultivation and finer development devoted to any object drawn into philosophical or historical
observation must affect it favorably. Nowadays, all linguistic studies find themselves incomparably better positioned and equipped
than at that time, indeed, one can say that only in our century
have they developed into a true science. The manner in which classical languages formerly were handled, and in truth are usually
still cultivated (as is not inappropriate also to the other goals of
philology highly respected by me), never or merely coincidentally
led to general and decisive conclusions about the relationships of
languages to one another. The effort was made to penetrate into
the essence of the Latin or Greek tongue as far as was necessary
to grasp the spirit of precious monuments admirable for all times
that those languages had produced and transmitted to us, and to
gain possession of this spirit takes a great deal. The very powerful
outer manifestation and form of language acted to serve such a
goal; to perceive in it what went beyond idiom, beyond the technique of the poets and the contents of the works was virtually of
no concern to classical philology, and of all observations in finer
detail, practically only those seemed valuable to it that were somehow able to help textual criticism to firmer rules. The inner texture of the language was not attractive for its own sake, and its
beauty and abundance was virtually presupposed, wherefore even
the most striking word formations remained mostly unregarded, if
they were presented clearly according to its concepts. Somewhat
as the poet, fully in control of and wielding his language, requires
practically no knowledge of its inner structure nor even less of its
historical changes, and only now and again chooses a strange word
to which he has allotted an opportune place; the grammarian too
was only as an exception on the track of a root of a word formation offensive to him, on which he was exercising this art. This
explains why for centuries the unremittingly continued observant
treatment of the Latin and Greek language, in schools as well as
in the studies of the scholars, advanced so little with simple study
of morphology and bore fruit almost only for syntax, lying halfway outside of grammar. Neither was it understood why these
two classical languages had to stimulate us so powerfully to hold
their figures sharply up to each other, and to discuss each one
reciprocally from the other with equal justification, since the Latin

language was wrongly considered to be the submissive daughter of the Greek; even less to raise up our native tongue, which had to perform the drudgery of an incompetent underling in our schools, let alone granting it the third place in esteem, although from three given points a figure can be drawn, from the relationships of three related languages a living law can be found.

The study of language has been compared often and not without reason to that of the natural sciences; they resemble each other even in the manner of the imperfection or the excellence of their conduct. For it strikes the eye that just as those philologists research the monuments of classical languages to gain critical rules for the emendation of damaged and spoiled texts, the botanists too originally designed their science in order to discover healing powers in individual herbs, the anatomists cut into bodies to become certain of the inner structure, upon the knowledge of which the restoration of damaged health could be supported. The subject matters were attractive as a means, not for their own sake. But gradually a change in views and procedures took place. Since it is natural and is confirmed by all experience that humans pass over what is native and meets their eyes daily, and are touched more strongly and are stimulated to observation by what is foreign and new; the assertion is thus permissible that through travels abroad as well as the importation of rare, foreign plants into our gardens and the resettling of various creatures from far continents in Europe, the sciences were given a new cast, and in examining these objects refrained from those practical goals and became involved in freer and therefore more scientific investigations. For that is indeed the true sign of science, that it cast its net for results from every angle and seize upon every perceptible peculiarity of things, set them down and subject them to the most stubborn testing, no matter what will issue from them finally. Linguistic science, it seems to me, on the same path that lifted the analysis of plants and animals from their narrower standpoint and raised them to a comparative botany and anatomy, has finally experienced an equally energetic upheaval. Without doubt, the Petersburg dictionary sponsored by Empress Catherine from 1787 to 1790, even though it was built upon very insufficient foundations, stimulated and furthered linguistic comparison quite effectively. But far greater influence on this field was exerted by the predominance of the Britons on all continents, firmly established primarily in India, through which the precise understanding of one of the purest and most venerable languages of the entire world, which earlier was virtually unknown, was awakened, secured, and spread. The perfection and powerful order of Sanskrit, although clearing a path to some of the oldest and richest poetry, had to tempt one to become familiar with it for its own sake, and after the ice was broken, and a magnet was found, as it were, to which those shipping out onto the ocean of languages could look, it shone such a bright and otherwise unsuspected light on the widely dispersed languages immediately connected and related to the Indian tongue, that from it a true history of these languages, as never before has met a linguist's eyes, in part already has issued, in part has been introduced, with deeply penetrating and surprising results. And since the effort was being made at the same time to unfold historically our own German language, incomprehensibly little regarded, just as the naturalist must recognize the same forces of the blades and nodules of native grasses that he perceived in foreign plants; so it could not fail that from our own most personal and most immediate standpoint, at the same time, a more lively glance was cast at the neighboring Slavic, Lithuanian, and Celtic languages, which have gradually been given the same historical significance and observation, or doubtless will be. In such a way most, if not all, the links in a great, almost limitless, linguistic chain have been found, which in its roots and inflections reaches all the way to us from Asia, fills almost all of Europe, and even now can be called the most powerful tongue on earth, upon which it progresses irresistibly and which it will someday fill everywhere. At the same time, through its inner structure, which can be followed clearly in it in endless gradations, if any other language is capable, this Indo-Germanic language affords us the most rewarding conclusions about the general course and progress of human speech too, perhaps about its origins.

I am authorized to present the feasibility of this investigation of the origin of human speech as a discrete problem, the success of which may still be doubted by many. If it should be capable of solution, then such doubters may object that our languages and our history should have reached back much farther than they do, for it is credible, indeed it has already been settled, that the oldest monuments of the Sanskrit or Zendic language, like the Hebrew or whatever one chooses to consider the oldest language, are separated by a long period, by many millennia, from the real origin of language or the creation of mankind on earth. How can the beginning of language be measured across such a chasm? Should not the entire question fall into the realm of the impossible?

This objection seems even more logical, when we consider the position and object of natural science, which as just illuminated relates similarly to linguistic research. The former researchers strive to penetrate the secrets of the life of nature, that is, the laws of the reproduction and lifespan of animals, to explore the germination and growth of plants. I have never heard that an anatomist or botanist conscious of his task would have wanted, beyond that, to prove the creation of plants and animals too; at most it can become clear to him that individual animals or plants, in order to attain their purpose completely, had to appear and be created first at a certain place. If then an analogy obtains between creation and reproduction, the two are essentially different from one another as a first and a second act. Eternally renewing reproduction takes place due to a force placed within the created creature, whereas the first Creation happened through a power operating outside of what was created. Reproduction, like steel striking against stone awakening sleeping sparks, calls forth new existence, the conditions and law of which were already created within what is doing the reproducing. But here there seems to be a turning point for precise thought, where natural and linguistic science essentially seem to part ways, and everything that follows will depend on whether we acknowledge language to be something created or noncreated. If it was created, then its origin remains as impenetrable to our gaze as that of the first created animal or tree. But in case it was noncreated, that is, not produced and shared immediately by divine power but through the freedom of man himself, then it may be judged according to this law, indeed, as ensues from its history back to its oldest branch, we are permitted to travel back over that unfilled chasm, over millennia, and, in thought, land on the shore of its source too. The linguistic scientist thus does not need to desist but can go further than the natural scientist, because he subjects a human work to his observation, one based in our history and freedom, not achieved suddenly but in stages, since by contrast created, unfree beings know no history at all and until today behave almost the same way as they did leaving the Creator's hand.

This does express in advance what I would like to have considered as the possible success of my investigation; nevertheless, a number of reasons must be enumerated for it, and moreover, it will not be unwise to precede them with whatever could be said in favor of an origin of language issuing immediately from the Godhead. Because such an origin would be thinkable in a double way, in that God created language as inherent in man or that He revealed it Himself only after the Creation, I will treat first a created and then a revealed language, and then explain more closely why neither is to be assumed.

To assume a created, naturally inherent human language seems attractive, at least from the surface. If we visualize its beauty, power, and variety, as it extends over the entire surface of the earth, then there seems to be something almost superhuman in it, hardly issuing from man himself, much rather something spoiled and impaired here and there under his hands. Do not the generations of languages equal the generations of plants, animals, indeed, of man himself in the almost endless variety of their changing form? Does not language flourish in a good location like a tree whose growth is blocked by nothing and which can spread out toward all sides, and, if neglected, does it not die out like a plant and would languish and wither, if lacking light and soil? The astonishing healing power of language, too, with which it quickly grows over and newly compensates for any damage undergone, seems to be that of true nature in general, and no differently than nature does language know how to make do with meager means, and to provide well: For it is sparing without being stingy, it expends generously and never squanders.

But let us step closer to the proper element of language. Almost all of nature is filled with sounds and tones, how should it not then have been bestowed upon man in the Creation? Do not animals communicate among one another with their voice, just as infinitely varied as that of man, does not the manifold song of the birds ring out through all breezes? Human imagination has attributed true language to animals. The saga even tells us that in the Golden Age the animals were still speaking intimately with humans, that since then they have only been holding back, but speak out in moments of urgency, like Balaam's ass spoke out when injustice was done to her and the Angel of the Lord had appeared. She spoke in the manner of man; other animals are supposed to have conversed with one another in their own language, or, as the saying goes, in their own parlance, which could be heard and understood by whoever had gained access to it through the use of a white snake or a dragon's heart. So after Sigurd slew Fafnir and dipped his fingertips into its heart's blood, the birds in the branches told him what still remained to be done.

We differentiate all of nature into the dead and the live, which is not the same as saying whether it is quiet or loud. Among the elements, only the inert earth is dumb, for air whistles and howls, fire spits, rustles, crackles, we attribute soughing to the sea, babbling, murmuring, splashing to the brook, indeed, its trickling seems to us a prattling and chattering. Like the earth, the rigid stones emit no sound, nor were the living plants, fixed to the ground, incapable of motion, endowed with it: When tree leaves whisper, it is the wind that moves them from the outside. All animals, in contrast, are endowed with movement and feeling, but not all with voice, for fish remain soundless, of the insects, only those make themselves audible that, whirring in flight, push air through their breathing holes or rub their hard wing cases against each other; no voice comes out from within them through their mouth. But a quite particular sound is always characteristic of every more perfect, warm-blooded animal, birds as well as mammals, with which it can announce its sensations of fear, desire, and of pain in turn, luring or warning; some of them, and, indeed, not the four-footed ones more closely related to us, rather birds above all, were granted a sonorous, generally charming, and joyful song. Do not all animal sounds parallel human speech? After all, hoarse, raw, hard human language has been compared to the crowing of the raven, the croaking of frogs, the barking of dogs, and the neighing of horses.

But this animal voice, equal to its animal form even when at its most varied, is visibly impressed within every animal and will be produced by it without having learned it. Let a newly hatched baby bird, taken from the nest, be raised by human hand, it will nevertheless be capable of all the sounds that are characteristic of its own kind, which it has never known. Therefore, the voice assigned to every animal remains always uniform and unchangeable: a dog still barks today the same as at the beginning of Creation, and a lark sweeps upwards with the same trill as it did many thousands of years ago. What was created inborn is ineradicable in character because it was created.

Thus, all animals live and act according to a mysterious drive placed within them that, in itself capable of no intensification at all, from the very beginning borne with its own natural perfection, sometimes unreachable by man. A spider's web is drawn as delicately and symmetrically from the body of the little creature and spread out as the self-grown ribs in a leaf. The honeybee shapes its six-sided cell skillfully time after time, without ever diverging a hair's breadth from its predetermined pattern and building plan. Nevertheless, outside of the dominant instinct of necessity, an analogue of freedom does dwell within animals, which touches them softly, from which they move back immediately into their nature again. When bees have flown out to collect nectar and settle down on a heath, from which they never miss the way home to their hive, surely and at the right time, there may be a few among the swarm that fly astray a few hundred paces and perish, lost: The little freedom has meant their ruin. There are docile animals that man trains for his own purposes, and it is easy to perceive that the more developed that drive towards art was in its development, the less such training can be accomplished. The honeybee or the ant would be insensitive to all human teaching, but the dog, horse, ox, falcon accept it to a certain degree and submit to the will of man. All of them, however, if they were relieved of that, would return to their natural spontaneity and forget what they had learned. All of animal life seems a necessity, from which quivering drills or glances of freedom are not capable of tearing them away; we free men ourselves do not escape it.

The voice with which the animal world was uniformly and unchangeably equipped for all generations accordingly is immediately antithetical to human language, which is always alterable, changes from generation to generation, and must constantly be learned. What man does not need to learn and entering life at once can do by himself, the whimpering, crying, and groaning that remains the same in all peoples, or any other outcry of physical sensation, that alone could be compared to the cry of an animal. But that is not part of human language either, and the tools of language can as little express that as they can the animal cry, it cannot even be precisely imitated.

Next to the case for the immutability of natural sound, we want to make another case for human language not being inherent, and posit that on a battlefield a newly born child of a French or Russian mother is taken up and raised in the middle of Germany; it will begin to speak not French, not Russian, but German, like all the other children among whom it grows up. Its language was not innate in it.

The selfsame humans who, born to us today, acquire all the sounds and peculiarities of our present language, would, having come into the world five hundred or a thousand years earlier, have come into possession of everything that differentiates the language of our forefathers from ours today. The uniqueness of every individual language is thus dependent on the space and time in which those who speak it are born and raised; space and time motivate all change in human language, from them alone can variety and divergence be comprehended of peoples arising from one source. The Tyrolean and Frisian of today will have trouble understanding each other's speech, although their ancestors must have stood closer together, belonging to one and the same stock. Even among people who understand one another, living together unseparated, according to generation and individual, peculiarities and divergences in language nevertheless tend to set in that now show evidence of a considerable volume and stock of words, now a poverty or lack of them, so that to them in general their language must seem a common possession, but at the same time as a particularly private way of expression to some individuals, vastly different from that uniformity of animal vocal ability.

No, language is neither innate nor acquired in man, and in all of its accomplishments and successes, it cannot be equated with the voice of animals; they must have only one thing more or less in common with each other, the basis underlying them, necessarily conditioned by the created body.

Every sound is produced by a movement and vibration of the air, even that elemental rustling of water or crackling of fire was conditioned in the powerful forcible striking together of waves that exerted pressure on the air, or in the consumption of fuels that excited the air. Vocal apparatus is unique to animal as to man, by means of which it is able to effect impressions on the air in various ways, the immediate consequence of which is a regular functional noise. The animal, like man, emits individual, similar sounds; man is capable of developing them far more richly and divergently. The orderly development of sounds we call articulation, and human language seems articulated to us, which coincides with the Homeric epithet for *man—hoi meropes, meropes anthropoi* or *brotoi,* from *meiromai* or *meridzo,* "those who divide their voice," "articulators." But this articulation of sound depends essentially on the upright walk and stance of humans, by means of which they are able to make the individual sounds heard calmly and evenly, whereas animals are bent to the ground:

> Whereas other animals hang their heads and look at the ground, he made man stand erect, bidding him look up to heaven, and lift his head to the stars. (from Ovid: *Metamorphosis*)

The necessary sequence and proportion of these sounds and tones is naturally conditioned, like the scales in music or the sequence and shades of the colors; nothing can be added to their law. For except for the seven basic colors, and the infinite mixing of them, no others are conceivable, nor can anything else be added to the three vowels *a, i, u,* from which *e* and *o* along with all the diphthongs and their compression to mere length arise, nor can the order of the semivowels and consonants, which occur in a countless variety of combinations, be expanded at its base. These primal sounds are inherent in us since, conditioned by the organs of our body, either they are cast from the full chest or breathed through the throat, or are produced with the help of the palate, the tongue, the teeth, and the lips. Some of their conditions are so palpable or physical that it would not be wholly impossible to imitate them through artificial, mechanical devices to a certain degree and to present them plausibly. But since the bodily organs of several animal species resemble those of man, it should not seem strange that precisely among the birds some are capable of grasping and repeating human words exactly; although the rest of their structure diverges further from ours than does that of the mammals, they are closer to us in the upright position of the neck, therefore also have more resonant singing voices, and that particular parrots, ravens, starlings, magpies, woodpeckers, can learn to speak. In contrast, not a single one of the mammals is able to do so; not even the monkeys, so frighteningly similar to us in other ways, although they attempt to imitate many of our gestures, ever hit upon the idea of aping our language. One would think that the species of primates that learn to walk upright would succeed in producing vowels, linguals, and dentals, even if labials were impossible for them because their teeth protrude: but not a trace of their attempting to speak.

Johannes Müller has recently investigated the throats of some songbirds for us and demonstrated what it is that raises and causes their singing. I do not know whether it would be possible for this dissection of the fully formed throats of human singers to grant us impressions that would predict a great development in the ability to sing; or to ask even more, whether an anatomist could succeed in discovering external signs of it in the speech organs of such peoples who use decidedly hard gutterals, or, like the Slavs, learn heavy, sibilant combinations. If that were the case, I would not be disinclined—because such traits can be inherited, as some gestures and shoulder movements pass unconsciously from father to son, or siblings frequently have received the same ability to sing—I would thus be inclined to believe that in the throats of children of specific peoples a physical predisposition for the pronunciation of characteristic sound production is already present, so that the Russian or French child born in Germany would still have trouble with some of our sounds. This would result in the opposite of the limitation of necessity in animals through freedom, to the extent that here the freedom of speech in man would seem to be impaired by an element of necessity, one that it overcomes easily. Anatomy still has much to learn before it can distinguish the speech organs of a North German accustomed to living on the plains from those of a South German Alpine shepherd. But our principal conclusion, that human language is not born into us, is not taken from us by that. The natural basis for sound, which requires voice as do the animals and presupposes it, as the structure of the human cranium does our soul, is nothing but the instrument upon which language is played, and this play occurs in humans in a variety that is com-

268 · Jacob Grimm

pletely at variance with the unchangeable animal sounds. The physiologist will be more attracted by the instrument itself, the philologist more by the playing upon it.

However, an assumption was posited other than that of the inherent nature of language just rejected, namely, that it was imparted to mankind by its Originator, not immediately in the act of creation, to be sure, but rather after the Creation, grasped by human memory and then passed on and worked out from generation to generation, with all the change and deterioration that it had to experience at the hands of man. That divine imparting or revelation of language, comparable to that of a divine law, would nevertheless have had to occur earlier than that, thus almost immediately after the completion of the creation of the first human couple; since they would have been unable to do without language for more than an instant, it would seem incompatible with creative omnipotence that its finished, most noble creatures lacked at the beginning what was later to be imparted to them.

This view would seem to differ essentially in its basis from that of the human origin of language to be opposed to it here, but seemingly only little in relation to the transmission of such a precious gift. Such a transmission occurs from generation to generation, since humans never all die at the same time, just as they come into this world gradually, and consequently those who survive leave to posterity what they themselves have received from their forebears, regardless of whether a language revealed by God or freely acquired by the first humans was being passed down. Revelation needed to occur only once, assuming that it never wholly died out again, but always had continued to cast its light, even if more weakly; invention by man could have been repeated several times. In the case of revealed language, it would be assumed that the first humans, closer to it, had been given preference by the divine power vis-à-vis later humans, who were at a disadvantage, which would contradict God's justice.

The notion of a revealed language, it seems to me, must be welcome to those who posit a condition of paradisical innocence at the beginning of all human history, after which the noblest gifts and abilities of man are ruined by the Fall; consequently, the godlike language, too, must have sunk from its peak and then only passed down weakened to posterity. Such a view could be appealing and gain support because the entire history of language, as far as we have penetrated it, in fact does seem to betray its decline from a perfect form to a less perfect one, and therewith seems to indicate that for language as well as for all of human nature, a restoration and resolution will have to set in and we will gradually have to return to the lost condition of initial perfection and purity on an intellectual path.

Yet we find this interpretation to be already in contradiction with the documents of our holy scripture, which nowhere makes mention of a divine revelation of language to man having taken place, much rather assuming the existence of language left unexplained by scripture itself, and does not have the confusion of language occur until a long time after the Fall. All linguistic discord in language was derived cleverly and movingly from a mighty sacrilege of prideful men who, like the heaven-storming Titans of Greek myth, undertook to move closer to the Godhead by foolishly building a tower, and in so doing lost the simplicity of their language, which, confused now, they carried from the site to all corners of the globe. Recently, a clever painter has attempted to depict, richly composed, this saga, which perhaps grew up from a mere misunderstanding of the Hebrew word *babel,* which means "to mix," "to mingle." But here art can only play, to no avail; since the splintering of language over the entire earth and its endless variety was a highly natural process and advanced the greatest goals of mankind, it can only be called beneficent and necessary, and by no means confusing, and it certainly occurred in a very different way than this tale, which is vulnerable to a loud objection from linguistic history, would have us believe.

Here my investigation touches upon a theological standpoint, which it does not need to fear.

By *revelation,* we understand a communicating or manifestation, the Greeks call it *apokalypsis,* "uncovering," the Romans *revelatio,* "unveiling," and all these words amount to the same concept: What has been made open was closed before, what has been uncovered was covered over or veiled. No one can doubt that a creating primal force also unceasingly continues to penetrate and sustain its work: The miracle of the world's duration matches that of its creation completely. This divine power, unceasingly manifesting itself, is not a perceivable revelation to any rational man. Since it penetrates all of nature and is contained in all things, it is present both openly and concealed and can be investigated through the means of things themselves. For it is within all things, and for that very reason not outside of them. Nature speaks ununderstood, as long as the seeker does not find its track, and it becomes understandable to him.

The childish imagination of antiquity, though, was accustomed to assume the immediate intercourse of the Godhead with man, the reality of which is as incomprehensible and as inadmissible to our reason as that of most other myths. For if the Godhead had shown itself visibly initially, why should it have stopped doing so afterward? This is contrary to the concept of constancy necessarily inherent in it; what is not created can have no history, it must always remain constant. One feels trapped in a circle of contradictions that, even if evident everywhere, hardly ever obtain more harshly than where a divine origin of language is asserted.

It does not disturb Greek poetry in the least that the gods appear and speak in the language of the country, as little as it bothers us on our stage today that heroes and men of all countries express themselves with one voice in the speech of today, since they become vivid only through the means of our own imaginations. But there must have been a reason present why in Homer, as well as in the tragedians, Apollo, Hermes, Athena, and other gods and goddesses do appear bodily and speaking to humans, but never Zeus himself. They present themselves only as his messengers, as it were, who are authorized to clothe and shape the highest will, in itself unutterable in human words; in rank polytheism nothing but obsequious underlings of the highest being appear, whose characteristics they represent, whose commands they proclaim and carry out, like Catholic angels or saints.

In the Old Testament, God appears bodily immediately and speaks with Adam, Eve, Noah, Abraham, Moses (Joshua), who understand his speech spontaneously and are portrayed answering it; nowhere is it said that a first revealing of this understanding took place or was deemed necessary. Yet even in Moses' time, God already begins to place Himself at some remove, to appear only on the mountain, to speak only from the cloud from which thunder and lightning strike, just as the thundering Zeus shows himself in the clouds. Gradually, He tends not to show up in person anymore; rather, the angel of the Lord does; in relation to Moses it is doubtful already on several occasions whether he has heard the voice of the Lord or that of His messenger. Later, God speaks to man only through prophecies and the mouth of angels, whose higher gift could be derived from a closer relationship to God, like the outpouring of the Spirit in the apostles' story (Acts 10: 44–46) loosens tongues immediately, but this does not make the simple origin of long-existing human language comprehensible, even if one wants to attribute the real inspiration of human linguistic practice to that outpouring beyond image. The book from which we take the name of the Apocalypse was sent to John by an angel of the Lord, and the Apostle Paul speaks of the tongues of men and of angels, as Plato has daimons implement the intercourse between gods and men; but all notions of daimons and angels is untestified to in the nature of the world, unfounded in history, no matter how hard the attempt to make it credible.

How should our reason grasp the origin of human language from divine revelation, which necessarily must have been not vigorous inspiration but only simple speech, and must have been passed down by means of this speech? If the first human beings were capable of hearing God's words, that is, of understanding them, then it seems to us unnecessary to disclose a language that they must already have possessed as the condition for that understanding. Yet we have previously proved that no language was born into them, in consequence of which that they were not within reach of a means upon which the understanding depended, that was indispensable to them. The nature of man at the time of the Creation was no different than it is today; he was capable of receiving sensations solely through his senses and through reason, with which he was equipped, sensations that would be inaccessible in any other way. Nowhere does a teaching descend to man so powerfully without an inner learning necessarily coming to meet it.

Even more, should and may we think of God as speaking? If He talked, that is, spoke human words, then we would also have to attribute a human body to Him, indeed all the human organs on which articulate speech is dependent. But it seems as perverse to me to imagine a complete human body without one of its parts, for instance without teeth, as the Godhead with teeth, consequently eating, since the teeth according to the wisdom of nature do help in speaking, but principally serve in chewing food. In such a manner, it would be quite impossible to deprive or attribute to the creating Godhead any of the other parts of the body, whose inner and outer harmony arouses our highest admiration.

But if any body at all, at least a human body, would not be appropriate for the Godhead, how could speech or the need for speech be attributed to it? What it merely thinks, that it also wills, what it wills, it has without delay and doubt, it has performed in more than lightning speed. Why would it have employed a messenger to convey slowly what it would have achieved with a gesture, if that had pleased its wisdom? Do not all those characteristics observed by us, omnipotence, original plan, and its execution run all together in the Divine Being? Without the like of itself, the Godhead rules unlonely everywhere in the endless abundance of nature; it has no need of the aid of any language even distantly comparable to that of man, just as its thoughts do not travel the path of human thought.

That an immediate word from God has ever penetrated to the ear of man as long as the world has existed can be proven by nothing in all of human history. His annunciation would not approach any human language; it would be a harmony of the spheres. Wherever it is written that God was speaking, the historian was following a saga that was making use of an image for the darkness of primitive times; who takes it literally when it is said that God wrote the Law on those stone tablets that Moses broke afterward? The Holy Scripture that we call the word of God is venerable to us because of its great age and the noble simplicity of its portrayal; but whoever it was who wrote it down already stood at such a distance from the beginning of Creation that he was unable to communicate anything but the image and the saga of it. What anyone will admit of heathen sagas, he must also be truth-loving and reflective enough to concede about those of the Old Testament. Arnobius inveighs against paganism with striking grounds, without suspecting that more than a few of them can be used against the new teachings.

The relationship of God to nature rests upon laws as firm and unshakable as the bonds of nature themselves, and since they carry their secret and miracles only within themselves and not outside of themselves, then any nonnatural means must be excluded from them. There is no such thing as a secret that works unnaturally.

It may strike us that neither Greek nor Indic antiquity made the attempt to pose the question of the origin and the variety of human tongues and to answer it. At least the Bible strove to solve one of the two puzzles, the variety, through the Tower of Babel. I know only one poor Estonian folk saga that could be compared to this solution. The old god, when their first home had become too crowded for the first people, decided to spread them over the whole earth, and to issue a particular language to each people, too. With this in mind, he placed a kettle of water on the fire, had the individual tribes step up in turn and listen to the sounds that the imprisoned tormented water was producing as it sang. So here humans were given, if not their first language, at least a new language by the natural sounds of an element.

I have demonstrated, as was the limit of my intention, that human language can as little be a revealed one as it was an inborn one; an inborn language would have made animals of man, a revealed one would have presupposed gods in them. Nothing else remains than that it was a human one, acquired by us ourselves with full freedom concerning its origin and progress: It can be nothing else, it is our history, our heritage.

That which we are, which differentiates us from all animals, bears in Sanskrit the significant, venerable name *manudscha,* which has been preserved to this very day preeminently in our German language, Gothic *manniska,* Old High German *mannisco,* New High German *Mensch,* and thus through all dialects; this word may indeed, with good reason, be traced back to a mythical ancestor Manna, Mannus, to which Tacitus already attests, to an Indian King Manas, the root of which is *man,* that is, "to think," and immediately next to which are found *manas,* Greek *menos, Mensch.*

Man, *Mensch,* is called that not just because he thinks, but he is also man because he thinks and speaks; because he thinks, this very close relationship between his ability to think and to speak indicates and guarantees to us the basis and origins of his language. Earlier, we saw Greek namings of man taken from his upright-positioned countenance, from his articulated speech; here he is named even more appropriately from his thought. Animals do not speak, because they do not think, and therefore are called the unspeaking, Old Norse *ómaelandi* (Danish: *de umaelende*), and the unreasoning, *bruta, mutae bestiae, mutum et turpe pecus;* the Greek *alogos* expresses both unspeaking and unthinking. The child begins to speak when it starts to think, and his speech grows as his thinking grows, both of them not additively but multiplicatively. Humans with the deepest thoughts, philosophers, poets, orators, also have the greatest power of speech; the power of speech shapes peoples and holds them together, without such a bond they would split apart, it is principally the richness of each people's thought that secures its world dominance.

Thus, language appears to be a progressive task, a work, an acquisition of man both swift and slow, to which they owe the free unfolding of their thought, through which they are at once separated and united. Man has God to thank for everything he is, himself to thank for everything he has acquired in good and evil. The inspiration of the prophet is only an image for the thought awakened and wakeful within him. But because language was at first imperfect, and its value was increasing, it cannot have issued from God, Who shapes only what is perfect.

The Creator placed the soul, that is, the power to think, within us, and the organs of speech, that is, the power to speak, as precious gifts, but we do not think until we exercise that ability, we do not speak until we learn language. Thought and language are our property, our nature's ascending freedom rests upon both of them, the *sentire quae velis et quae sentias dicere;* without them, like animals, we would be subject to sheer necessity, and with them we have scaled the heights.

But this language, this thinking, is not isolated for individual humans, rather, all languages are a community that has entered history, and they interconnect the world. Their variety is destined to multiply and to animate the course of ideas. From generations of man eternally changing and renewing, the precious acquisition afforded to all of us is transmitted to our descendants, a possession that posterity is obliged to maintain, to govern, and to increase. For here, teaching and learning interlock immediately and unnoticed. The infant hears its first words at his mother's breast, spoken to him by the mother's soft and gentle voice, and they nestle into his pure memory before he has even gained control over his own organs of speech. That is why it is called the mother tongue, and thus with years its scope is filled in quickly widening circles. It alone conveys homeland and fatherland to us the most ineradicably, and whatever of the individual generations and tribes receive a common linguistic idiom impressed upon it must be valid from then on for all of human society. Without language, the art of poetry, and the invention of writing and the printing of books that occurred at the right time, the best forces of mankind would have wasted away and would have faded. Writing, too, has been called the gods' gift to man; but its convincingly human origin, its growing perfection, if it were necessary, would have to confirm and complete the proof of the human origin of language.

Herodotus reports to us that Psamtik, the king of the Egyptians, in order to investigate which people and which language had been created first, gave two newborn children to a shepherd to raise alone, with the order not to speak a word in their hearing, and to notice what sound they would then produce. After some time elapsed, when the shepherd approached these children, they had called out *bexos* with outstretched hands, and then repeated the same word frequently in the presence of the king. But when inquiries were made, it was learned that the Phrygians call bread *becksos;* therefore the conviction set in that the Phrygians were the oldest people on earth.

If it were possible, for the whole tale sounds highly fantastic, even to undertake such an experiment and to carry it out in that manner, exposing newborn children gruesomely on a remote island and having them raised by silent servants, one would, to be sure, hear no words of the oldest human language, which could by no means have been inborn in them, but these miserable creatures torn from their human heritage could well have invented a language for themselves with their awakening ability to think, starting from the beginning, like the first created humans, and in the case that their isolation could continue, to impart it to their progeny. Only at such a price—which, however, probably would never be paid as long as the earth lasts because numberless hindrances would get in the way—could linguistic research gain immediate confirmation of what it is justified in concluding on other grounds.

I am approaching my actual task, or at least that part of it most attractive to most of my listeners, which is to give the answer to how one should think the first humans effected the invention of their language.

Yet we must first consider briefly whether, quite apart from the problem still remaining peripheral here, to what extent the fundamentally different languages of the earth can be traced back to one formation or to several formations; whether there too, where a single original language is present, widely distributed, and later dividing into many branches, one is to posit only one human couple or more than one through which it was produced and passed on.

It is to be assumed that man and woman together were created mature and capable of reproducing, for the bird does not presuppose the egg, nor the plant the seed, rather the egg presupposes the bird, the seed the plant; child, egg, seed grain are products, consequently not originally created: Thus, the first man was never a child, but the first child had a father. Who would believe that from things noncreated, elements of a secret, silent power combining and working with one another had gradually struggled up toward life? The animating bond, at the disappearance of which life always recedes back into dead substances, must have preceded. But that only one pair and not more was created of every animal, of every plant, that all grasses in their abundance were multiplied from the prodigality of a single blade, has little to be said for itself. The creative force making one pair come into being could have created several at once unimpeded, as it had already been required to bring forth something similar twice in the first couple. Against the issuance of all of animal life from one pair of every species, the social instinct of the ants and bees has been interposed, not without reason, for it must have been inborn in them, and not have developed slowly, and consequently not have waited for the development of the mass. Applied to man and to language, it is even probable that more than one pair was created, even for the natural reason that the first mother could have given birth to nothing but sons or nothing but daughters, which would have stymied all further procreation, even more for the moral reason of avoiding the inbreeding of siblings, which is abhorrent to nature. The Bible passes over the fact in silence that, if Adam and Eve stood alone, their children had to mate with one another.

The origin of language is also explained much more easily if two or three human couples were shaping it immediately, and then their children, so that all linguistic relationships were able to multiply plentifully on the spot; the unity of the resulting rules runs no danger from this because with a single couple, too, man and wife, two individuals had to invent language, and after that their children would be participating. Especially when there were many pairs, one can willingly and from early on even attribute to women, who after a few generations took up customs and positions different from the men, peculiarities in dialect coinages for those concepts familiar primarily to them, as Prakrit attests most precisely for us vis-à-vis Sanskrit. But in all old languages we see masculine and feminine inflections differentiated next to one another, which by no means can have happened without the influence of women on the formation of language itself.

From the relationship of languages, which offers us more certain conclusions about the relationship of peoples than all the documents of history are able to, we can draw inferences leading back to the original condition of man in the era of the Creation and to the formation of language among the first men. It affords the human mind considerable joy to intuit what it can sense and infer by reason, beyond palpable means of proof, for which the external verification is lacking as well. In the languages whose monuments have come down to us from a distant time, we perceive two different and divergent directions, from which a third, preceding them but lying beyond reach of our evidence, must necessarily be deduced.

Sanskrit and Zend, and for the most part Greek and Latin, present the old type of language to us; it shows us a rich, agreeable, admirable perfection of form, in which all sensual and intellectual components are interpenetrated full of life. In the continuations and later manifestations of the same languages, as in the dialects of present-day India, in Persian, modern Greek, and the Romance languages, the inner power and flexibility of the inflections has mostly been given up and disturbed, in part reintroduced through external means and aids. In our German language too, the sources of which, now weakly trickling, now flowing powerfully, can be traced over long periods of time and weighed, the same decline from the earlier high point of greater perfection of form is unmistakable, and the same means of replacement are followed. Let us place the Gothic language of the fourth century next to our present-day language; there we find euphony and adroitness, here, at the cost of them, a much more intensified development of speech. Everywhere, the old force of language appears diminished to the extent that something else has taken the place of the old gifts and means, the advantages of which should not be underestimated either.

These two directions by no means stand sharply counter to one another, and all languages display themselves on manifold, similar, but unequal stages. The diminishing of form, for example, had already begun in Gothic and Latin, and for the one language as for the other one may posit a preceding, older, and richer shape that relates to its classical state as these languages do to New High German or French. Put differently and more generally, a peak of formal perfection attained by the old languages cannot be established historically at all, as little as the contrasting intellectual development of present-day language has reached its completion; it will not have done so for a vast amount of time. It is admissible to posit an older linguistic state even before Sanskrit, in which the abundance of its nature again would have been more purely shaped, which we cannot reach historically at all, but guess at from the relationship of the Vedic forms to the later one.

It would be a damaging mistake, and it seems to me to have had an inhibiting influence precisely in the investigation of the primal language, to place that perfection of form even farther back, all the way into a supposed paradise. Rather, comparing the last two periods of language, it turns out that, just as a dissolution of inflections takes its place, inflection itself must have arisen sometime from a combination of analogically related parts of words. Accordingly, three and not merely two stages of development of human language must necessarily be posited: (1) the formation and growth, as it were, and establishing of the roots and words; (2) the blossoming of a complete inflection; (3) the urge toward thought, whereby the inflections are dropped again as not yet satisfying, and what happened naively in the first era was splendidly prepared in the second; the connection of the words and strict thoughts is effected with clearer consciousness. These are foliage, blossom, and ripening fruit that, as nature demands, appear in unalterable sequence one after the other. Through the sheer necessity that a first, invisible period precedes the two visible to us, it seems to me that the delusion of a divine origin of language is wholly eliminated, because it would contradict God's wisdom to place constraint in advance on what should have a free human history, just as it would have been against His justice to let a divine language bestowed upon the first men sink down from its peak for their descendants. Whatever of the divine that language bears in itself, it has because in our nature and soul something of the divine has also been extended.

With an observation of language only as it appears in the last era, one would never have approached closer to the secret of its origin, and those researching the etymon of a word in the present linguistic state usually fail, since they are capable neither of purely separating out the formative parts from the root, nor of ascertaining the sensual content of it.

Initially, it seems, words developed unhampered in idyllic ease, without any confinement but their own sequence, measured by feeling; their impression was pure and unsought, but still too full and overladen, so that light and shadow could not be distributed correctly. But gradually an unconsciously operating linguistic spirit lets less weight fall upon the subconcepts and thins and shortens them. This is the principal notion as codetermining parts are added on. Inflections arise from the upgrowth of guiding and moving modifiers, and now, like half-covered and almost wholly covered drivewheels, are dragged along by the noun that stimulated them; they have passed over from their originally partly sensual meaning into an abstract one, through which the former is glimpsed only occasionally. At last, when the inflection has worn out, too, and become reduced to a mere unfelt sign, then the lever inserted begins to loosen and, more firmly determined, to be set once more from the outside; language loses part of its elasticity but wins proportion and rule everywhere for the infinitely increased richness of thought.

Only after the successful analysis of inflections and derivations, through which Bopp's insight has won great appreciation, were the roots exposed, and it became clear that, for the most part, the inflections are compressed from the material added to the same words and notions that in the third era usually precede them, unattached. Prepositions and clear compounds are appropriate to this third period, inflections, suffixes, and bolder composition to the second, the first allowed free words, sensual notions, to follow one after the other for all grammatical relationships. The oldest language was melodic bit diffuse and drifting, the intermediate one full of compact poetic power, the new language seeks to compensate for its diminished beauty through the harmony of the whole, and with smaller means is nevertheless capable of more.

The veil cloaking the origin of language is parted but not fully raised. It is neither practicable here nor is it my purpose to present all or most of the proofs for the views propounded, which would demand a heavy book in itself, I am attempting to present only the essential foundations of the investigations.

Nothing in language, just as in nature, which takes it on her lap, as it were, happens in vain; everything, as I say above, is sufficient without squandering. Simple means achieve what is strongest; originally not a letter stands meaningless or superfluous.

Every sound has its natural content, based and coming to application in the organ that produces it. Of the vowels, *a* keeps to the pure middle, *i* the height, *u* depth; *a* is pure and rigid, *i* and *u* are fluid and capable of consonantalization. Obviously, overall a feminine basis must be attributed to the vowels, a masculine one to the consonants.

Of the consonants, *l* designates what is gentle, *r* what is rough. It can be perceived that in many words of the oldest language, *r* rules, where the younger employ *l*, whereas the *s* of the older yields to the *r* of the younger. But never do *s* and *l* mingle. Either the spirit of language intended to fill in a gap that had arisen, or, which seems more likely, both *r*'s are already different in their pronunciation, the former close to *l*, pure and rolling, the latter related to *s*, hoarse and impure.

All consonant geminations are to be denied to the oldest language and only gradually arose through the assimilation of various consonants and especially frequently through an adjacent *i*. Consonantal gradations, which took place most clearly and two times in the sound shifts of the German language, customarily put all the unvoiced sounds back into right place, however, with a marvelous instinct, after displacing them. If natural drive and free force have worked together anywhere in language, then it happened in this most striking phenomenon.

E and *o* were foreign to the original language. If diphthongs and modifications are appropriate to the second era, and umlauts and still other vowel coloring to the third, then one will have to attribute predominantly almost only short vowels and simple consonants to the first. (Every diphthong resulted from two syllables, *au* from *a-u*, *ai* from *a-i*, as especially the history of inflection teaches. Consonantalization appears in between, *av* or *va*, *aj* or *ja*. All modifications presume earlier monosyllabicality; *baira baurans ein bira burans*.)

Yet to discuss the nature of the individual sounds is not my obligation here; this would be more in place where that physical capacity of our organism is to be applied carefully to language.

Pronouns and verbs appear to be the levers of all words. The pronoun is not merely the representative of the noun, as its name could make one believe, but is precisely the start and beginning of all nouns. As the child whose capacity for thought has awakened utters "I," I find it expressly acknowledged in the Yajurveda that the original being speaks "I am I," and that man, when he is called, answered "I am it." All verbs and nouns designating the personal relationship in itself, insert pronouns, as they are expressed externally for that purpose in the third period. When man spoke his *I* for the first time, which in Sanskrit is *aham,* he ejaculated it from a full chest with a throaty breath, and all originally related tongues have remained the same in this, only that they weaken the pure *a* or displace the guttural stage. In the oblique case a half-declining labial *m* appears. The identifying *t* of the second person spoken to, in contrast, remains lodged in the nominative and oblique cases. The farther third person, though, demands greater variety than both the first persons, which stand facing one another, and its principal identifying mark was either *s* or *t*, the former primarily for designating the fluid reflexive concept, which also suffixes onto verbs.

Except for the animating pronoun, the greatest and most specific power of language is in the verb, which exemplifies almost all roots in itself.

All verbal roots, the number of which in the first linguistic era does not have to have exceeded a few hundred at the beginning, but which grew extremely rapidly, contain sensual notions from which analogous and abstract buds, too, were able to open up immediately, as, for example, the concept of life sprouts from that of breathing, that of dying from that of exhaling. The proposition that light and sound flow from the same root is momentous.

But all verbal roots were invented with the simplest outlay of means, by the consonant following or preceding the vowel. Whether roots can consist solely of vowels can still be doubted, since from what was said above concerning the nature of vowels and consonants the generation of a root seems to be dependent on the marriage of both genders. Sanskrit knows no root formed solely from the short *a,* whereas the short *i* is assumed to be the root for *to go* (which is evident in the Latin *i* too, which, however, is long), and short *u* as the root for *to resound;* but consonants could have fallen away from both of them. Among those formed with consonant and vowel, the ones with consonants in initial position seem to precede in age those that have consonants in final position, because those with vowels in final position also tend gradually to add a second consonant, but not to prefix [those with vowels in initial position], for instance, next to the root *ma* a second root *mad* results, which corresponds to Latin *metire,* our German *messen* ("to measure"). It is something different that the breathy initial sounds *v, h,* and *s* tend now to occur in front of liquids, now to fall away; which should one consider the older: the occurring of it, I think.

What vowel and what consonant the inventor wanted to use for a verb, aside from the organic power of the sound breaking out and asserting itself naturally, lay mostly at his will, which would not have happened at all, had it been always and wholly dependent on that influence, but itself could be practiced with finer or coarser feeling. In these simplest laws of formation, we thus see here too necessity and freedom interpenetrating one another. If in, for instance, Sanskrit the root *pâ,* in Greek *piein,* Slavic *piti* expresses *to drink,* then nothing stops a different inventor of language from reaching for *kâ* or *tâ* for it. A great part of Indo-Germanic roots has merely a primal historical right, which only organic determinants can alter. Yet instinctively it was provided that in the individual languages none or few roots identical in sound are chosen for different notions, that is, that the same sounds were not chosen several times by the inventors for basically different notions, which would be vastly confusing. From this we must carefully distinguish, though, the unrecognized and dark relationship of various sensual and abstract concepts that grow out of the letters of one and the same root.

Whether and to what extent roots that have double unvoiced consonants in initial and in final position one might allow in the first era, previous investigations still leave undecided.

For every verb in the second era person, number, tense, mood, and gender can be designated, the persons by added personal pronouns, the tenses mostly through auxiliary words that, originally merely attached, gradually grew on as inflections. Aside from the designation of the past through such an auxiliary verb, repetition of the same root, or reduplication, set in, since what is past naturally finds its expression in repetition. But after the extinguishing of the reduplicating syllable, the German ablaut still is connected intimately with such reduplicating form, and as diphthongs are contracted into a long vowel, the reduplications are into ablauts. In our German preterites formed with the ablaut, one therefore must not think of auxiliary verbs having been assimilated.

All nouns, that is, the names attributed to things or characteristics, presuppose verbs, the sensual concept of which was applied to those, for example, our *Hahn* ("rooster"), Gothic *hana*, designates the crowing bird, thus presupposes a lost verb *hanan* that corresponded to the Sanskrit *kan*, Latin *canere,* and the ablaut of which, Gothic *hon*, Old High German *huon* at the same enlightens us about *huon*, about *pullus gallinacaeus*, New High German *Huhn*. In the same way, the Slavic name of the rooster, *pjetel*, leads back to *pjeti*, "to sing," the Lithuanian *gaidys* to *giedmi*. The wind, Latin *ventus*, Slavic *vjetr*, Lithuanian *vejas*, Sanskrit *vâju* means "the blowing one," from *vâ*, Gothic *vaian spirare*, just like *animus*, to Gothic *anan spirare*, our spirit (*Geist*) belongs to an old *geisan vento ferri; ventus, wind, vjetr* as well as *Geist* ("spirit") have inserted the lingual sound disappearing from *vâju, vejas*, as happened countless times, for example, in our *Hund* ("dog"), too, as against Latin *canis,* Greek *kuon*. Examples stream towards us endlessly from all sides. Our *Bohne* ("bean"), obscure today, stands there rootless like the Latin *faba,* but it is easy to see that *faba* must have issued from *fagba, Bohne* from Old High German *bôna*, consequently, a Gothic *bauna* from *bagbana, bagbuna*, to which Slavic *bob* may be added; to *fagba, bagba* the Greek *phagein* teaches us the correct root: *fagba* was "edible fruit," as was *fagus;* our Old High German *puocha,* New High German *Buche,* and Greek *phake,* "lentil" (German *Linse*) betray the same root.

It was most human and natural that the fashioning of language assigned a gender to every name, either as it was obviously evident in the thing itself or could be attributed to it in thought. In inflections, however, the masculine gender was shaped the most completely and actively, the feminine gender more peacefully and heavily, so that more consonants and short vowels suit the former, long vowels the latter; a neuter generated from both of them, however, shares the peculiarities of both. Through differentiation by gender, rule and clarity is imposed on all situations in which the noun must be placed, in one most fortunate turn, as if by a jolt.

These situations are especially relationships of case and number. Whereas a pronoun designates a nominative case dominant in a sentence, the oblique cases must express their spatial concepts through particles, which are added to the noun like the auxiliaries are to the verb, in time growing together with it and generating various inflections. On account of such narrowing and contraction, long vowels and diphthongs are attributed predominantly to those inflections when they were generated, and as the vowels thinned out, the inflection faded. In the newer languages, we finally see that the faded inflection has disappeared completely or almost completely and been replaced from the outside by articles or prepositions, which make us suspect that the inflection once must have issued from similar components. If the French *le loup* and *du loup* equals the Latin *lupus* and *lupi,* and probably demonstrably comes from *ille lupus, de illo lupo,* then it follows that the final sound *s* contained a pronoun and the inflection *i,* traced back to a full, original form, will produce a particle.

But since the particles themselves, with the exception of the half-animal interjections inherent in the organism, originally were living nouns or pronouns, to which in the course of time abstract functions are attributed, then the living cycle of the language has been completed.

Language can dispense with individual, great advantages, for example can give up the middle and the passive, the optative, many tenses as far as form is concerned, and can make do with clearer circumlocutions instead, or replace the sensual expression with nothing at all, too, for instance, the fine, efficient dual form. For a time, we still reached the Sanskrit *tschakšuší,* the Greek *osse* by means of "both eyes," the Greek *keroin* by means of "with both hands," and the addition proves the naturalness of the old dual; finally "eyes" and "hands" sufficed.

In this address, I have touched upon rich, inexhaustible linguistic relationships only in broad outline, in order to leave room for a general observation of the three periods I have posited. It turns out that human language is in decline only seemingly and in examining some details; overall it must be seen as constantly progressing and increasing in its inner strength.

Our language is also our history. Just as the foundation of a people, of a realm, was laid by individual generations who united, took up common mores and law, acted in league, and expanded the volume of their property; convention thus also demanded a founding first act from which all ensuing ones were derived and to which they could relate. The duration of the community imposed myriad changes afterward.

The state of the language in the first era cannot be called a paradise in the sense usually associated with this expression of earthly perfection; for it lives through practically a plant life, in which the high gifts of intellect are still slumbering or have only half awakened. I may summarize its depiction in the following traits.

Its appearance is simple, artless, full of life, as blood circulates swiftly in a youthful body. All words are short, monosyllabic, formed almost exclusively with short vowels and simple consonants; its stock of words is compressed quickly and densely, like blades of grass. All concepts issue from sensual, unsullied perception, which itself was already a thought, and into which easy and new thoughts enter from all sides. The relationships of words and notions are expressed naively and freshly, but unadorned by other words following in a sequence. With every step that it takes, the chatty language develops in abundance and capability, but in general it seems without proportion and harmony. Its thoughts have nothing permanent, constant, therefore this earliest language contributes no monuments of the spirit and lingers without a trace in history, like the life of those earliest humans. Countless seed has fallen into the earth, which prepares for the second period.

In this period, all phonetic laws of sounds have multiplied and have opened brilliantly. A euphonic alteration arises from splendid diphthongs and their moderation into long vowels, next to the still prevalent abundance of the short vowels; in this way, consonants too move up to one another, no longer separated everywhere by vowels, and increase the strength and power of expression. But as the individual sounds close more firmly together, particles and auxiliaries begin to move in more closely, by the sense that dwells within them gradually weakening; they begin to unite with the word that was supposed to determine them. Instead of special concepts, difficult to survey, and the vast realms of words expected when the sensual power of language is weakened, beneficent accumulations and rest points result, which make the essential emergence from the coincidental, what rules from what is subordinate. The words have become longer and polysyllabic; masses of compounds are formed now from the loose order. As the single vowels merged in diphthongs, the single words merged in inflections, and as the doubled vowel did in dense compression, the components of the inflections also became unrecognizable, but all the more applicable. New permanent endings that remain clear join up with those that have become unfelt. The whole language is still sensually rich, to be sure, but more powerful in thoughts and in everything that connects them; the suppleness of the inflections guarantees a prospering stock of living and orderly expressions. At this time, we see language most highly suited for meter and poetry, for which beauty, euphony, and variety of form are indispensable, and Indic and Greek poetry indicate a zenith in immortal works reached at the right moment, never to be reached again.

But since the entire nature of man, and consequently language too, is nevertheless involved in an eternal, irresistible upswing, the law of this second period of linguistic development could not suffice forever but had to give way to the striving for an even greater freedom of thought, which seemed chained even through the grace and power of a perfect form. No matter with what power words and thoughts are interlaced in the choruses of the tragedians or in Pindar's odes, the feeling of a tension that impedes clarity arises in the process, which becomes even more strongly perceptible in the Indic compounds that pile image upon image; the spirit of language strove to deliver itself from the impression of such truly overwhelming form by giving in to the influences of vernacular idioms that rise to the surface again and again in the changing fates of peoples, fructifying language. As opposed to the Latin language, declining since the introduction of Christianity, the Romance languages developed, on a different level and basis, and next to them, in the course of time, the English and German languages expressed themselves, not through their oldest means, but through that mixture conditioned by the sheer force of the present. The pure vowels had long since blurred through umlaut, fracture, and other ways unknown to antiquity, and our consonantism was destined to be displaced, distorted, and hardened. One may regret that the purity of the entire phonetic system weakened, almost fell out of joint; but no one will deny that from the resultant intermediate sounds unexpectedly new devices had been brought about that could be manipulated most freely. A mass of roots was obscured through such phonetic changes, from then on no longer maintained in their original sensual meaning, good only for abstract notions; of the former inflections, most were lost and replaced by richer, freer particles, or rather outdone because thought, aside from certainty, also can gain flexibility. Just as the four or five Greek or Latin cases in themselves appear less capable than the fourteen of Finnish, the latter nevertheless achieves less with such more apparent than real flexibility; thus, in general, our newer languages are less handicapped than one would believe, by their either leaving the overly rich form of the Greek verb unexpressed or, where it counts, having to use circumlocutions.

As far as the weight and the result of this discussion is concerned, I may be finished with them with a single but decisive example. None among all of the newer languages has gained more strength precisely through relinquishing and destroying old phonetic laws, through the falling away of almost all inflections, than the English language, and a substantial power of expression has become dependent on the abundance of its intermediate sounds, which are only learnable, not even teachable, a force that perhaps has never before been at the disposal of any human tongue. Its entire, thoroughly intellectual, and marvelously successful potential and structure resulted from a surprising marriage of the two noblest languages of later Europe, of the Germanic and the Romance, and it is known how the two relate to one another in English, in that the former provided the sensual foundation in great measure, the latter added the intellectual concepts. Indeed, the English language—by which not by chance the most superior poet of modern times in contrast to the old, classical poetry was generated and borne; naturally, I can only mean Shakespeare—can by all rights be called a world language, and, like the English people, seems to have been chosen to rule in the future even to a greater extent in all corners of the earth. For no other living language can compare with it in richness, reason, and in pliant structure, not our German language, either, which is split the way we ourselves are split, and would first have to shake off many defects before it too entered the arena: yet it will afford us some beneficent memories, and who would want to cut off its hopes? The beauty of human language did not blossom at its beginning but in the middle of it; it will not offer its ripest fruit until sometime in the future.

But who can espy the secret paths of this future? It was appropriate to a great world order that in the course of time dense forests withdrew before climbing grapevines and grain-bearing grasses, which took up more and more space as the land was cultivated; thus too, of the languages diverging in all directions, exhausting themselves over broad spaces, touching one another again later, finally only those that had provided and borne nourishing intellectual fare seem to become master of the field. And instead of all human languages walking away obscured and ruined down the steps of that Babylonian tower, which reached for the heavens, as do the Egyptian pyramids, the Greek temples, and the vaulted churches of the Christians, they could some day, at a vast distance in time, flow together clean and pure, indeed take up within themselves many a noble thing that now lies as if shattered in the languages of wild tribes.

Languages had not reverted to rigidly and externally functioning natural law, like that of light and of gravity, but rather were placed in the warm hand of human freedom, furthered through the blossoming strength of peoples as well as held down through their barbarism, now prospering cheerfully, now faltering on fallow ground. Only to the extent that our generation succumbs to inescapable influences of a power ruling outside of it itself in the clash with what is free and necessary will vibration, muting, or gravitation in human language too become perceivable.

But wherever its history directs our glance, life is stirring, there is a firm foothold, soft, yielding joints, unceasing stretching and folding of wings, never-quieted change that has never yet let the final conclusion be reached; this all guarantees to us that language is the deed and work of humans and bears the virtues and defects of our nature within itself. Uniformity in it would be unthinkable, since an area for play had to remain open for what was newly added and what grew from it, which only what continues to exist calmly has no need for. In long, vast usage words are fixed and smoothed, to be sure, but have also been worn and used up, or have been lost through the force of coincidental events. Like the leaves from a tree, they fall to the ground from their stem, and are overgrown and supplanted by new creations: Those that maintained their status have changed their coloration and meaning so often that they can scarcely be recognized. Usually, a replacement and compensation for most such damages and losses are offered almost on the spot. That is the quiet eye of that protective spirit of language, which heals all of its wounds overnight and makes them scar over, orders all its concerns and protects them from confusion, except that it has shown its highest favor to some individual languages, and its lesser to others. This is, if one will, also a basic force of nature, which bubbles forth inexhaustibly from the primal sounds inborn and planted within us, mated with the structure of human language, taking every language in its arms. But that capacity for sound stands in relationship to the capacity for language as the body does to the soul, which the Middle Ages appropriately called the mistress, the body, the chambermaid.

Of all that humans have invented and thought up, preserved among themselves and passed on to one another, of what they have produced in association with the nature that was placed within them and created in them, language seems to be their greatest, noblest, and most indispensable possession. Having climbed immediately upward from human thought, clinging to man, keeping step with him, it has become the general property and heritage of all humans, which fails no one, and no one would be able to do without it, anymore than the air to breathe, an acquisition that is both easy and difficult for us. Easy, because from the cradle on, the peculiarities of language are imprinted on our being, and we master the gift of speech imperceptibly, just as we imitate gestures and expressions from one another, the gradations of which are infinitely similar and different, like those of language. Poetry, music, and other arts are the property only of favored humans, language is the property of us all, and yet it remains very difficult to possess it completely and to probe it to its core. The masses make do with about half of the stock of words or with still less.

Music, awakened from a dead instrument with its wavering, gliding expression, more felt than understood, stands opposite to articulated language, which grasps all thoughts clearly and certainly, but in song it joins spoken words and gives them a solemn accompaniment. One may compare such heart-lifting human song to that of the birds, which expresses deeply lasting sensation beyond the need for animal cries, just as some tamed birds learn tunes often repeated to them and whistle them. Nevertheless, as inspired as it seems, the sweet call of the nightingale is always the same and only an inborn, immutable skill, but our music has issued from the feelings and imagination of humans, different everywhere. Set down in notes, the song can be sung again, the music played again, as the word can be read from a book. The speech machine that I was talking about above set about to reproduce human language less in thought than in the sound of words, and to get to the bottom of the mechanism of the basic sounds physiologically.

But to look for evidence of the godlike origin of human language in poetry or music, because a higher inspiration is attributed to them and they are called divine or heavenly, seems inadmissible even if only because language, in the case of which such an assumption fails, necessarily preceded both of them. For song arose from stressed, measured recitation of words, the rest of the art of poetry from the song, all the rest of music from song through intensified abstraction, which after relinquishing words soars winged to such heights that no thought can follow it surely. Whoever has now become convinced that language was the free invention of man will also not doubt the source of poetry and the art of music in the reason, feeling, and imagination of the poet. Much sooner could music be called a sublimation of language than language a precipitate of music.

In faith, mysterious and wonderful is the origin of language, but surrounded all around by other wonders and mysteries. The wonder is hardly small that lies in the saga, a wonder that thrills and surfaces among all peoples over the whole earth in the same boundless variation; grown up through the long communality of humans it must have been broadly transmitted. Not so much in its own essence does the mystery of language rest, as much more in our weak knowledge of the first era of its appearance, when it still lay in its cradle, which I strove to elucidate to myself by adjudging artless simplicity, sensual unfolding, as its characteristics: My whole view turns on that hinge; this is what separates me from my predecessors. Was not the essence of the inflections veiled in darkness to us before one layer after another was drawn away from it? Countless events, even from historical times, have become clear only to the eyes of the historian; the oldest history of the human race is slumbering in secret, like that of its language, and only linguistic research will cast beams of light upon it.

One language is more beautiful and appears more productive than the next; this does not bother the poet, and he knows how to entice great effects from meager means, as a charming voice warbles from gray feathers. The Nordic skalds too were masters of artful song forms, and piled volume on volume, image on image: If one has penetrated their poetry, it soon leaves one empty because it sings of nothing but battle, victory, and clemency, but Pindar touches all the strings of the soul. One myth is deeper and more lovely than the next, but that myth grasps us most strongly around which the greatest abundance of poetry has grown up; the Eygptian myth loses compared to the Greek one, the basis of which it is often supposed to form, because it offers almost nothing but seed and fruit, the foliage and blossoms of the art of poetry are lacking to it entirely. But in all of poetry nothing is as close and as equal to language according to its potential and development as the epic, and it too must have swung up from simple ground to the heights that we admire in it. Whoever thinks that he sees in it and in the most noble monuments of human poetry and language only weakened reflections of more powerful creations that have disappeared from the world would have explained less than nothing by that, because whatever he was shifting the source back to, if it could somehow be reached, would cry out even more loudly for explanation.

I planned to raise the question here, at the end, of the extent to which the Indo-Germanic language, on which we concentrated almost exclusively in what has gone before, and the other tongues of the earth may be derived from one and the same source. That would change nothing essential about the results we have gained about the general origin of them all; but my strength would have to fall short of the extraordinary bulk of such an almost unlimited investigation, even if touched upon; for example, even if I limited it to the relationship of the Finnish language to that one about which I gave my various thoughts. In the course of historical research, when it has turned to all the significant language families of the earth, important conclusions for what has been discussed here, and hopefully in favor of what I have found, will one day result. But now I would only have muddied the water for other fishers.

I cannot conclude without paying tribute to the genius of that man, who, compensating for what he lacked in depth of research or scholarly rigor by thoughtful tact, by an active feeling for truth, had already disposed of the difficult question of the origin of language, like so many others; that answer he gave us still remains pertinent, even if the answer is to be strengthened and confirmed with other reasons than he had at hand.

Translated by Ralph R. Read III

ACKNOWLEDGMENTS

All reasonable efforts have been made to locate the parties who hold rights to previously published translations reprinted here. We gratefully acknowledge permission to reprint material from the following publications:

From Adam Müller, *Twelve Lectures on Rhetoric: A Translation with a Critical Essay,* trans. Dennis R. Bormann and Elisabeth Leinfellner, University Microfilms International, 1978. Copyright © 1978 by Dennis R. Bormann and Elisabeth Leinfellner.

From *Dialogue on Poetry and Literary Aphorisms* by Friedrich Schlegel, translated and annotated by Ernst Behler and Roman Struc. 173 pages. Copyright © 1968 by The Pennsylvania State University Press, University Park, Pennsylvania 16801.

"On Poetry in General" and "On Romantic Poetry" reprinted from *Horn of Oberon: Jean Paul Richter's School for Aesthetics,* ed. Margaret R. Hale. English translation copyright © 1973 by Wayne State University Press, Detroit, Michigan 48202.

On the Different Methods of Translating by Friedrich Schleieracher, translated by Andre Lefevere, copyright © 1977 by Van Gorcum BV. By permission of Editions Rodopi BV, Amsterdam.